Western Lands and Waters
XIII

Other books by Briton Cooper Busch

Britain and the Persian Gulf, 1894-1914

Britain, India, and the Arabs, 1914-1921

Mudros to Lausanne: Britain's Frontier in West Asia, 1918-1923

Master of Desolation: Reminiscences of Captain Joseph J. Fuller

Hardinge of Penshurst: A Study in the Old Diplomacy

WILLIAM DANE PHELPS, MASTER OF THE SHIP "ALERT"
By permission of the Houghton Library, Harvard University.

ALTA CALIFORNIA
1840-1842

The Journal and Observations of
William Dane Phelps
Master of the Ship "Alert"

Introduced and edited by
Briton Cooper Busch

THE ARTHUR H. CLARK COMPANY
Glendale, California   1983

Contents

Illustrations and Maps

Acknowledgements

No original manuscript, no matter how intrinsically interesting or historically valuable, finds its way into print without the assistance of many people. Initially, the project would not have been feasible without the full cooperation of the Houghton Library of Harvard University, owners of the Phelps collection, and I am very grateful for their permission to publish the following account.

In the course of tracing the career of Captain Phelps and the ship *Alert,* I owe much to the helpful directors and staffs of the following institutions in California: the Bancroft Library, the California Historical Society, the Huntington Library, the Santa Barbara and San Diego Historical societies, and the Monterey Public Library. In Massachusetts: in addition to the Houghton Library, the Pusey Library map collection and the University Archives of Harvard University, the Gloucester Public Library, and the Lexington and Massachusetts Historical societies. To good friends who gave their warm hospitality, my equally warm thanks: in Massachusetts, Ken and Sandra Martin; in California, Art and Barbara Balinger, Jack Hunter, Bea and Winston Miller, and Sue and Niven Busch. The long-standing interest of the latter (my father) in California's history has not been totally without influence. Rose Novak, for the second time, provided critical comment along with expert typing; the Colgate

University Research Council helped with preparation
costs. Above all, I owe a special debt to Adele Ogden,
who generously gave of her time and wide expertise
on California's maritime history by reading and com-
menting upon the entire manuscript, thus saving me
from those errors which I would rather forget, though
I take full responsibility for those that remain.

HAMILTON, NEW YORK
JANUARY 1982

Introduction

"We have now reached a period in the annals of California when the doings of foreigners become a more important element than those of natives or Mexicans," wrote Hubert Howe Bancroft in opening the fourth volume of his extensive *History of California* – a volume which devotes a substantial 700 pages to the years 1840-1845.[1] Captain William Dane Phelps, the author of the pages which follow, was one of these foreigners, and one of the few to leave a detailed record of his movements and observations. Phelps was master of the ship *Alert,* trading along the California coast for hides and tallow in the years 1840-42. The voyage of the *Alert* to and from California was not particularly notable, but the months spent in California fell in an interesting and fluid era. As a sea captain, Phelps was of course accustomed to keep a daily log, but these particular journals display a curiosity and willingness to record which is exceptional among nineteenth-century masters, and which make his account well worthy of preservation.

William Phelps was born in Gloucester, Massachusetts, in 1802, third of nine children born to Henry Phelps and Mary Forbes Coffin. Henry Phelps traced his ancestry to another Henry Phelps who arrived at

---

[1] San Francisco 1886 (Works, vol. XXI). The following general remarks on California, where otherwise uncited, are based upon the seven volumes of Bancroft's *History* together with his *California Pastoral, 1769-1848* (San Francisco, 1888).

Salem from London on the ship *Hercules* in the year
1634. Henry the descendant was born in Salem in 1765,
the son of a Salem merchant captain. Despite the disa-
bilities of a club foot and an imperfect formed right
arm and hand, Henry studied at Harvard (class of
1788), although he seems to have had serious financial
difficulties after his father was lost at sea in 1786.
Henry graduated nevertheless, and then studied with
a well-known Salem and Gloucester doctor, Joshua
Plummer, and was assisted by the good doctor in es-
tablishing an apothecary shop in Gloucester in 1790.
Henry was well liked, and, although he soon gave up
doctoring, his apothecary shop on Front Street became
the resort of the town's leading citizens. In 1792, a post
office was established in Gloucester, and Henry became its first postmaster (1792-1809); for some time
he was also the principal acting magistrate of the town.
Mary, his wife, was the daughter of Peter Coffin, a
well-known landowner of Gloucester; her grandfather
was Reverend Eli Forbes, prominent in Gloucester's
history as pastor of the First Church. William Dane
Phelps, in other words, came from well-established
Gloucester origins.[2]

In his volume of published memoirs, *Fore and Aft;*

[2] Henry Phelps, William's father, is discussed in John J. Babson, *History
of the Town of Gloucester, Cape Ann, including the Town of Rockport*
(Gloucester, 1860, reprint 1972), p. 560 (and see pp. 276-9, 403-3); William
Richard Cutter, *Genealogical and Personal Memoirs relating to the Families
of Boston and Eastern Massachusetts* (N.Y., 1908), II, pp. 867-69; William
Bentley, *The Diary of William Bentley, D.D., Pastor of the East Church,
Salem, Mass.* (Gloucester, 1962), III, pp. 307-08; James F. Pringle, *History
of the Town and City of Gloucester, Cape Ann, Massachusetts* (Gloucester,
1892), p. 323; Charles Hudson, *History of the Town of Lexington* (Boston,
1913), II, p. 376; and file on Henry Phelps, class of 1788, Harvard Records,
Pusey Library, Harvard University.

or Leaves from the Life of an Old Sailor,[3] which appeared in 1871 under the pseudonym "Webfoot," William Phelps was rather reticent on his background,
saying only that he hailed from a seacoast town in the
Boston area, attended school during the War of 1812,
spent a year in the printing tráde, presumably as some
sort of apprentice, and went to sea in 1816 as a cabin
boy. Perhaps Phelps was eager to get on to his story
of sea-going adventure and thus avoid discussing his
father's antipathy to his son's chosen career. Henry
Phelps apparently had no wish to see his son go to
sea (at least according to William Phelps' daughter),
but rather preferred that he follow his own steps to
Harvard.[4]

However, William Phelps was one of those people
who find the call of the sea irresistible. As a cabin boy
on the brig *Corporal True,* Phelps witnessed a dis-
abling storm which sent his vessel (intended for England) into St. Barthélemy in the West Indies in
distress. Phelps later termed this voyage the worst
suffering from hunger and thirst that he experienced
in forty years at sea, but it did not discourage him from
sailing again the following year as a cabin boy in the
brig *Pickering,* bound for the far South Atlantic to
take seal skins from the Falkland Islands and South
Georgia for the Canton market.

In this second voyage, Phelps found a hard master
to match the hard work and conditions. His fate was
to be left with a small gang for two years (with food

---

[3] Boston, 1871. Data on Phelps' career, unless otherwise cited, are based
on this account.

[4] Alice D. Goodwin to Mr. Currier, Harvard Library, 4 June 1927, William
Phelps Papers (MS AM W 84), Houghton Library, Harvard University,
vol. 10.

for only one) on the Indian Ocean's desolate Prince Edward Islands killing elephant seals for blubber. Eventually reaching Cape Town, Phelps and another disillusioned hand applied to the local authorities to force their discharge; the *Pickering's* captain had refitted at Cape Town and was prepared to remain away from home indefinitely. Phelps was fortunate to escape (though he never was paid for his two years), for the rest of the crew was left high and dry on the beach at Java – and the master in the end was charged with the crime of barratry.

Now Phelps tried coasting voyages out of Cape Town on local brigs and even, when times were particularly hard, signing on a British sloop-of-war on the St. Helena station for a three year tour of duty – only to desert at Simon's Bay in 1821. He soon tired of the alternative, pressing hay for a local farmer, and signed on a trader for Van Dieman's Land, Australia, and South America. Eventually he was paid off in Valparaíso. His visit to Chile was made memorable by four months' service in the Chilean navy in a war against Peru. Restless again, he deserted to sign on the *Nautilus* of Boston, a crack China trader bound home. When at last he saw his family in 1823, they had already given him up for lost.

Not surprisingly, he was soon off again, this time before the mast on a merchantman bound for the Mediterranean. The next years were spent in many similar voyages, and Phelps' persistence and experience soon brought promotion to the rank of mate. After four or five years of service on voyages to Europe and the Caribbean, at last in 1831, after fifteen years at sea, he was made master of the brig *Mermaid,* a smart

Boston vessel trading to the Barbary coast for wool
and to Smyrna for tobacco and other Turkish products.
As his own supercargo, Phelps made good profit for
his owners. Through the 1830's he made several similar trips, generally profitable, and usually uneventful.
Phelps had his encounter with disaster, however, in
a tragic wreck in the winter of 1836. Bound into Boston
from Smyrna on the brig *Regulator,* of which he was
master, Phelps was driven ashore on Brown's Island
near Plymouth. A fierce winter gale was raging, and
the rigging was covered with ice; the crew could
steer only by hauling on the braces, since the rudder
was choked with ice. Letting go all his anchors, Phelps
managed to keep the vessel off the beach for one ghastly
night, but of his ten crewmen, five perished – three
in a boat which had been launched into the storm,
and two crushed on deck by falling wreckage. In the
morning, Phelps and the surviving five men were res-
cued by the crew of the brig *Cervantes,* shortly before
the *Regulator* dragged her anchors and was pulled
into the surf and total destruction. Phelps and the
others suffered severely from the cold (in Phelps'
case, a badly frozen foot).[5]

A few of Phelps' journals from his early days as
mate and master survive in the Phelps collection at
Harvard, and they show an active curiosity to record
his observations on the habits of Smyrniot Turks or
the physical charms of Benghazi. Always an interested
observer, Phelps made good use of his impressions,
comparing Turkey's grapes with California's, or New
Zealand facial tattooing with that of California Indians. Whenever possible, he did his best to preserve

---

[5] Boston *Daily Evening Transcript,* 8 February 1836.

anything new – this unusual form of shrimp, that albatross captured at sea. That he might lack for an immediate audience seems not to have disturbed him, for
he early decided that there was value in recording
observations over and above the obligatory deck log.
As he explained many years later in *Fore & Aft:*[6]

> Perhaps some of my seafaring brethren may treat as ridiculous
> the idea of an old sailor's giving to the public an abstract of
> his voyages, with observations on places, people and things, which
> are commonplace and familiar to him, who has travelled over the
> same ground, and is so well acquainted with similar scenes him-
> self. To such I would say, Brother, I write not for your amuse-
> ment or edification, but the great majority of the reading public
> desire to have just such information as you and I can impart to
> them, of "matters which we say, and part of which we were."
> Instead of sharply criticising and finding fault with *Fore & Aft,*
> please to sit down yourself and write out your own experiences
> in your own way; the world may be the wiser for it. A man
> who has passed thirty or forty years in roaming over the globe
> must be laden with rich experiences, unless he has passed with
> his eyes shut, which, if imparted to the many who have not been
> much abroad, cannot fail to interest and enlighten them, and
> especially the young.

Clearly, Phelps learned more than the art of command at sea during his ventures; one cargo of 115 tons
of ice taken to Malta on the brig *Herald,* for example,
landed him in the Maltese courts (he had impinged
upon a local monopoly for ice – from Mt. Etna).
According to *Fore & Aft,* on his return from Malta,
in 1838 or 1839, Phelps bought a "snug little farm"
in Lexington, on the outskirts of Boston. The choice
of Lexington was probably dictated by the fact that
his second wife (his first wife, Mary Ann Cushing,

---

[6] *Fore & Aft,* p. 175-6.

died in 1831; the date of the marriage is not certain), Lusanna Tucker Bryant, hailed from there. The location of Phelps' property is not clear; he owned several houses at different times in that town. Between August 1838 and January 1840, however, he was the possessor of a famous dwelling, the Jonathan Harrington house, which faces Lexington green, and from which Ruth Harrington saw her husband shot by the British in the battle of Lexington in 1775 (he died on the doorstep). In January of 1840, a good opportunity arose when Phelps was offered command of the Bryant, Sturgis & Co. ship *Alert,* bound for California in the hide and tallow trade. Phelps apparently sold the Harrington house at once, lodged Lusanna and their two daughters (Lusanna, born in 1836, and Alice, born in 1838; a son, Edwin, was born in 1845 and died four years later) in another less elaborate building, and made for Boston. The stage from Lexington, his daughter Alice remembered years later, was always the worst part of the voyage in the eyes of Captain Phelps.[7]

In the 1820's and 1830's, the hide and tallow trade was the mainstay of California's external commerce.[8]

---

[7] Hudson, *op. cit.;* Helen Clark Fernald, *The Jonathan Harrington House* (n.p., 1937); "Recollections of Mrs. Goodwin [Alice Phelps Goodwin]," undated typescript, Lexington Historical Society, Lexington, Mass. (My thanks to Larry Whipple, Curator, for this reference.)

[8] Remarks on the hide trade are based upon the following sources, in addition to the works of Bancroft: Robert Glass Cleland, *The Cattle on a Thousand Hills* (San Marino, Calif., 1941); Sherman F. Dallas, *The Hide and Tallow Trade in Alta California, 1822-1846,* unpublished Ph.D. thesis, Indiana University, 1955; Bruno Fritzsche, " 'On Liberal Terms': the Boston Hide-Merchants in California," *Business Hist. Rev.,* XLII (1968), 467-81; and Adele Ogden, "Boston Hide Droghers along California Shores," *Calif. Hist. Soc. Qt.* VIII (1929), 289-98; "Hides and Tallow: McCulloch, Hartnell and Company, 1822-1828," *Calif. Hist. Soc. Qt.,* VI (1927), 254-64, and "New

By that time the brief rush for otter and fur seal skins was over due to the dwindling supply, but the seals had led Bryant, Sturgis & Co., among other Boston firms, to the Pacific and eventually to California. When the furs ran out, the merchants turned to the extensive cattle herds of the California missions and ranches, trading finished goods for hides, tallow and whatever remaining otter pelts the padres and others could find. The hides went to Boston for leather; the tallow to South America, Boston, Mexico, or Hawaii for soap and candles. Such profits as existed came from the markup, normally 200-300%, on New England goods. The profits were sufficient to keep first McCulloch & Hartnell, which firm dominated the trade in the years 1822-28, and then Bryant, Sturgis & Co., in the trade for a generation. In the years when the trade was of major significance, 1822-48, these firms together shipped some half million hides. The vessel did more, however, than carry away hides: they brought news and fashions from the outside world beyond what filtered through from Mexico; they provided essential communication for local residents separated long distances but possessed of little significant indigenous maritime industry (it will be observed, for example, how often the *Alert* carried passengers from one point to another); they even served the local government, by carrying away political exiles or moving official goods and persons.

By 1840, however, a sizeable vessel such as the *Alert* (398 tons), in order to collect a full cargo of 40,000

England Traders in Spanish and Mexican California," in Adele Ogden, ed., *Greater America: Essays in Honor of Herbert Eugene Bolton* (Berkeley, 1945), 395-413.

hides was required to spend longer and longer on the coast. The trade was in serious decline, for several reasons. At the head of the list was the political situation in California. An ancient Arab proverb on Spain, rudely paraphrased, remarks that Allah gave to Iberia rich lands, salubrious climate, handsome inhabitants and indeed all things requisite for man's enjoyment. But perfection would be paradise, and there is only one Paradise. So one exception was made: Spain was denied good government. Had the Arabs conquered California, they might well have applied the same rubric, for California was perpetually troubled in the early 19th century by faction quarrels — ancestral (Mexican versus Californio vs. Indian), regional (Monterey and environs versus Los Angeles and San Diego), or administrative (centralizing governors versus local-minded petty despots), the whole overridden by the often impractical attempt to apply irrelevant Mexican laws to a remote and distinct California setting. To these factors must be added outside foreign intervention. The Russians at Fort Ross were on the point of cutting their losses and selling out, but British and French annexationist schemes each had their proponents, while meanwhile the United States presence increased steadily as more vessels appeared on the coast and immigrants trickled in from the interior. The dangers of involvement in conflicts real or potential were all too clear, as Bryant, Sturgis & Co. pointed out to Phelps:

> From Mr. Robinson [Phelps' experienced supercargo] you will get such information & advice as will enable you to act discretely when you get on the Coast. Be very careful not to interfere, or take any part in any political or other party move-

ments among the Inhabitants, & do nothing that may be deemed a violation of the laws or regulations of any place you may visit.[9]

Any commerce may be disrupted by political disturbance, but the trade in hides in particular had been altered by the secularization of the missions, a process begun in 1833. The rights or wrongs of such measures need not be discussed here, but with the breakup of mission lands, the occasional reflexive slaughter of mission herds in angry response without consideration of the hide market, the desertion of neophytes (as the convent Indians were called) – who after all did the work, and the assumption of control over mission finances by lay *administradores,* who did not necessarily have in mind the best interests of either mission or converts, all insured that the supply of hides from the missions was at once smaller and more subject to individual whim rather than long-range plan. Administradores, like other lay customers, were far more interested in the vagaries of fashion, meaning that the trade goods of a vessel in its second or third year on the coast lost favor compared to newly arrived items. At the same time, individuals were less reliable in the payment of debts for goods purchased than the mission padres had been; it was nearly impossible to collect cash from either source, as cash was scarce in California, and the cattle could only be killed in season when

[9] Bryant, Sturgis & Co., to Phelps, 17 January 1840, Bryant, Sturgis & Co. Papers [BSP], Baker Library, Harvard Business School, MS 766, vol. 11. On other interests, see E.D. Adams, "English Interest in the Annexation of California," *Amer. Hist. Rev.,* 14 (1909), 744-63; Sheldon G. Jackson, "Two Pro-British Plots in Alta California," *Southern Calif. Qt.,* LV (1973), 104-40; and Russell M. Posner, "A British Consular Agent in California: the Reports of James A. Forbes, 1843-1846," *Southern Calif. Qt.,* LIII (1971), 101-12.

they were fattest. For that reason, credit was normally extended over a year.

It was in the interest of Bryant, Sturgis & Co., therefore, to urge quick sale at high prices – any merchant's normal desire, of course, but at the same time, to avoid giving credit where possible, for the firm was well aware of "the risk of keeping property in a country liable to political convulsions," property meaning both cured hides and hides still on the hoof.[10] Letter after letter from the firm to its agents and masters stress the necessity of speed and the increasing cost of doing business in California. To Thomas Shaw (supercargo on the *Monsoon*) they wrote in September 1839:

> In times when money is worth from 1 to 2% a month, as it has been for the greater part of the time for the last three years, the great length of the voyage renders the business hardly worth pursuing, and increases the importance of getting home a portion of the property [in other words, as soon as possible].[11]

To Phelps, in January 1840: "the *utmost economy* will be necessary in expenditure of stores & provisions."[12] Or to Henry Mellus, Robinson's successor, in June 1840: "The depreciation in value, the loss of interest, the heavy postage bills and a thousand other expenses eat up all the profit on one of these long voyages."[13]

Richard Henry Dana, who as a sailor worked for the same firm some years earlier, correctly recorded in *Two Years Before the Mast* that the normal markup was high and that costs kept all firms but those with

---

[10] Bryant, Sturgis & Co. to Thomas Shaw, supercargo, ship *Monsoon*, 15 November 1838, BSP, vol. 11.

[11] *Ibid.*, 10 September 1839, BSP, vol. 11.

[12] *Ibid.*, to Phelps, 17 January 1840, BSP, vol. 11.

[13] *Ibid.*, to Henry Mellus, 17 June 1840, BSP, vol. 11.

heavy capital support from the trade. He leaves the
impression, however, that profits were high.[14] But, as
Bruno Fritzsche has shown, an acceptable but hardly
usurious 10% was a probable return.[15] But that figure
assumes normal conditions, and in the late 1830's and
early 1840's, normal conditions did not apply. In addition to political uncertainties and predictable costs,
regulations governing the operation of foreign vessels
on the coast had a maddening habit of changing suddenly, for example, prohibiting coasting, or the use of
ship's boats in San Francisco Bay, or some such per-
verse interference (as viewed by master or supercargo)
in free trade. At the same time, duties were commonly
so high (over 40% of invoice), that for many lesser
merchants smuggling was mandatory to turn any profit
at all. Finally, the trade was temporarily broken, at
least at the level at which it had been conducted in
the 1830's, by a sudden glut of hides in Boston in the
early 1840's.

In part this glut was caused by outside competition
– hides from the Sandwich Islands (Hawaii) or South
America – but the sudden arrival of three vessels from
California (*Barnstable, California,* and *Tasso*) in
1843 brought prices for hides down from the average
11-13¢ per pound to a low 9.75-10¢, too low to turn
a profit. Since a hide was bought in California for $2
cash or $2.25 worth of trade goods, a hide averaging
twenty-five pounds and sold at 9.75¢ returned only

14 Throughout, I have used the edition of *Two Years Before the Mast*
edited by John Haskell Kemble from the original manuscript and the first
edition (2 vols., Los Angeles, 1964). References to *Two Years* have been
made to chapters rather than pages so that they may be located in any
edition. Dana's remarks on profits occur in Ch. XIII.

15 Fritzsche, *op. cit.*

$2.44, simply not enough margin to cover the cost of two or three years in California. Bryant, Sturgis & Co. had tried to preserve some optimism, writing to Robinson in October 1840, "In reference to any future operations we can only say, as we have said heretofore, that we are disposed to continue the business as long as it can be made profitable. . . ," but clearly they had doubts already.[16] When the news of yet another round of obstructive California regulations arrived, William Sturgis, writing for the firm, told Robinson in July 1841 that the partnership was dissolved: "We at once concluded to abandon the business while these regulations exist, & sold the ship [*California,* just arrived in Boston] for upwards of $12,000 to a concern who have more energy than ourselves," though they were willing to continue if the next vessel brought news of a repeal.[17] It did not, and the hide glut of 1843 found Bryant, Sturgis & Co. already out of business, although the trade continued at a lower level of profit under others, as described below, until the gold rush totally disrupted California's economy.

Until the convulsive years of 1846-49, however, when California became part of the United States and the wave of fevered gold hunters arrived, the methods of the hide trade had remained fairly stable for twenty years. Phelps gives few details in his journals, perhaps because he kept separate account books for that purpose, and the journals were meant for the more general reader (in particular, his wife), but the procedure has been set forth by Dana and several successors. Generally, missions and their successor ranchos killed steers

---

[16] Bryant, Sturgis & Co. to Alfred Robinson, 22 October 1840, BSP, Vol. 11.
[17] *Ibid.,* to Robinson, 13 July 1841, BSP, vol. 11.

at the *matanza* or killing time – usually August, after the cattle had fattened up on spring and early summer feed, though rainfall and feed supply could alter this.

The hides were locally dried, or, less often, salted. Supercargoes or resident agents visited every important source, seeing to the collection of this year's hides for last year's debts, and with luck, obtaining the ranchero's commitment for the following year's business. Much time was by necessity spent on horseback, particularly when the vessel clawed its way northward against the prevailing winds (hence ports of call to he north lay to "windward," and any point to the south was to "leeward"). Although agents could list items for sale, normally the ranchero (or his wife) or mission representative visited the vessel itself as it moved along the coast, for in it was fitted out a "trade room" displaying a wide variety of clothing, fabrics, tools, metalware, and furniture (Phelps' list of trade items for 1840-43 is given in Appendix II).

When the hides were ready, they were moved to a suitable collection spot by mule or wagon or small boat, then collected by the vessel, and taken to be stored in a depot known as a "hide house" in San Pedro or San Diego (where the climate was more congenial to the drying process than any port to the north) until the total cargo had been assembled. Work in the hide houses was difficult and tedious, for the hides had to be beaten and folded and moved innumerable times, as so colorfully related in Dana's account. Finally they were loaded aboard, a process that could take weeks, as every possible hide was squeezed in by every conceivable steeving process. Block and tackle, energetic shanty-singing, and brute human force could push in a hundred hides where it seemed that only a handful would fit. Again, Dana describes how it was done, though he may not have realized that those extra hides represented the difference between profit and loss for the owners. The owners knew it, in any case. Phelps, for example, whose instructions were more comprehensive than usual, perhaps because he was new to the coast, was advised not only that the *Alert* could hold 40,000 hides (she had not brought so many home her last trip) without riding too low in the sea, but that, if necessary to complete the number, Phelps should fill the space allotted as a dining cabin for the officers.[18]

Since the Captain's pay normally included at least some incentive on shares, his motives – within the limits of safety, hopefully – were the company's. This meant, however, that each voyage of every company vessel differed in the details of shares of ownership and profit. Thus even though several Bryant, Sturgis & Co. vessels might be on the coast at once, their several accounts were kept strictly separate. Phelps' share of the *Alert's* voyage is not known, but Robinson, the supercargo, who through investment held an unusually high stake, received for his efforts 6.5% on the net proceeds returned after sale in the United States of the cargo he sent home in any of the company's vessels.[19]

Dana says little of such financial details, but his readily available description of the curing and loading process needs no repetition here. Phelps himself felt that it hardly could be improved upon. As he wrote in *Fore & Aft:*

I read [Dana's] book some years since, and was impressed with

---

[18] *Ibid.,* to Phelps, 17 January 1840, BSP, vol. 11.
[19] *Ibid.,* to Robinson, 18 January 1840, BSP, vol. 11.

the correctness of his description of the manner of collecting and curing a cargo of hides; therefore anything I could now say of that business would only be a repetition. The author of that work is charged with stating that the ship's crew had to skin some thirty thousand bullocks to obtain the cargo. I think Mr. Dana does not make such a statement. I will only say, that the crews, on these voyages, kill and skin only the animals required for the supply of beef for ship use.[20]

This remark is given in full because a curious question arises as to the date at which Phelps did in fact read *Two Years Before the Mast*. Obviously as of 1871, when *Fore & Aft* was published, it had indeed been "some years," or Phelps would not have had any doubt regarding Dana's supposed claim that the ship's crew did the killing (Dana makes clear that they did not). More important, however, is the fact that *Two Years* is referred to three times in the journals, beginning with a remark entered on February 1, 1842, regarding Dana's relationship to Henry Fitch. Dana was one of the few to be critical of this well-known merchant, and Phelps explains that Dana was really reacting to his own ouster from Fitch's establishment for just cause (drunkennesss). John Haskell Kemble reproduces Phelps' explanation in his definitive edition of *Two Years* but does not raise the point that Phelps sailed on the *Alert* from Boston in January of 1840, but *Two Years* first appeared for sale only in September of the same year.[21]

How then did Phelps come by Dana's work? The answer can only be guesswork. One possibility is that

20 *Fore & Aft*, p. 236.

21 Dana, *Two Years*, Kemble edition, p. 234, note 45. Remarks on *Two Years* in general are based upon Robert Francis Lucid, *The Composition, Reception, Reputation and Influence of "Two Years Before the Mast,"* unpublished Ph.D. thesis, Univ. of Chicago, 1958.

Phelps' journals were written after the fact – fabricated, as it were. This is most unlikely, since Phelps did publish his memoirs, based upon these same journals, and anonymously. There would seem to be little need to falsify the same materials, nor is there any evidence that Phelps planned publication of the journals as such. In *Fore & Aft,* in fact, he discusses only the highlights of this California trip, such as his visit to Sutter's fort or his role in the "Jones War" of 1842.[22]

Second, internal evidence, such as names given in several forms, conflicting estimates for the size of the same estate, or confusion in dates or days of the week, all quite understandable over a three years' voyage, would hardly be valuable additions to a manuscript prepared for publication: clever forgeries for a master swindler, perhaps, but not likely to win a publisher's favor for a sea captain's journal in an era when there were, after all, a great many retired sea captains about. Nor does it seem logical to assume that Phelps read Dana's manuscript before sailing; Dana only just finished it in late 1839, and it is not likely that Phelps had access to the draft manuscript. Moreover, it seems safe to assume that Phelps might have made more references to *Two Years* had he had the volume in hand, or in mind, for the whole of his stay in California. It remains to presume, therefore, that Phelps read the book while in California, and probably read it fairly close to the time of his first reference, that is, early in 1842. Surely a copy of this work, which was quite popular from the first, would have been sent by an interested friend or relative to some American in

---

[22] On Commodore Jones' premature seizure of Monterey in 1842, see Bancroft, *History of California,* IV, Ch. XII.

California in contact with the east and known to
Phelps. It would be natural for Phelps, a literate and
reasonably well-read man himself, to borrow such a
volume. Just as naturally, he would be critical, for
Dana viewed matters from the forecastle, not the quar-
terdeck – to say nothing of the fact that Phelps had
the opportunity to see far more of California and Californians. It is not impossible, too, that jealousy played
a role; Phelps would not have known that *Two Years*
would win a reputation as a literary classic, but he
shows in his claim to be the first to go up the Sacramento River and in other matters that he had pride,
pride enough to wish to be the first to write a sea-going
account of the hide trade in California.

There is one other reason for assuming the best of
Phelps regarding Dana's book, and that is Phelps' out-
standing reputation throughout his career for integrity
and reliability. This is demonstrated not only by the
position of authority in which his owners placed him
– shown most by making him supercargo *and* master
in a subsequent voyage to California – but also by the
respect in which he was held by the elite of California.
Any reader of his journals will soon encounter his
prejudices, not to say bigotry, regarding religious and
moral matters (considerably modified, not surprisingly,
in *Fore & Aft*). That there could be spiritual value
in Catholic "trumpery," or that native custom and
tradition (burial mounds, for example) merited respect never occurred to him. He was ever scornful
of the low agricultural productivity of the rich lands
he visited, ignoring the fact that since captains like
himself had little use for surplus grain or similar
crops, there existed no market for such commodities.

His contempt for flea-ridden beds or other hardships of the road – taken pretty much for granted by experienced travelers such as Robinson – comes out clearly.[23] Yet when one of his crew was beaten up by locals, Phelps assumed he deserved it.

More important, his views never prevented him from making good friends of local citizens – above all those of American origin – not least because he seems to have been a fair trader, and was in addition well known as an excellent shot with a rifle who kept his own and his friends' tables well supplied with choice game. He had a considerable reputation as an epicure and raconteur, not surprising given his many travels, but in his story-telling it was necessary to surmount what appears to have been a speech defect. As William Heath Davis (himself entertained by Phelps' account of his visit to Jerusalem) explained it, "Captain Phelps had a curious peculiarity of hesitating and stammering as he commenced to talk, his right cheek quivering rapidly until he got along further in his speech and warmed up a little, when his language came fluently and the pulsation of the face ceased." [24]

Davis was one of Phelps' admirers ("a good observer and a man of excellent judgment"), but he was not alone. Thomas Oliver Larkin, the most prominent American in Monterey (and the only American Consul to be appointed to California) had many dealings with Phelps in this voyage and a subsequent visit of 1845-48. When Larkin found himself languishing as a political prisoner in Southern California during the political

[23] Alfred Robinson, *Life in California during a Residence of Several Years in that Territory* (N.Y., 1846), 108ff.

[24] William Heath Davis, *Seventy-Five Years in California* (San Francisco, 1967), 152.

upheaval of 1846, he advised his wife Rachel that if
anything should happen to him, she should turn to
Phelps: "You will look on him as as [sic] a good and
honest man as there is in this country." [25]

It was high praise indeed, but Phelps' relations with
Larkin were always fairly formal. Nathan Spear, on
the other hand, a leading pioneer San Francisco merchant, was a good friend, as an 1842 letter of Phelps
bears witness. The passage serves to demonstrate, as
well, that Phelps could be prolix in everyday correspondence as well as his journals.

> So much for sentiment. – now let's talk about something we
> can *eat,* and I know that this will be a theme on which you will
> dwell with much delight. Already in imagination I hear that
> slap of the right hand on the thigh and that hearty smack of the
> lips peculiarly your own. Nathan, my dearly beloved sympathiz-
> ing friend, if you have tears prepare to shed them now (not of
> sorrow, but of joy unspeakable) while I tell you that *those
> lobsters*!!! those much talked of oft promised and long expected
> lobsters have at last been persuaded to quit their vile crawling
> among slime and sea weed, and at the urgent request of my
> steward put off their dirty brown coat for one of scarlet, and
> still farther to throw off this crustaceous covering when its bright
> hues no longer pleased the eye but tickled the palate, and quietly
> reposed their mortal parts in a pot of vinegar for the gratifica-
> tion of your palate. You will receive by Capt. Snook the above
> mentioned remains and I trust you will do them justice by
> having them decently intern'd (as *Nye* says) after being prop-
> erly embalmed with the oil of gladness and perhaps some other
> "substitutes" which your well known taste in such matters may
> suggest. I will probably be absent. . .[26]

---

25 Thomas Oliver Larkin to Rachel Larkin, 14 December 1846, in George
P. Hammond, ed., *The Larkin Papers* (Berkeley, 1955), vol. V, p. 313.

26 Phelps to Nathan Spear, 14 June 1842, Spear Papers, Bancroft Library,
C-B 106. Joseph Francis Snook and Gorham Hayden Nye were both ship
captains on the California coast.

Phelps was not done with these friends when he sailed for home in 1843. Although Bryant, Sturgis & Co. had dissolved, some of its principals were prepared to carry on. Samuel Hooper, one of the junior members, joined with several other investors to form William Appleton & Co., which took charge of some Bryant, Sturgis & Co. interests, including the ship *Barnstable*.[27] Henry Mellus, with Robinson's assistance, acted as agent for the new firm, and the *Alert* took home some of the *Barnstable's* first hides in 1842; thus was one firm transformed into another without any great trauma, though Appleton's activities were considerably shorter lived than Bryant, Sturgis & Co., Phelps, however, was approached by a rival of both firms, Joseph B. Eaton, who owned the *Tasso, Sterling,* and *Moscow.* In September 1845, Phelps sailed from Boston as master and supercargo of the bark *Moscow,* possessed of the customary financial interests in the vessel, and with instructions to take charge as well of the *Sterling,* in California at the same time.[28]

Arriving in California four and a half months later, he found himself in the midst of the revolutionary events through which the United States acquired California. Phelps' very interesting relations with Frémont and the other leaders gave him a unique eyewitness view of the process, on which he has much to say in *Fore & Aft.* There is little need therefore to retell the story here; suffice it to say that Phelps, not content to remain on his vessel out of touch, took to horse to

[27] The *Barnstable* accounts are found in the papers of William Appleton, Houghton Library, vol. 29. Robinson held 2/22, Henry Mellus, 1/22, and Bryant, Sturgis & Co. 7/22 of this vessel.

[28] Phelps Papers, vol. 7 (Journal of the Bark *Moscow,* 1846); and Phelps to Joseph B. Eaton, 6 and 21 November 1846, and 21 November 1847, vol. 1.

ride with Commodore Stockton's forces sent to do
battle with Californians defending the pueblo of Los
Angeles. Although Phelps resumed his mercantile activities before the two forces could come to grips,
clearly he was one of those who helped nudge California permanently into the United States. His account
in *Fore & Aft,* however, skips over a few points – for
example his grounding of the *Moscow* at Bodega,
which so injured the vessel that it began to sink later
at Santa Barbara (with help, Phelps' crew patched it
together). Nor does he discuss his financial concerns,
including the charter of the *Sterling* to Frémont
(Phelps charged him a substantial fee, but collecting
it was another matter). The financial side was under-
standably prominent in Phelps' mind – for which
reason he continued to sell to his old customers, including shot and shell for the struggle against annexation (but Phelps assumed, rightly, that the Californians
would do little with such armaments).[29]

Alas for trade, however; these years were not the
best for mercantile success. The *Moscow's* voyage was
only moderately profitable, though Phelps did surprisingly well considering the wartime conditions. Phelps
was at the same time trying to straighten out the affairs
of the *Sterling,* whose supercargo, Thomas B. Park,
had proved most inefficient. A problem of a different
sort was the *Moscow's* condition; old and unseaworthy
to begin with, the grounding at Bodega completed the
process of deterioration despite emergency repairs and
the vessel was condemned at San Diego in June 1847.
Phelps now sailed north on the *Barnstable* to San Francisco, taking the remaining cargo from the *Moscow*

29 Phelps Papers, vol. 7.

(though he had already sent some of the hides she had collected home via the *Sterling*). In September 1847, with John Paty & Co. he purchased at Monterey the *Malek Adhel,* a former Mexican brig taken as a U.S. prize of war, but sold her at auction less than a year later, by which time Phelps and his crew had gone off to the gold mines. Mining was not to Phelps' taste, however; he longed for home, and his eyes were giving him trouble. In September, he left San Francisco as a passenger on the *Tasso* for Valparaíso, from which port he took an English steamer for Panama, crossed the Isthmus, and boarded a schooner bound for Charleston.[30]

When he reached South Carolina in early 1849, it was to make for home and the snug little farm where he was reasonably content for the next five years. Once again, the sea called, and Phelps set out to fulfill a long-standing ambition, a voyage to China. "I had enjoyed the comforts of home for over five years, felt I was getting rusty and lazy. . ." On Christmas day, 1854, he left Boston in the medium clipper *Arcadia,* bound for California and Canton: "The long route was always my choice." [31]

One hundred and twelve days later, he was in San Pedro, the main problem of the voyage being the initial recruitment of a crew which could be expected to work the vessel and not run for the gold fields. Much had changed in the six years since Phelps last saw California, little, to his eyes, to the good. "I was grieved to find that not a few of the people who, when I was

---

[30] My thanks to Adele Ogden for providing me with the account of Phelps' movements in 1845-48.

[31] *Fore & Aft,* p. 322.

last here, were well to do in lands and cattle, had parted
with their property and become poor, not from any
fault of their own, but through the bad faith of our
government in the action of its Attorney-General [re-
garding land titles] and the sharp practice of newcomers." [32] Since Phelps complained loudly in his
journals of the unproductivity of those same former
owners, obviously he had somewhat moderated his
views over the years.

His California interval was brief, however, for with
one visit to Santa Barbara to discharge cargo, and sad
farewells for friends whom he knew he would see no
more, Phelps and the *Arcadia* were bound away for
China in mid-June 1855. After a necessary call at
Honolulu to replace crew desertions in California, he
pushed on for China. Three months in Shanghai produced a cargo of tea bound around the Cape of Good
Hope. When he docked at New York in March 1856,
it was to retire from the sea and live a peaceful life
in Lexington.

Phelps in his later years lived in a large house on
Massachusetts Avenue; as a man of substance in the
community, he was active in such institutions as the
Five Cent Savings Bank and the Lexington Savings
Bank, of which latter he was a trustee and which first
operated out of a room in his own house. Although
failing health handicapped his last years, Phelps seems
to have enjoyed life, summering each year at Magnolia
on the coast near Gloucester. On April 19, 1875, the
centenary of the battle of Lexington, Phelps like other
home-owners in the town decorated his house from top
to bottom with patriotic pictures, slogans, flags and

[32] *Ibid.*, p. 329.

bunting. This splendid ceremony, attended by President Grant and an estimated 100,000 visitors (another 100,000 attempted to get into the town without success), was the last such celebration for Phelps, for he died that August in Magnolia and was brought back to Lexington for burial.[33] Phelps was survived by his daughter Alice, who married a successful wholesale druggist named Goodwin, and was well known in Lexington society until her death in 1936 at the age of 97.

After retirement, Phelps had not abandoned his literary pursuits. The year 1871 saw the publication of *Fore & Aft,* his entertaining memoirs, which reproduced only selected sections of his California journals. The volume focused upon the Frémont years, but in summary form also described those incidents which he considered to be of interest to the general reader, such as his visits to Sutter's fort at New Helvetia, or the way in which Californians conducted a rodeo. Although often hazy on dates, particularly regarding his own early career, Phelps' book still holds interest as a colorful account of an interesting life. Bancroft, in preparing his *History of California,* found the book most useful (he did not have access to the original journals) : "besides being a most interesting and oft-quoted narrative of personal experiences, [it] contains much useful information about Cal., yet it must be noted that the captain, with all his honesty and zeal, was not on all points an accurate witness." [34]

[33] *The New England Historical and Genealogical Register* (Boston, 1875), XXIX, p. 446; Beverly Allison Kelley, *Lexington, A Century of Photographs* (Lexington, 1980), includes photographs of Phelps' house on April 19, 1875, complete with decorations (p. 85) ; pp. 20-21 provide a picture of Meriam Hill, a well-known mansion in the Lexington area in which Phelps' daughter Alice (Mrs. Charles C. Goodwin) lived until her death.

[34] Bancroft, *History of California,* IV, pp. 775-76.

Although published under the penname "Webfoot," there was no doubt of the author's name to anyone who really cared to know. More questionable has been Phelps' authorship of an unpublished survey of the history of New England's early trade with the northwest coast, entitled "Solid Men of Boston in the Northwest." The manuscript, some seventy-seven leaves, unsigned and undated, is held by the Bancroft Library. The author gives a most useful recapitulation in particular of the activities of Nathan and Jonathan Winship, whose vessel the *Albatross* was important in the Northwest fur-Hawaiian sandalwood-China tea trade. The *Albatross'* voyage was chronicled by Captain Nathan Winship's clerk, William A. Gale. The manuscript also includes valuable information on the sea-otter trade in both Alta and Baja California.

"Solid Men" is without doubt from Phelps' pen. Phelps was a close friend of Gale's, and his access to the log of the *Albatross* is referred to in *For & Aft.*[35] Moreover, several letters to or from Phelps make mention of the manuscript, as for example one to Hubert Bancroft in 1872: "You will see in my account of the early men of the NW that. . ."[36] The manuscript has proved of considerable value to more than one historian, including Samuel Eliot Morison, and the question of authorship should be laid to rest.[37]

---

[35] *Fore & Aft,* p. 354.

[36] Phelps to Bancroft, 5 May 1872, Bancroft Papers, Bancroft Library, C-E 65/24. The Bancroft Library card catalog entry for "Solid Men" notes as well a letter from Samuel Hooper to Phelps, 29 November 1868 (Phelps Papers), from which Adele Ogden had already determined Phelps' authorship.

[37] Samuel Eliot Morison, "Boston Traders in the Hawaiian Islands, 1789-1823," *Mass. Hist. Soc. Proc.,* LIV (1920), 17, n.1; Morison notes that the manuscript "was apparently prepared about the time of the Civil War by

The various journals and papers which Phelps had saved clearly were of service in preparing his undated historical account and his published memoirs, but after Phelps' death, they remained quietly in the family's possession until presented by his daughter to Harvard University in 1927. The collection, some ten volumes of assorted logbooks and account records now in the Houghton Library, has remained unpublished since that time, although used by occasional enquiring scholars.

The two volumes which form the log of the *Alert* are written in commercially-sold leather-backed, lined notebooks, rather than the patent ship logbooks which were available with spaces for recording watch changes, latitude and longitude, and the like. The first, and shorter volume (as Phelps makes clear, he concluded it in order to send it home to his wife when opportunity arrived), begins with the *Alert's* departure from Boston on January 22, 1840. The voyage out to California was not unusual in any way, and the short daily or weekly entries have not been reproduced until June 27, when Phelps made his landfall at Monterey. Aside from a list of his crew (twenty-two all told including Phelps, his first mate G. C. Everett, and his supercargo Alfred Robinson) which approximates that given in Appendix I, Phelps merely records sailing conditions: "Variable winds with heavy rains. Ship making but slow progress. . . ." His course took him to the westward of the Falkland Islands and then between Staten Land and Diego Ramirez. Damage to the rudder forced the *Alert* to put in to Valparaíso for repairs, but

someone who knew the Winships well, and who had access to their records," but does not name Phelps.

the job was soon done and after that it was clear sailing.

The journal account of the passage home which concludes Part II has been omitted for the same reason. After his departure on December 30, 1842, Phelps soon found that his vessel was rather "crank" running before a wind, since his cargo of hides had settled a good deal. Presumably they had not been squeezed in with maximum efficiency, but shifting a few hundred from his 'tween decks to his hold and striking the guns down off the deck improved the *Alert's* sailing qualities. Aside from one mishap off the Brazil coast, when the *Alert,* ghosting along with all studding sails set was taken full aback by a sudden squall (the only cost was smashed cabin windows and a cabin full of water), this passage was equally unremarkable. Phelps' final entry is for May 4:

> 5 PM Nausett Light bore NW dist about 12 miles. At 7 PM the sun set in splendour behind Yankee Land, a sight we have not seen for years. Of course all on board as in high glee at the prospect of being in Boston Bay tomorrow morning which we shall be if the breeze continues (please God). After the decks were cleared up (the Tarring and Painting being finished) the crew cleared out their old duds overboard, Jackets, Shirts, &c which a few days ago were valuable to the owners were now thrown away and for about a mile ornamented the ships wake.

Phelps' handwriting, through both volumes, fortunately is normally quite clear, though on occasion, when in a hurry, or running short of ink, or simply to squeeze a word in at the end of a line, readings of particular words are questionable. Whenever this is the case, I have so indicated by a bracketed question mark or explanatory note. Brackets denote words or phrases added by the editor; parentheses are Phelps' own. I have attempted to keep the flavor of Phelps' language throughout, retaining his rather erratic capitalization (typical of the era in which he wrote) and spelling. Punctuation, however, is usually guesswork, and it is often impossible to tell periodization from imperfections in the paper. I have supplied commas and periods where they seemed appropriate, therefore; apostrophes, however, were generally foreign to Phelps and they have not been added. Chapter headings are also supplied by the editor.

A word remains to be said about footnotes. I have adopted the policy of indicating in a note any aspect of the text requiring explanation, regarding either the form of the manuscript or any word, name, or term which may be unfamiliar to readers. I have attempted to give a brief sketch of each individual mentioned in California for whom I have more information than that given by Phelps, though I have not so treated such well-known figures as Sutter or Frémont. Data on vessels encountered on the coast will be found in Appendix III; for clarity, vessel names have been italicized throughout although Phelps did not follow this practice. Place names are noted only when particularly obscure (the editor, born and raised in California, has used his own subjective judgment on what constitutes "obscure"), but all are indicated where possible on the maps. Beyond that, however, I have tried to preserve the flow of events – an attitude which I think Captain Phelps, who delighted in storytelling, would have approved.

Volume I

On the California Coast
June 1840 to April 10, 1841

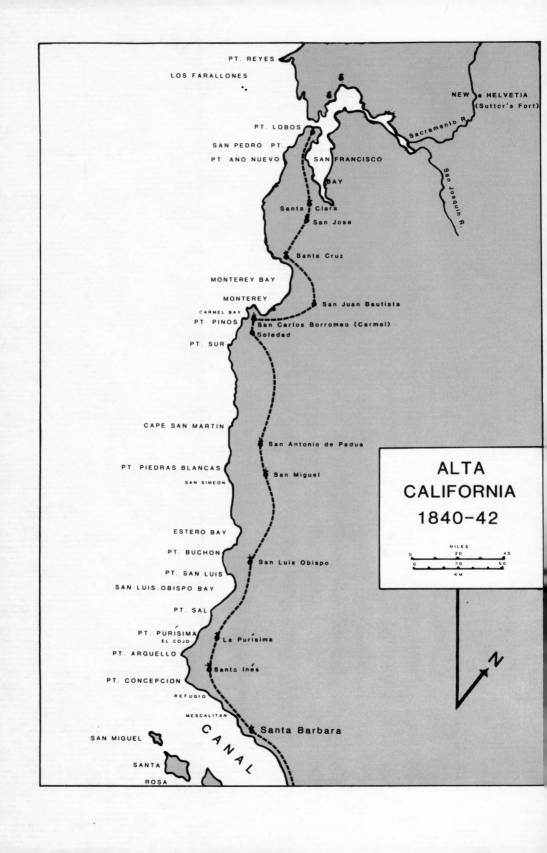

PT. REYES

LOS FARALLONES

NEW • HELVETIA
(Sutter's Fort)

Sacramento R.

San Joaquin R.

PT. LOBOS

SAN PEDRO PT.

PT. AÑO NUEVO
SAN FRANCISCO

BAY

Santa Clara

San Jose

Santa Cruz

MONTEREY BAY

MONTEREY

San Juan Bautista

CARMEL BAY

PT. PINOS
San Carlos Borromeo (Carmel)

Soledad

PT. SUR

CAPE SAN MARTIN

San Antonio de Padua

PT. PIEDRAS BLANCAS

SAN SIMEON
San Miguel

ESTERO BAY

PT. BUCHON

PT. SAN LUIS
San Luis Obispo

SAN LUIS OBISPO BAY

PT. SAL

PT. PURÍSIMA

EL COJO
La Purísima

PT. ARGUELLO

Santa Inés

PT. CONCEPCION

REFUGIO

MESCALITAN

CANAL

SAN MIGUEL
Santa Barbara

SANTA

ROSA

ALTA
CALIFORNIA
1840-42

MILES
0   20   40

0   20   60
KM

N

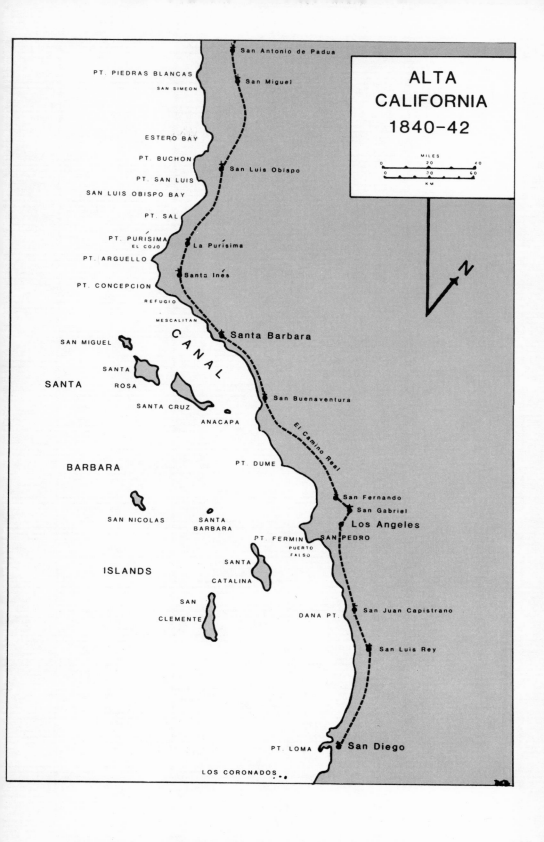

ALTA
CALIFORNIA
1840-42

MILES
0   20   40
0   30   60
KM

N

PT. PIEDRAS BLANCAS
SAN SIMEON

San Antonio de Padua

San Miguel

ESTERO BAY

PT. BUCHON

San Luis Obispo

PT. SAN LUIS

SAN LUIS OBISPO BAY

PT. SAL

PT. PURISIMA
EL COJO
PT. ARGUELLO

La Purísima

Santa Inés

PT. CONCEPCION

REFUGIO

MESCALITAN

CANAL

Santa Barbara

SAN MIGUEL

SANTA
ROSA

SANTA

SANTA CRUZ

ANACAPA

San Buenaventura

El Camino Real

BARBARA

PT. DUME

SAN NICOLAS

SANTA
BARBARA

San Fernando
San Gabriel
Los Angeles

PT. FERMIN

SAN PEDRO

PUERTO
FALSO

SANTA
CATALINA

ISLANDS

SAN

CLEMENTE

DANA PT.

San Juan Capistrano

San Luis Rey

PT. LOMA

San Diego

LOS CORONADOS

The First Coastal Passage

Monterey to San Diego and Return to San Francisco, and a Visit to the Pueblo of Los Angeles

JUNE 27th [1840]. Judging Cape New Year which forms the West side of Monterey Bay to bear E b N Dist 21 Miles at Midnight. Shortened sail to stand off & on until daylight when we found ourselves about seven miles WNW of the above Cape. The land high & covered with wood. Made sail and kept away across the Bay.

SUNDAY 28th. Moderate Breezes & foggy. At 9 A M saw the shipping in Monterey Harbour, & at 10 anchored in 5 fathoms water, the flag staff on the Fort bearing WbN. Found lying here the Ship *California* belonging to our owners, the U S Ship of War *St. Louis* cmd. by Capt Forest [Forrest] and a French Corvette, and a Mexican Schr. The men of War are here in consequence of the Californian Government sending the foreign residents away from the country in an arbitrary and illegal manner. There were about forty of them here, some were men who had assisted the Govt in their troubles and fought and bled in their service. Some – American trappers who had found their way across the mountains and remained here, others were discharged seamen, American & English, mostly poor

but many respectable. These have been sent away in
irons to Acapulco, wihout a hearing or trial of any
kind. The news of this outrage was conveyed to St
Blass [San Blas] were [where] these Ships of War were
lying. They immediately got under weigh & proceeded
to this place to investigate the matter. An official correspondence is going on, and depositions being taken
of the foreign residents who remain (for they have not
troubled the higher classes) and it is uncertain what
the consequence will be. The Frenchman is prepared
to demolish the town if he finds that one Frenchman
was among those sent away. The American is not vested
with such high authority, but the Californians appear
to feel quite ill at ease, with two ships of war lying
within pistol shot of their town demanding redress.[1]

WEDNES. JULY 1st.   The entry having been made, and
the cargo having been examined by the Custom House
officers, we are now filling up the shelves and preparing the Trading Room for business. Received some
visits from Traders to day & effected sales to about
$2,500. Also transhipped some goods to the *California*

---

[1] Phelps here refers to the "Graham Affair." In April 1840 Isaac Graham
and some 50 other foreigners were arrested for plotting to overthrow the
Governor, Juan Bautista Alvarado, and sent off to San Blas, Mexico, most
returning over a year later. Charges of general troublemaking by the foreigner element – in addition to the supposed plot – were answered by charges
of brutality towards the prisoners. It is not necessary here to enter into the
details of the case; Phelps' one-sided account, however, should be corrected
by a reading of Hubert Howe Bancroft, *History of California,* vol. IV, Ch. 1
(San Francisco, 1886, reprint Santa Barbara, 1969). The French vessel
referred to was the sloop-of-war *Danaïde,* which arrived on 11 June, and,
as Phelps reports, sailed again on 2 July, after finding no Frenchmen were
involved. Governor Alvarado, in deference to obviously superior firepower,
retreated to his rancho at Alisal, 25 miles away [near present Salinas],
for the duration of the intervention.

Data for ships, encountered by Phelps on the California coast will be
found in Appendix III.

for the Windward Ports. The Governor finding himself pressed pretty hard by the American Cap'ns, with officios [official communications], had cleared out upon pretence of an insurrection among the Indians in the interior demanding his presence – he had backed out. The Frenchman finding there were no subjects of France sent away, had nothing further to do here, and sails tomorrow for the Sandwich Islands.

THURSDAY JULY 2d. The weather at this season of the year cannot be said to be pleasant at Monterey. The winds prevail at from West to NW and blow fresh during the middle of the day, but is moderate at night. The mornings always foggy, clearing up about 10 or 11 AM and remaining pleasant untill about 4 PM when the cold fog again sets in and continues through the night.

The French Ship of War sailed to day for the S. [Sandwich] Islands. It is said that she has the money on board that was extorted from the Gov't of the Islands a few months since with orders to refund it. The Governor of California still absents himself. He is said to be at the Mission of San Juan, where he will probably remain till the *St. Louis* sails. The Amer. officers are highly indignant at his conduct. A statement of facts will be made to the Commander on the Station and it is expected that the American and British ships in these seas will soon be here to settle the business. As it is now, there is no security to foreign residents.

FRIDAY 3rd. We have been engaged in trading to some considerable amount the last two days. All [engaged] in repairing sails & etc. *California* sailed for Sd. Isds.

SAT 4th. The cutter was sent to fish this morning off

Pt. Pinos and returned at 10 A M with an abundance
of cod, large red rock fish, and a variety of others. At
11 A M the *St. Louis* got under weigh for St. Blass
at noon being about a mile to the N W of the anchorage she fired a National Salute in honor of the 64th
Anniversary of the Declaration of Independence. We
returned the salute, both ships having the national flag
at the Main & Mizen & Peak, with the English at
the Fore, there being an English Ship in the bay with
her national colors displayed with the Stars and Stripes
at the Fore. The *St. Louis* had left without her Capt
having any interview with the Govr. in the meantime
Mr. Estabrook [2] of the *St. Louis* had been left, vested
to act as Consular Agent. Gave part of the crew liberty
on shore. Dined in company with a number of American & English gentlemen at the house of Thos. O.
Larkin Esq.[3] an American resident here.

SUNDAY 5th. The Starboard Watch on liberty on
shore. The big Church of the Presidio is the only place
of Public worship in Monterey. The Catholic the only

2 Ethan Estabrook was left as Consular Agent in 1840, but was not recognized by local authorities as possessing any particular authority; he sailed
for Mazatlán in 1841. Bancroft, *History of California,* II, p. 792; further
references to individuals, unless otherwise noted, are to be found in the
Pioneer Register located in Bancroft, vols. II-V.

3 Thomas Oliver Larkin, born in 1802, arrived in California in 1832, to
join his half-brother in commercial activity. By the time of his death in 1858
in San Francisco, he had become one of the leading Californians of his era,
active in every sort of enterprise from flour mills to lumber to real estate,
in addition to being the first and last American Consul in California. See,
in addition to the applicable volumes of his papers *(The Larkin Papers,*
vol. I-V, Berkeley, 1951-55), Robert J. Parker, "Larkin, Anglo-American
Businessman in Mexican California," in Adele Ogden, ed., *Greater America:
Essays in Honor of Herbert Eugene Bolton* (Berkeley, 1945), 415-29, and
Reuben L. Underhill, *From Cowhides to Golden Fleece: a Narrative of
California, 1832-1858, Based Upon Unpublished Correspondence of Thomas
Oliver Larkin* (Stanford, 1939).

religion tolerated of course we protestants are termed heretics. During the stay of the French Man of War here, the officers were more or less of them continually on shore and with that gaity and ease peculiar to the French, visited at every house laughing chatting and dancing with every pretty girl in the place, and of course found great favour in the eyes of the fair sex. One morning during some service to the Holy Virgin performing at the Church of the Mission by all the virgins of the place, in came a bevy of young officers to assist them in their devotions. The old priest ordered them out, saying that they only came for the purpose of coquetting with the girls. Thereupon rose a tumult, the virgin devotees exclaiming let them stay, they came with pious feelings and are better Christians than we. Let them stay – they did – and afterwards escorted them home. The watch on liberty returned on board at sundown, and the remainder of the crew were permitted to go on shore for recreation.

MONDAY 6th.   It being the first opportunity they have had for six months. They all returned on board at proper time and in good order.

TUES. 7th.   Sales were effected to a considerable amount, and some hides were taken on board. Mr. Everett went on shore with the cutter & killed a Bullock for ships use.   4 P M the yawl was sent to cut some light spars, permission to do so being first obtained of the Alcalda. Part of the crew employed in watering. The streams are mainly dry at this season, and the only way we can obtain good water is to bail it up with dippers.

WED. 8th.   Employed in making sales of goods, filling

water & repairing sails. The Carpenter commenced cauking [sic] the Decks. Among our customers to day were an Old Lady, housekeeper to the Govern. and her Daughter of about 18. Their purchases were small but was not completed without a great deal of tact. The young lady no doubt thought herself a Beauty, judging from her coquettish manner. They both evidently came to spend the day, and after dinner keeled themselves upon the Cabin lockers and went to sleep. At sundown they were whipped [4] over the side & went on shore.

THURS. 9th.   This day some sales of cargo have been effected, and a ton of hides taken on board. The carpenter caulking the deck. Took my gun and started on a ramble over the hills, found some strawberries & blackberries; the season for them is nearly over, but whortleberries are abundant, but not quite ripe. Bagged nine Partridges and three Pidgeons [sic] and returned on board about 4 P M. The country about Monterey is agreeably broken by hills & vallies having a verdant appearance. The hills are crowned with trees mostly of the pine tribe, with clumps of scrub oaks & the surface of the vallies & plains covered with rich feed for cattle, but I have not seen enough of the country yet to speak of its character, soil, & productions. I can only say now, that its general appearance is pleasant.

This day has been the warmest we have experienced since being here. The C 74 in the shade. Employed in filling water, repairing old sails & making sales of goods.   5 P M went upon the Hills & picked a considerable quantity of Berries. Got the Launch in & stowed. Employed in restowing the Hold & getting ready for sea. Sent the cutter a fishing at daylight and

[4] Author's note: "hoisted over in a chair."

4 Boys a berrying. At 11 A M the Cutter returned with about 200 fine Large Fish, and the Boys returned at dark with a good lot of berries. Part of the crew were permitted to go on shore to wash their clothes at the watering place.

SAT. JULY 11th. Pleasant & Warm. Unmoored Ship and dropt out in fair way. The 2nd officer was sent with the cutter & a crew to fish & returned with a large quantity some of which resembled the cod of our own coast. Went on shore myself and was again successful in getting a mess of pidgeons. The Govr returned to Monterey immediately after the departure of the *St. Louis.* Mr. Eastabrook [Estabrook] the Gent. left by Capt. Forest as Vice Consul, dined on board of our Ship to-day, and informed me that officios are passing between his Excelly, and himself and that as yet the Gov. refuses to acknowledge him in his public capacity.

SUN 12th. Sailed for Sta. Barbara with a breeze from West and beat about in the Bay all day & night without being able to weather Point Pinos.

MON 13. Foggy with SW winds. Ship beating to windward without gaining much.

14th & 15th. The wind prevailing from the Southern quarter with thick heavy fog. 6 P M passed Point Conception.

THURS 16th. Anchored at Sta Barbara in 7 fathoms found the *Monsoon* lying here just arrived from the Leeward ports. At 9 AM went on shore Dined at the Commadants Don   Noreiga.[5] Found at his house

---

[5] Phelps here left spaces to fill in the other names of José de la Guerra y Noriega, a leading resident of California, who had arrived in a military capacity in 1801, retiring from a long life of service in 1842, but remaining

an American Lady, A towns-woman of my own. Mrs.
Stevens,[6] wife of Cap'n S. now at San Francisco. The
Comat. has a very large family and has one daughter
married to Mr. Robinson [7] my supercargo, another to
an English Gent. Enjoyed an excellent dinner and a
number of hours conversation with Mrs. S. and returned on board towards sundown. Sent the 2d officer
& 4 men to kill a bullock. Met Mr. Shaw [8] supercargo
of the *Monsoon* on shore & gave him the latest news
of his family.

a grand patriarch of Santa Barbara until his death in 1858. Unusually, he
was called "Captain Noriega," an affectation adopted by at least one of
his sons; the name is that of his mother's family. Bancroft, *California,*
III, 769-71; William Heath Davis, *Seventy-Five Years in California* (San
Francisco, 1967), 312.

6 Mrs. James Stevens clearly was a favorite among the leading foreigners
along the California coast. Married to Captain Stevens, master of several
vessels including the *Leónidas* and *Bolivar,* Mrs. S. was often to be found
in the company of Larkin, Robinson, Phelps, and others in the early 1840's.
She seems, however, to have become something of a liability; by 1841, it
was suggested to her that she should return to the east coast. By 1845,
Larkin, offered to pay half her passage; in 1846, she reached the point
of loading her baggage aboard a vessel bound home, but changed her mind
at the last minute, sailing finally on the *Admittance* in 1846 – with Larkin
paying half, and John Coffin Jones the other. (Robinson to Larkin, 18
August 1841; Larkin to J. C. Jones, 26 August 1845; John Batista Rogers
Cooper to Larkin, 18 January 1846; and Jones to Larkin, 26 January 1846;
Larkin Papers, I, p. 111; III, p. 324; IV, pp. 167, 185.)

7 Alfred Robinson, or Don Alfredo as he was known in California, played
an important role in California-Boston mercantile associations. Arriving
in 1829 at the age of 22, Robinson served for many years as clerk and
supercargo for Bryant, Sturgis & Co. A convert to Catholicism, he married
a daughter of José de la Guerra y Noriega, Ana Maria; the gala affair
was attended by Dana, and is described in *Two Years,* Ch. XXVII. Robinson
later was an investor in Bryant, Sturgis vessels, and in 1839 returned to
California on the *Alert* to take charge of the company's interests. His journal
of the voyage is in the Bancroft Library (74/116/c.27-8). It provides cor-
roboration of all important details, but few observations of the sort made
by Phelps.

8 Thomas Shaw reached California in the 1820's, and was clerk and supercargo for several vessels, including the *Monsoon,* 1839-41.

FRIDAY 17th. The weather at this place is much pleasanter than at Monterey there is but little fog and on passing Pt. Conception one feels that he has changed climates. To-day some sales of goods were effected. 500 hides were taken on board. The carpenter employed caucking decks. Sent the boat after Lobsters 25 was successful. Went on shore and visited a number of American risidents [sic] found them all very hospitable & friendly. Rode up to the mission of Sta Barbara. Of these missions more hereafter.

SAT 18th. Employed variously: viz: selling & discharging goods & taking in hides, repairing sails, caucking the decks &c. Part of the Crew on liberty.

SUN. 19th. All Hands at Rest. The *Bolivar* from Windward arrived today.

MON. JULY 20th. Continuation of warm & pleasant weather. Employed as usual, Trading &c. Many visiters [*sic*] on board during the day.

TUES 21st. Sent the 2d officer & 4 men to cut wood on shore. Killed a Bullock for Ships use. Went a shooting towards evening & met with good sport, returned with a good bunch of Pigeons, Partridges & Curlews. The cutter was also successful in Lobster fishing. Received on board a quantity of hides.

WED 22d. This day part of the Crew employed in cutting wood others filling water. The Lady & Daughter & Son of the Comadent [sic] also Mrs Stevens dined on board to day. The day was pleasantly spent. The *Bolivar* sailed in the afternoon for Sta Pedro, and the *Monsoon* in the evening for St. Louis [Luis]. One of our woodcutters left his work in the morning & probably deserted. The 2d officer in charge of the gang saw an Indian woman clearing out with his axe which was the first intimation he had of the Man's being missing. She was overhauled however & the axe recovered. The natives are great thieves.

THURS 23rd. All hands engaged in Wooding, Watering & repairing Sails. One man injured by a fall from a tree. The deserter of yesterday returned Hungry & Humble, & was accepted.

FRIDAY 24th. Employed as yesterday. Got an Indian with a Bullock Cart to draw the wood that had been cut to the beach. Took my gun in the afternoon and visited the wood cutters & while there shot a number of Pidgeons & Quail, and a Fox.

SAT. 25th. Wooding & Watering & restowing the Hold. The firewood we obtained here is scrub oak which grow in the vallies & on the hill sides, the limbs of which we chop off to leave the trunk standing. The trunks are very knotty & would not pay for the trouble of felling the tree. The wood we bring in a bullock cart about two miles to the boats. The carts are the most miserable concerns. A description of these vehicles & their manner of working cattle will be given hereafter.

SUN. 26th. Part of the crew on liberty, the remainder at rest. Receiving an invitation to visit the Commadent's garden, I went on shore in the afternoon for that purpose (although I always prefer remaining on board my ship on the sabbath unless I can associate with those on shore who keep the day Holy and in this country I expect to find none such among the foreign residents). On my way to the house of the Commandant I noticed that a number of the stores of the foreign residents were closed. I was glad to see it and thought I should find that the owners paid more respect to the Lord's day than I had imagined they did. I was glad to indulge in the pleasing hope that New Englanders (and there are quite a number there) however far they have wandered from the homes of their childhood had not lost the sabbath day feelings inherited from our Pilgrim Fathers by the way. But alas seeing one store open I thought I would look in and see how its inmates were occupied, and here were the persons (I wish I could call them Gentlemen) whose stores were closed, playing at cards, and hailed my entrance with blasphemous expressions of joy as one that would join them in their impious pastime. I need not say that I soon left them, or with what feelings. In company with the Comdt Sr Noreiga, the Padre President of the Missions,[9] & Don Alfredo Robinson, visited the gardens of the first named Gent. situated near the edge of the valley and covering about 10 or 12 acres. There were many grape vines with decent clusters of green grapes, but so thickly cultivated that about ½ of them are spoiling for the want of sun and air. There are many Pear trees of an inferior kind with some dwarf apple trees, but for the want of pruning and thinning are of no value. The Fig Tree also would apparently be very productive here if properly cultivated and in short the whole garden presented a confused mixture of Fruit trees, vegetables, & Flowers set out with-

9 The Padre President, or supervisor of the missions, was presumably Padre Joaquín Jimeno, president of the southern missions as of 1838. Phelps might mean, however, the more widely known Franciscan, Padre Narciso Durán, who was president before 1838, and remained prefect of the southern mission (both resided in Santa Barbara). See Bancroft, IV, p. 63.

out order or taste and growing without care or cultivation, unprofitable to the owner, and unpleasing to
one who has been accustomed to a better state of things.
I could not praise any thing ·in the Don's garden, but
some beautiful olive trees, these were straiter [sic] and
handsomer than any of the kind I ever saw in the
Mediterranean, and were in good bearing, but these
were not much indebted to air for their thirsty appearance, and would have been much improved by
trimming. Weeds similar to those that would grow in
the gardens & fields of a yankee farmer (if he would
let them) were here very abundant and thrive to admiration in all parts of the premises, & with none to
molest or make afraid!

The liberty men returned on board at sundown in
good order. The Cmdt. has prohibited the selling of
ardent spirits from the shops here on the Sabbath for
which he ought to receive the grateful thanks of every
Ship-Master visiting the place.

MONDAY 27th.   Employed in Wooding & taking on
board Hides. Killed a Bullock for Ships use. Sent the
cutter after Craw Fish & was successful in obtaining
about 40 they taste similar to our Lobsters, and resemble them in size & formation with the exception
that they are destitute of the two large claws which our
Lobsters possess.

The day has been warm & pleasant.

MONDAY JULY 28th.[10]   Took on board some Hides &
Tallow. Discharged some cargo & got ready for Sea.
Latter part foggy.

---

[10] Phelps here repeats the day of the week twice; the 27th was in fact
Monday, and Phelps catches his error only on August 5th, by giving both
Tuesday and Wednesday the same date.

TUES. 29th. Ready for sea but waiting advices [i.e., news or instructions]. Carpenter repairing the Yawl. A Mexican bark arrived this forenoon. Heard to-day that the S. Sea Expedition [11] had arrived at Monterey. Shot two beautiful large Birds to-day of the Stork species, about two feet high and of a damask colour, spoon bill.

WEDNES. 30th. Made some sales of Goods & got some Hides.

THURS. 31. Weather very warm. Killed a Bullock.

FRIDAY AUG 1st. 3 P M Sailed for St Pedro.

SAT 2d. 4 P M Came too [sic] at St Pedro. Blowing strong from NW. The Chain got foul & the anchor dragged hove up & stood out to sea. Latter part calm.

SUND. 3rd. 9 A M fresh breezes from NW beat up and at Noon came to anchor in 5 fathoms, paid out 70 fathoms chain. Mr Robinson started for the Pueblo. Found the *Bolivar* here.

MON 4. Went up the creek & killed a fine mess of curlew. Sent the 2d officer & some men to kill a Bullock. Strong winds & clear.

TUES 5th. Nothing transacting on board. Sent our boat a filling & went with the cutter myself on an excursion up a creek that makes up from the Bay of St. Pedro passing the Bar on which there is about 9 feet of water at high tide we came into water deep enough for a large Ship, and room enough for 12 ships to lie at secure anchorage in any winds, completely

---

[11] Phelps refers to the exploring expedition of six ships led by Charles Wilkes, 1838-42. See William Stanton, *The Greater United States Exploring Expedition of 1838-1842* (Berkeley, 1975).

landlocked. The channel runs up for a number of miles, but having no lead & line in the boat did not get much as much [*sic*] acquaintance with its channels as I intend to hereafter. Shot a number of curlew Rabbits & a Hair Seal. The 2d cutter was successful in fishing.

WEDNES. 5th. Employed in surveying the Bay & Creek of St. Pedro. Found a small island in the Bay a solitary grave which I presume to belong to some wanderer of ocean whose bones after his life of hard toil has ended are left to bleach on a foreign strand [Dead Man's Island; now removed].

THURS. 6th. Completed the Survey of the Creek. Caught some fish & killed a number of curlews. A number of traders came in from the Country to-day and made some considerable purchases.

The Wind every afternon since we have been here has been strong from WSW. moderating at Sundown.

FRIDAY AUG 7th. Employed in selling goods. Taking on board Hides & Tallow, & various other work. Went in the afternoon to shoot Rabbits, returned with 5 & 1 Plover.

SAT. 8th. This day spent much the same as yesterday. Sold & landed some goods & received some Hides. Among the visitors today were two women who had come 30 miles in a Bullock cart bringing a Quantity of Hides & Tallow which they bartered with us for goods.

Sent the Yawl a fishing & was successful.

SUNDAY 9th. The day observed as circumstances permitted, but not to my own satisfaction. The Sabbath is not observed by Foreigners or Catholics in this country enough to distinguish it from other days of the week.

MON 10th. Landed some Cargo & took on board a quantity of Hides & Tallow. Killed a Bullock.

TUES. 11th. Employed in Trading, landing goods &c. Received 291 Hides & 4 Bags Tallow.

WED. 12th. No Traders off. Sent the Yawl fishing & went up the Creek myself in the Cutter gunning. Shot 19 Rabbits & a Large Wolf.

THURS. AUG 13th. No business doing on board. Mr Robinson started at 4 PM for the Pueblo, The Village of the Angels (Pueblo de los Angeles). It is about 30 miles from the port of St Pedro & is represented to be a pleasant & very fertile place. I have not visited it yet but intend doing so on my return from St. Diego. The country in the near neighbourhood of the port is dry & steril without wood or vegetation. The ground is covered as far as the eye extends with a kind of wild mustard which grows as high as a mans head. It is now dead and dry. Here is but one house and that at the landing place which is kept as a stopping place for traders and a depot for Hides & Tallow. All the goods that are landed are carried up a steep bank & all that are taken off thrown off the bank, or lowered down.

FRIDAY 14th. The cutter was sent to fish at daylight and returned at noon successful. Took an excursion up the creek & shot some Rabbits & Birds. No business done to day.

SAT. 15th. No Traders to day. Had little party on board to dinner consisting of Mr. Foster [Forster] & Wife, Mrs. Warner, a Sandwich Island Lady, wife of an American, their children, & Capt. Nye of the *Bolivar*.[12]

SUNDAY 16th. Part of the Crew on Liberty, the remainder at rest. At sundown the liberty men returned.

MON 17th. No Traders down. Killed a Bullock. In the afternoon with Capt Nye went up the creek in pursuit of game. Returned at dusk with 22 Rabbits, some squirrels & Birds.

TUESDAY 18th. Employed in making sails for the Pinnace and overhauling the Ships Stores.

WEDNESDAY 19th. Nothing doing in the business line, no Traders making their appearance. This month is what is called the Mantanza season, or the time of slaughtering. The cattle are fattest during this month, and are slaughtered in great numbers. Most of the meat is left for the Birds & Beasts, the Hide & Tallow being all that is considered of any value. The Hide brings $2 in goods and the Tallow $8 per 100*d* [hundred weight]. The Bullock produces about 50 lb. The price of a good Bullock is from 6 to 8 dollars (in goods) making it about $4 [i.e., in real value of goods], a first rate cow & calf from 3 to 5 dollars.

Sent the 2d officer with the Cutter a fishing in the morning, and she returned in the afternoon having been very successful.

One of the seamen deserted last night taking his

---

12 John Forster reached California in 1828 as a sea captain. For some years he was a shipping agent and sometimes captain of the port of San Pedro. From 1840 to 1844, he was manager of Abel Stearns' properties and business at that port. In 1844 he settled on an ex-mission estate in San Juan Capistrano, where he lived for many years. Married to a sister of Pio Pico, a prominent Californian (Governor, 1845-46), Forster was a man of considerable wealth and eminence.

Jonathan T. Warner came to California in 1831; sometime agent for Larkin, he was principally a trapper and land grantee in the San Diego area.

Gorham Hayden Nye was well known as a master of several vessels including the *Bolivar* (1840-43) and the *Fama* (1843-46).

clothes & stealing others, His name on the articles as John Williams, a poor miserable creature whose appetite for ardent spirits which could not be gratified on board ship was the only cause that can be assigned for his desertion. He ran away at Sta Barbara, and staid two days untill nearly starved when upon promise of amendment I received him on board again, but I hope now he has gone for good. I am almost discouraged in trying to benefit seamen, by advice or persuasion. They are convinced while they abstain from the use of liquor that they are better off, and at sea, or when going on shore they will promise to not touch it, but at night they will often return on board, beraft [sic] of reason, such I am sorry to say has been the case with a number of my best sailors and from whom I had reason to hope for better things. Reason with them the next morning they say. We were urged to drink by landsmen, and could not refuse. If left to their own wills I do not believe they would seek for strong drink, but in all sea ports there are a class of Brute to be found who seem to think that poor Jack has no right to act for himself when on shore and very kindly take the trouble of him themselves and with the strongest assurances of friendship ply him with Rum untill they can make whatever use of him they like, which generally is to rob him of his money strip him of his clothes & turn him a drift.

THURSDAY AUG 20th. This is a *granda festa* [fiesta] *day* with the Catholics in honor of some Saint or other, I don't know who and is to be celebrated by Horse racing and gambling at the *Pueblo*. Feeling no desire to be present I went on an exploring trip with the 2d Cutter up the creek and discovered a new inlet from

the Sea about 8 miles from the only one heretofore
supposed to exist. The wind was blowing strong on
shore, with much swell, preventing from ascertaining
the soundings, but to all appearance there is sufficient
to allow a small vessel to enter. The middle of the entrance bore from Point Fermin SSW per comp. about
9 Miles dist.

FRIDAY 21st.   The principal Race at the Pueblo yesterday or the one that was to have taken place, was a
grand failure. One of the horses had been groomed
by an Englishman and put in proper trim for running,
but it seems that the owner of the horse (a Californian)
believed the Englishman had put some charm on him
by which he was to be beaten, and the Priest of the
Mission was sent for to bless the Horse & remove the
charm. The ground was also consecrated on which the
race was to take place and many holes were dug around
the enclose and filled with salt (previously blessed by
the Priest) and many wax tapers burnt about the legs
of the poor animal to counteract the evil doings of the
Heretic Englishman, by which last act of piety the
horse was so badly burnt as to completely cripple him
& of course would not run. Others were run but of less
amount. The distance is about 300 yards. The Natives
are fond of the sport & bid high. One of the bets yesterday or stakes were 300 Cows 50 Pair of Oxen 40
Mares 100 Horses & 100 bbls of Arguadente [Aguar-
diente] (Rum).[13]

---

[13] *Aguardiente* is referred to several times in Phelps' journals; "rum"
is a somewhat misleading translation, however, for what would better be
called brandy. Distilled from fermented grapes, it was a colorless clear
liquor, rather like pure alcohol at first, but took on patina and thickness
with age, and reaching – according to Davis (*Seventy-Five Years*, 92) –
at age 10 a "fine amber color, and was then a rich, oily liquor, very pal-

SAT 22d. Took on board 150 Hides, some bags of Tallow & killed a Bullock for Ships use & in the afternoon sailed for St. Diego.

SUNDAY 23d. Running down the coast with a light breeze from NW. At Night becalmed off Pt. Loma.

MONDAY 24th. At 9 AM a light breeze from SW bore away for the Port of St. Diego. @ 10:30 came to anchor in 5 fathoms water. Furled sails, discharged some hides, and landed all the spare spars. Found laying here the Schr. *Moss* formerly U.S. Rev. Cutter.[14]

TUES. 25th. Delivered 1800 Hides at the Hide House to be cured, & landed part of our live stock to remain & increase while the Ship remains on the coast.

WEDNES. 26th. Restowed the Hold & cleaned Ship. The sein was drawn for fish but without success. Got ready for sailing.

THURS. AUG 27. Fine breezes & pleasant. Killed a Bullock for Ships use. Unmoored Ship & got ready to sail in the morning, but was detained upon business. In the afternoon, went a gunning but had poor luck. Killed a very large Rattlesnake having 13 rattles in his tail. I am told that they are very numerous on this coast but although I have been much in the woods and about on the Hills & Plains this is the only one I have met with as yet.

FRIDAY 28th. Sailed with the band breeze at 10 A M in company with the *Moss* for St. Pedro. At 10.30

---

atable." Needless to say, it could be drunk well before reaching the age of ten.

[14] Phelps' manuscript says here and below very clearly *"Moss"* but no vessel of that name has been traced; Phelps undoubtedly meant the Schooner *Morse* (renamed *Nymph,* but had the name slightly wrong).

passed Pt. Loma. At dark about 15 Miles to the NW of the Pt. The *Moss* 2 Miles to WSW.

SAT. 29. Beating to windward against light winds from NW, The *Moss* in Company.

SUNDAY 30th. At 4 PM came to anchor in St. Pedro, the *Moss* anchored about the same time.

MON 31st. All Hands cleaning Ship inside & out & painting the Gig.

TUES. SEPT 1st. Received some Hides & Killed a Bullock for Ships use. Varnished the Decks.

WEDNES. 2d. Sent the Cutter fishing. People employed in Varnishing Decks &c.

THURS 3d. No business doing in buying or selling. Hides are scarce, and hardly any goods in demand. Went up the Creek hunting, shot 16 Rabbits, 1 Wolf & 2 Rattlesnakes.

FRIDAY SEPT 4th. Some sales effected today and a few Hides & some Tallow received. Among the Traders on board to-day were three Ladies, one of them young & pretty. The Californian Ladies do not come up to the Yankee Ladies in beating down prices of goods. They are generally willing to pay the prices asked and they are not *slow.*

SAT 5th. Received some Hides & Tallow. Took in the Launch & Stowed her. Started for the Pueblo.

SUN 6th-WED 9 [15]

THURS 10. Returned from the Pueblo de los Angelos or the Village of the Angels, containing about 200 Houses & about 2500 inhabiants (native Foreign &

---

[15] Phelps here gives the dates, but no entries.

Indian), is about 30 miles from the Port, has a good road leading to it and a extensive plain, the most part of it covered with wild mustard among which Herds of cattle which formerly almost covered the plains find abundant feed, about 15 miles from the Port. The country presents a more fertile appearance, the vegetation which is dry & yellow at this season of dryness in the vicinity of the port is at this distance abundantly watered. The ground is covered with perpetual green and spotted with cattle grazing in all directions. About 1 League from the Village we stopped at the Vineyard of a Yankee by the name of Wolfskill and partook of some refreshment.[16] At 8 P M we stopped at the house of Don Abel Sterns [Stearns] a native of Boston but long resident in this country.[17] At his hospitable house we were entertained during our stay at the Pueblo & received much information from him with regard to the condition & prospects of California. He computes California to contain 400,000 square miles & being capable of supporting 7 or 8 millions of inhabitants. He was one of the principal actors in the late revolution which resulted in their ridding themselves of a Mexican Governor and electing a Native to the office.

---

[16] William Wolfskill (1798-1866), originally a Kentuckian, settled in the late 1830's in the Los Angeles area, and became one of the leading vinyardists in California on a tract lying in the heart of modern downtown Los Angeles. See Iris H. Wilson, *William Wolfskill* (Glendale, 1965), and below, entry for 11 September 1842.

[17] Don Abel Stearns arrived in California from Massachusetts in 1829. By the time of his death in 1871 he had become one of the most important merchants – and subsequently landowners – in the Los Angeles area (see Doris Marion Wright, *A Yankee in Mexican California: Abel Stearns, 1798-1848* (Santa Barbara, 1977). The "revolution" referred to by Phelps was the overthrow of Governor Manuel Victoria in 1831; see Bancroft, III, Ch. VII. Victoria ordered Stearns, a naturalized Mexican citizen, to leave the country.

Mr Sterns came to this country from Mexico as a
Trader, lost his property and almost his life, was ordered out of the country, & in order to secure himself
he with others got up a revolution in which they were
successful. After many vicissitudes he at length was
fortunate in trade & is now wealthy.

The day after we arrived at the Pueblo was the Pa-
tron Sts. day of the Village & of course a Granda Festa
and duly observed by the inhabitants in the usual manner of the Catholics, by Bull fights, Bear dances &
other Buffoonary, ringing bells, firing guns during the
day, & Fandangos & Fire works in the evening. The
Bull fight consisted of a wild Bull being drove into
a large enclosure and tormented by about 50 horsemen.
Many feats of good horsemanship were exhibited, but
altogether it was a very miserable affair. The fandango
to which we were invited in the evening was also a
miserable get up and otherwise than giving us an opportunity of seeing the female beauties of the place
afforded but little gratification.

There are many good vineyards here among others
we visited that of Don Luis Vigne [Vignes][18] containing about 17000 vines all in good bearing this year and
nearly ripe. Mr. Vigne is a Frenchman & understands
the culture of the vine. He says that were it not for the
vermin this would be a first rate wine growing country,
but they are so much troubled by the Wolves, Foxes,
and a species of ground squirrel that destroys the
Grape, that it is difficult to protect their vineyards

---

18 Jean Louis Vignes settled in the Los Angeles area in 1829. A neighbor
of Wolkskill's, Vignes was also a leading wine producer, importing cuttings
from his native France to improve the stock. See Leonce Jore, "Jean Louis
Vignes of Bordeaux, Pioneer of California Viticulture," *Southern Calif. Qt.,*
XLV (1963), 289-303.

from being stripped by them. Mr. Carpenter [19] a Yankee farmer settled here has also about 15000 vines & some fine fields of Indian corn, also a great many apples & Pears, Peaches, Quinces, but not much variety. I observed in the garden vegetables similar to those we have at home but not so well cultivated & of course inferior to ours.

There are 7 to 8 Americans at the Pueblo. Traders, or Farmers, most of whom are doing well (i.e.) they are making money, but the Laws of the country afford so little security to life or property that there is but little inducement to enterprise. I saw & heard much of the miserable policy of the Govt., but of this hereafter. When I have been longer in the country, I can speak with more certainty. Don Able spoke of Hall T. Kelly [Kelley] [20] being some time at his house during his tour through this country, has not seen any of his writings but says all the information H.T.K. has of the Columbia River & the country thereabouts was communicated to him by himself & a Mr. Warner a man in his employ who had been an otter hunter in that region, thought that Mr. K. was not in the same state of mind while at his house.

Left the Pueblo for the Ship Wednesday afternoon. Rode about 20 miles and stopped for the night at the house of Don Manuel Dominguez; [21] was kindly entertained and provided with a good Horse to complete

---

[19] Lemuel or Samuel Carpenter seems to be little known, but had a vineyard and orchard on the San Gabriel River.

[20] Hall T. Kelley was a New England school master and Pacific coast enthusiast and propagandist who visited California in 1834. See Bancroft, III, 409-11.

[21] Don Manuel Domínguez was a leading citizen of the Los Angeles area, holding numerous official posts.

the journey. Arrived at the port about 10 o'clock A M found that 2 vessels had arrived during my absence, the *Roger Williams* (the vessel that carried the Foreigners prisoner to Mexico) and the Barque *Index*.

SEPT. 11th.   Employed in taking on board Hides & getting ready for sea. Killed a Bullock.

SEPT 12th.   Sailed for Sta Barbabara [sic], but owing to calms & light winds did not arrive at the above place untill

SEPT 17th.   We anchored about 4 PM. Found here the Ship *Alciope* of Boston loading for Sandwich Islands & the Brig *Bolivar*.

SEPT 18th.   Took on board some Hides & Tallow. Carpenter making spars for the Launch. The Crew repairing sails.

SEPT. 19th.   The crew variously employed. The *California* arrived in the morning last from St. Luis. Has been successful at the windward ports in making collection but unfortunate in losing her pinnace and two Boys by the boats capsizing. In the afternoon heavy Thunder & sharp lightning with heavy showers of Rain & squalls of wind, something very unusual at this season.

SUND 20th.   Pleasant throughout the day. One watch on Liberty.

MOND. 21st.   Calm & Foggy. Delivered all the Hides to the *California*. Carpenter employed on the Launch.

TUES. 22d.   Employed in filling water & various other work.

WED. 23rd.   Employed as yesterday. Let the *Califor-*

nia have our 1st Cutter in lieu of the one lost. Recd. some packages of goods from her & took Mr. Mellus's [22] baggage on board. Mr Robinson leaves us here for a season & Mr. M. takes his place to do the trading.

THURS 24th. Ships company variously employed on board. Took the Carpenter & one Man on Shore & repaired and put in operation Don Noriega's grist mill, horse power.

FRIDAY 25th. Pleasant weather. Understanding that there [was] a gentleman passanger on board of the *Alciope* attached to Sandwich Island Mission, I called on board in the morning to see him and found him to be the Rev. Benj. W. Parker, taking a short voyage for his health. Spent an hour & invited him on board the *Alert* to tea. 6 PM sent a boat for M. P. and spent a very pleasant evening in his company. Supplied him with some Books & Papers. Knew some of his Classmates at Andover, and was happy in being able to give him information of some of them that was new & gratifying to him. The *Alciope* is commanded by the Capt. Blinn who formerly commanded the Ship *Parthian,* the ship which took a number of Missionary families from Boston to the Islands a few years since and this same Capt. B. rendered himself famous or rather infa-

---

[22] Henry Mellus first arrived in California in 1835, before the mast with Richard Henry Dana on the *Pilgrim.* Leaving the ship to become an agent's clerk (not altogether unusual for one of good family, such as Mellus was), he made numerous trips along the coast and at least one to the east again, as clerk and supercargo. Settling first in Los Angeles, he later was a prominent merchant in San Francisco, with branch operations in several California cities. In 1860 he was chosen mayor of Los Angeles, but died the same year, aged 45. As a supercargo for Bryant, Sturgis & Co., and six vessels of Appleton & Co., he is often referred to in Phelps' pages. Phelps and Mellus' father had been mates on the same vessel; Francis Mellus Diary, Huntington Library, San Marino, p. 24.

mous (if reports were true) by his mistreatment of
them. He was decisively turned out of his ship in consequence and has been wandering about these parts
ever since, sometimes employed and sometimes not.
He obtained charge of the *Alciope* a few weeks since.
I do not like to grudge any person, but from the appearance & conversation of the man I should think
he was a person likely to conduct in the manner that
he was charged with.

On board the *California* is another somewhat celebrated character, not however for mistreating his passangers, but as being one of the first navigators in these
seas, and being also one of the old class American
seamen, Capt. Wm. Smith [23] a native of Virginia, but
a Bostonian by adoption is now 74 years old has been
to sea ever since he was eleven years of age and commenced his sea life on board an English gun boat before the war of the Revolution and during that war
in various Ships under the flag of the U. States. After
that period he came to the N W coast of America, and
pursued the fur trade for many years. He also was very
successful in sealing and in commerce at the Islands &
Canton and by exercising a very little economy & pru-
dence, could have been very rich, but it seems he had
not the remotest acquaintance with either of these virtues and although he has been constantly afloat he now
finds in his old age that he is poor, & dependent on
strangers for his daily bread. Mr. Sturgis one of my
owners was many years in the NW & Canton trade,

---

[23] William Smith first arrived in California in 1810 as mate of a fur-
sealing and ottering vessel (the *Albatross*) of which he became master
several years later. After many adventures, he returned to California in
1836 to make his home on Boston vessels visiting the coast, as Phelps
describes. See Dana, *Two Years,* Ch. XXIV.

and was intimate with Capt. Smith and in kindness to the old gentleman, desires his Capts. if they fall in with him to give him a home on board their Ships while on the coast, consequently he is transferred from one to the other, having spent so much of his life at sea, he can only live on Ship board. Has a most sovereign contempt for the land, and every body that lives on it, and wishes to die on board ship and be buried in his hammock in blue water. Ruschenberger (in his "3 Years in the Pacific")[24] speaks of him as being a remarkable specimen of an old seaman, and relates his conversation with Capt. Smith in which the old man says that but two things ever chafed him, "A Californian Sadle [sic] & a Missionary." As to the first I can fully agree with him in deprecating the above named article, as the most uncomfortable machine I ever stradled. But as to the ill feeling he professes towards the Missionaries I cannot participate in and am convinced that it is only because through the instrumentality of the Missionaries, there now is exhibited a more moral state of things at the Islands and the old visitors there, being now debarred of their former indulgences, they have similar feelings to the authors of this change that a Bear would have to the person depriving her of her prey. I have invited the old gentleman to spend the day on board of the *Alert* & intend having Mr. Parker also to dine.

SAT. 26th.   Pleasant weather throughout the day. The crew employed in getting ready for sea. Killed a Bullock..

The old Sea Dog & the Missionary, both on board

---

[24] William Samuel Waltham Ruschenberger, *A Voyage Round the World . . . in 1835, 1836, and 1837* (Philadelphia, 1837).

and both appeared to enjoy each other's conversation. The old Capt has a most excellent memory, and likes to be questioned of the events of olden times. He is a man of good information and from what I gleaned from himself and have heard from others respecting him, should think he was one who had been accustomed to rely on himself alone in the face of warring elements and who knew that a Ship could not safely have more than a single will, and that, the will of her Master. It appears however that he was somewhat tyranical [sic] to his crews and that while he was determined to sail his own ship, firmly convinced that a ship should have but one Capt., he at the same time believed the rest of mankind to be little better than asses; took his own observations, and cared not a fig for those of his mates, and was never more bent on following his own views than when all hands grumbled & opposed him. But however successful he may have been in steering his ship on the trackless ocean, he now finds that he was ill fitted by his headless·improvidence to secure a port of comfort for his declining days. Capt Smith was well acquainted with the celebrated Navigator & Discoverer, Vancouver, and was frequently in company with him in these seas. During the last war, he commanded the Ship *Albatross* of Boston on the N.W. was frequently in port with and on terms of intimacy with Com. Porter and tells some very amusing stories of events that occurred in those days & especially of his being chased by the *Essex* junior whom he took for a British cruiser and during the chase threw most of his papers overboard, & much other property. The old man has a home now offered him at the Pueblo by Don A. Sterns, and as it [is] thought to be best for him to be there, he has been given to understand that it will be inconvenient for him to remain on board either of the Ships, although it is but 30 miles inland he cannot bear the thoughts of going and says, "They are going to send me to die on the Rocky Mountains." We parted with him in the afternoon and to all appearance, not in the least chafed by being in contact with a Missionary.

In the afternoon walked with Mr. P. up to the Mission of Santa Barbara. Were welcomed by the Priest, who showed us the large & fine gardens of the Church, which were well stocked with a great variety of Fruit Vegetables & Flowers. Went over the Church and its numerous appendages exhibited to us the Plate & Jewels of the altar, and the costly Robes of the Priests &c., &c. but I had seen so much tumpery of the kind before that my imagination was not much wrought upon. My chief object was to obtain some of the Indian skulls that I supposed were in the charnal house and on expressing my desire to·him he immediately took us there but unfortunately about six weeks before, the house was cleared out, being full of bones, & the skulls buried. The priest said over 2000 skulls were interred at the time. There were about 1500 Indians belonging to this Mission when in its prosperity. It had then 25,000 head of cattle, but is now poor and going to decay. There are now about 400 Indians here.

SUNDAY SEPT 27th. Got under weigh at 1 P M and made sail for St. Francisco. Latter Part strong breezes. Ship beating to windward in the canal [25] of Santa Bar-

---

[25] The Santa Barbara Channel, which runs between the coast and the Channel Islands, was generally called the "canal," following the Spanish usage. Dana, *Two Years,* Ch. IX.

bara. 5 PM carried away the Main Top Gallant mast in the wake of the cap. Sent the wreck down upon deck. Found the mast decayed.

MON 28th. Stopped at the Island of Santa Rosa and landed one of a gang of otter hunters from Sta Barbara with a lot of provisions for the party. Afternoon strong breezes from W. Ship off Pt. Conception. Carpenter making a new T.G. Mast.

29th TUES. Beating to windward with strong Winds from WNW.

WED. 30th. Winds light & Variable. Got up a new M. T. Mast.

OCT. 1 to 5th. Light winds and variable with much Foggy weather. Crew variously employed in repairing sails, making Sails for the Launch & Tents for the Boats Crews &c.

TUES. 6th. Ship off Pt. Carmelo. Evening squally 6 PM tacked off Shore & double reeft the Topsails. Morning foggy. Spoke brig *Joseph Peabody* from Nootka Sound bound to Monterey.

WED. 7th. Still beating to windward. Wind from WNW. At 6 PM tacked off Shore; Pt. Anno [Año] Nuevo ENE 3 miles. The mountains on fire and the Forests in the Valleys in a broad sheet of flame & presenting during the night a spectacle sublime & awful. During the Night the wind increased to a Gale from NNW. Ship under Close Reefs.

FRIDAY OCT. 9th. Strong Gales from NNW. Ship under Close reeft Fore & Main Topsails, Main Spencer & F T Staysail. A heavy Sea running. Latter Part of the Day wind abating. Made Sail.

SAT OCT 10th. At daylight passed near the Farralones [Farallon] & at 7 PM entered the Bay of St. Francisco & anchored at Yerba Buena (or Sweet Herb) Cove, and moored with both bower anchors.

SUNDAY OCT 11th. Pleasant weather; part of the crew on liberty on Shore, the remainder at rest. There are now lying here the Ship *Monsoon*, Brig *Miguel*, Schr. *Moss* & *California*.

MON. OCT. 12th. Variously Employed in fitting the Boats for service &c.

TUES. OCT 13th. Mr. Mellus & 4 Hands left with the Pinnace for Santa Clara. Latter Part Strong breezes & clear.

WEDNES. 14. Variously Employed on the Rigging & Sails. Carpenter repairing one of the Quarter boats. at 7 PM the Pinnace returned with a load of Potatoes, Pumpkins, & Beans.

THURS. 15th. Got up the Stump F. & Mizzin T. G. Masts. The Pinnace was despatched in the morning to St. Leandry [Leandro] for Hides & Tallow.

FRIDAY 16th. Pleasant & Warm. Went a hunting about the entrance of the Bay. Returned at sunset with 1 seal, 10 Wild ducks & 2 Teal. Mr. M. returned from the Mission. Latter strong winds from W.N.W. & clear.

SAT 16th [17th] OCT to 21st. Nothing of consequence has transpired. Some Sales of Goods have been effected. The Carpenter employed in new planking the 2nd Cutter. The Crew variously employed in wooding, watering &c.

SAT 24th. Sent the Launch with goods to St. Leandry.

SUNDAY 25th. Sailed the *Monsoon, Duxbury* & *Nymph.* Part of the Crew on liberty. Mr. Mellus started for the interior.

MON 26th. Cloudy with [intervals] of fine weather. People employed cutting wood, painting ship &c.

TUES. 27th. Foggy & calm in the morning. Afternoon pleasant with fresh NW winds. People variously employed. Carpenter repairing the Gig.

WED. 28th. Started at 7 AM in the Cutter for an excursion to St. Leandry. Arrived at the entrance of the creek about 11 AM, proceeding up a winding passage, the left bank being crowned with a fine forest of wood, principally Oak & Butternutt [sic] without any underwood & the opposite bank rather low & without wood, being one vast plain affording all the year round excellent grazing for cattle, but now having recently been overrun with fire (the work of the wild Indians). The feed has been destroyed many leagues round the Bay of St. Francisco, but as it is hoped the Rainy season will set in soon. The immense herds of cattle which now are hardly able to subsist may yet be saved, the low lands now abound with Wild Geese & Brant, the ponds & creeks with Ducks of which there are said to be about 20 difft. kinds. Hair Seal are also numerous in the various creeks. Proceeding 5 or 6 Miles up that passage, shooting Ducks & Plover on our way, we came too [sic] at a convenient spot for encamping. Here we pitched the tent & while some were picking the birds for dinner, & getting ready to cook them, I took a stroll with my gun and returned to camp in about an hour with a fine allotment of game. Found at the camp Don Jose Estiedillo [Estudillo],[26] the owner of an extensive tract hereabouts & whose house was at about 2 Miles distant. At his urgent request I went home with him to dinner, to which I did complete justice. Found him to be a jolly old gentleman of Falstaff proportions with a numerous progeny around him, his wife a fine motherly woman, was very attentive to me, likewise a blooming young Miss who is by far the prettiest & most agreeable female I have yet met with in California. After dinner took another look after game, promising to return to sleep at the house. Shot a large wolf & a number of ducks. Supped at 8 PM, and retired to bed (but alas not to sleep). At 10 tired & sleepy I promised myself a night of rest & sound sleep, to strengthen my assurance of the same, I saw with pleasure that my kind hostess was putting clean sheets & pillow slips on my bed which stood in the corner of the room we were sitting in, and I gladly availed myself of the first overture towards retiring, to bid the family "Buenas noches." [27] None can appreciate the comfort of a good bed & clean sheets better than the one who has been all the day in pursuit of game, sometimes climbing the mountain side, or pursuing his object across quagmires, and through brush & briar, untill he is glad to be able to drop on his bed at night, too weary to undress, thus fatigued was I, & such were my feelings when the bed was ready for me, but to enjoy the clean snow white sheets & the embroidered fringed pillow slips which were drawn over pillows of wool in red silk ticks, I made a successful effort and divested myself of my garments, leapt into bed and after indulging in a few thoughts of --

[26] Don José Joaquín Estudillo was a native Californian (1798-1852), and a well-known land and office holder of the San Francisco area. As of 1842, he held the San Leandro Rancho (Oakland).

[27] Author's note: "good night."

Home – composed myself to rest, but I soon found I
had bed-mates & their name was *legion*. I had blown
out the light & could not see the beseigers who seemed
determined to drive me from my quarters, but I felt
their assaults in all directions. If I had worked hard
during the day, I was compelled to work harder during the night, for I found myself literally covered by
a host of the most industrious & blood thirstly fleas it
was ever my lot to lie down amongst. I could not account for their being so numerous when I knew that
the sheets were quite fresh & clean, but after an hour
or two's worrying, kicking & scratching I found that
under the sheet was placed a very thick blanket probably taken from some other bed and this blanket had
in all probability afforded a birth place & home for
fleas of many generations, it was in vain I threw the
vile article across the room, turned the bed over &
shook the sheets scattering regiments of the light troops
over the floor, they had tasted fresh blood & they were
not a foe to be turned from their purpose easily. They
quickly formed again, and a few moments march
brought them back to the field of battle, where for
the live-long night the conflict continued, & much blood
was shed. I thought once I would let them make their
own terms & allow them to draw on me for what
amount they pleased, hoping they might at length satisfy their demands & leave me to a little rest, but no,
they seemed to be like the "daughter of the horse leech"
continually crying, "more, more." I wished myself
almost any where else, and nothing but the darkness
of the night & the howling of the wolves kept me from
retreating to the boat. The night was passed however
without a wink of sleep, and with the earliest peep of

day I slipped on my clohes, caught my gun and sallied forth, grateful that my veins were not wholly drawn, and determined to avoid as much as possible for the future, Californian lodging.

29th.   In the afternoon returned across the Bay, having as passangers Don Jose, Wife & Daughter (named Maria Conception) the last being now rigged out in her best for a visit, has improved very much in appearance. The passage across the bay was at first pleasant, but the latter part rough, the ladies were sick & frightened, and it was some time after dark before we reached the Ship. We found a good supper ready for us, after which the company were provided with good beds (without fleas) and I believe all spent a comfortable night (I can answer for one).

FRIDAY OCT. 30th.   The Ships company employed in wooding. The Launch returned from Santa Clara with a load of Hides.

Don Jose & family remain on board, they were dissappointed in not finding the family at home, whom they came to visit, and therefore accepted my invitation to take up their quarters on ship board. A Russian Man of War arrived yesterday having on board the Gov. & family and other families of the Russian settlement of Sitka, on their way home to Russia.[28]

SAT 31st.   A strong Gale from NNW the passangers spent the day on shore & returned at night.

SUN. NOV 1st.   Pleasant with strong breezes from NW. Part of the crew on liberty.

---

[28] The governor was Ivan Kuprianov (1835-40); the vessel the *Nikolai*. Kuprianov stayed a month in San Francisco, dealing with various Russian-Californian questions, including the sale of Fort Ross. Bancroft, IV, 174-81.

MON. 2d.   Sent the Launch to St. Leandry with Don
Jose &c. and went with the cutter myself & 5 men up
the Bay to take some goods to the Ranch or Farm of
Don Hosea [José] Sanchos [Sanchez].[29] Arrived at the
creek at sundown, pitched the tent discharged the
goods, and supped with the old gentleman at his house
about a mile from the camp. At 10 returned to camp,
declining a pressing invitation to sleep at the house,
and passed a comfortable night in the tent.

TUES 3d.   Started early to shoot Geese; they are very
numerous here, but difficult to get at. Shot only 4. Don
Sancho's Farm consists of a tract of land 12 miles long
& 4 wide is well situated & if cultivated would yield
large crops, but it is only used for the raising of cattle,
of which he has 8000 head. Near his house lie the car-
casses of 2 or 300 cattle which were killed about 2 mos.
ago from which nothing had been saved but the Hides
& Tallow. The beef is left for the crows & vultures
of which there are thousands around every matanza
(or killing place) and are so shocking tame as to suffer themselves to be taken by hand. Left in the forenoon, stopped at a pleasant place about 2 PM to cook
dinner & take a siesta under the trees & arrived on
board at 7 PM.

WED. 4th.   Pleasant & warm. Calm in the forenoon &
fresh breezes from NW at night. Launch returned
from St Leandry bringing a load of wood. One of the
crew unable to do duty in consequence of a beating
received from the Spaniards last Sunday on shore,
probably caused by drink & his own misconduct.

---

[29] Don José Antonio Sánchez, a famous Indian fighter, arrived as a soldier
in 1791. Retiring in 1836, he lived either in Monterey or on his rancho of
Buri-Buri (modern San Mateo), described below at page 119, note 44.

THURS. 5th.   Pleasant & warm. Employed in stowing the Hold filling water. Received a visit from the Russian officers. Later Part Strong Breezes from NW.

FRIDAY 6th.   Morning calm & fine weather. Received on board a lot of Hides & Tallow. Took in the Launch & stowed her. Afternoon Strong NW winds. Weather coolish.

SAT. 7th.   Unmoored & got ready for sea. Weather pleasant.

The Second Passage

San Francisco to San Diego and Return, with a Letter to His Wife

SUNDAY, NOV. 8th [1840]. Fresh breezes from South. 9 AM got underway and beat out of the Harbour. At Noon passed the Fort. 10 PM Ship outside the Farallones. Squally with heavy rain through the night. Ship under double reeft Topsails. Midnight split the Mizen Topsail & furled it. Wind shifted suddenly to West. This is the first rain we have had for nearly six months.

MOND. 9th. Strong Westerly winds & pleasant throughout the day. At 1 PM Anchored at Monterey with the Best Bower in 8 fathoms water.

TUES. 10th. Moderate & pleasant throughout. Recd. 140 hides & made some sales of cargo. 8 PM noticed the Barometer to 30.50 being much higher than it has been since leaving Boston. The T. [temperature] at the same time 62°.

WED. 11th. Light winds & fine weather throughout the day. Crew making new Mizen Topsail & F. [Flying] Jib.

THURS. 12. Morning calm & Pleasant. Received a boat load of Hides & Potatoes. Ends with fresh NW breezes & clear.

FRIDAY 13th. Moderate & pleasant. Ends foggy.

SAT. 14th.　Begins calm & pleasant. 11 AM moderate breezes from NW. Got under weigh for Santa Barbara in company with the *Monsoon* for St. Luis. Weathered Pt. Pinos & bore away. Fine breezes & pleasant through the night.

SUN. 15th.　Pleasant, & fine breezes from NW. 8 AM Ship off Mt. [Point] Buchon. At sunset passed Point Conception.

MON. 16th.　Ship becalmed about 12 miles from Sta. Barbara. At 11 PM anchored in 6 fathoms water in Sta. Barbara.

TUES. 17th.　Pleasant. At daylight hauled the Ship farther out & anchored with a slip rope & buoy on the chain. Took on board 400 Hides. Killed a bullock.

18th & 19.　Changeable weather with some Rain. Employed in filling water & taking on board Hides. Arrived the *Monsoon* & *Index*. All Ready for sea.

FRIDAY NOV 20th.　Got under weigh from Sta. Barbara at 2 PM with a breeze from NNE. Midnight ship becalmed of [sic, off] St. Buenaventura.

SAT. 21.　First part gentle Breezes & fine weather. 6 PM Calm & continued through the night.

SUN 22d.　The morning light variable winds & calm. Got the Pinace & Cutter ahead and towed the Ship into the Port of St. Pedro. Ends pleasant.

MON 23rd.　Morning foggy. Recd. a lot of Hides & Tallow. Ends fine.

TUES 24th.　Morning pleasant & warm. Continues the same through the day. Crew variously employed. Evening threatening appearances from NE. Single Reeft the Topsails and got ready for slipping the cable.

WED 25th. Begins with light breezes and considerable swell from the Eastward. 3 AM fresh breezes & Squally. Wind E to NE. Clear sky. 5 AM strong Gale. Ship started her anchor & commenced dragging towards the rocks. Set the topsails & slipped the Chain. Close reef'd the Topsails & stood to the Wd [Westward]. 10 AM Moderating. Tacked Ship & stood in for the port. Noon calm. 2 PM breezes from the SW. 3 PM picked up the ship buoy & hove in the chain. Sighted[30] the anchor, and came too, with 60 fathoms cable in 8 fathoms water.

THURS 26th. Westerly winds and fine weather throughout the day. Killed a Bullock for ships use. After breakfast I started with one of the Boys and two Horses to shoot wild geese at a place about three miles from the landing. At this we were joined by a number of California boys, half breeds and Indians on horseback, who hung in our rear waiting for sport of some kind. The scamps are always ripe for mischief and on the present occasion I could see they had fun in view, but I warned them to "cui da" [cuidado].[31] they are all very expert in the use of the lasso (a small rope made of hide, about 6 or 7 fathom long with a running noose in one end) which they will throw when at full gallop over the horns of a bullock or round one of his legs, with the greatest precision. A Californian spends two thirds of his life in the saddle & of course [they] are excellent horsemen; even a boy of 8 years of age will lasso a wild Bull & bring him to the ground. I was uncertain what was the object of my present com-

---

[30] To "sight" the anchor is to heave it up to see if it is clear; in this case, Phelps was mooring to an anchor already in position.
[31] Author's note: "Beware."

pany, untill I fired into a flock of geese on the plain, two had their wings broke and made off on their legs. And now the shout was raised from the "muchachos" [32] and away they started full speed swinging their lassos over their heads in pursuit of the wounded geese, and which the never failing lasso soon dragged to my feet. These gentry stuck to us, and in fact made themselves very useful auxiliaries, as on one occasion when swinging a bunch of geese over the back of one of my horses, he took fright, broke adrift and cleared out over the hills and was soon out of sight. The troop was at a short distance off & saw the occurrence, and with the speed of the wind, away they scampered in pursuit, and in the course of a hour & an half they returned with him, which they might have done in half an hour but it would have been too little sport for them. They like nothing better than to give chase to a horse and alarm him all they can by their shouts & frequently catching him by his long tail and taking a turn with it round their saddlehead heave him flat on his "beam ends" after harassing the poor creature till they are tired and the horse wild with fright, they throw the noose over his neck and take him in tow.

At 12 N. having taken 20 geese & killed others which we did not get, returned to the Ship well satisfied with the days sport. Ends calm.

FRIDAY 27th. Moderate & pleasant throughout the day. Received a few hundred hides on board. Sent a boat to fish but was unsuccessful. Ends calm.

SAT 28th. Morning Calm & pleasantly warm. Killed a bullock. Took on board some Hides & Tallow & at

---

[32] Author's footnote: "Boys."

1 PM got under weigh with a light breeze from SW for St. Diego. Ends Calm.

SUNDAY, MONDAY, & TUES. Light airs, or Calms all the time.

WED. DEC. 2d. At 1 PM anchored in the Lower Harbour of St. Diego. Ends Calm.

THURSDAY 3rd. Moderate & pleasant. At daylight hove up the anchor & kedged the Ship to the anchorage abreast the Hide House & Moored with both bowers, with 45 fath. on each.

FRIDAY & SAT. Continuation of fine weather. Employed in landing Hides & Tallow.

SUNDAY 6th. Pleasant throughout. Part of the crew on liberty.

MONDAY 7th. Morning foggy. Latter part pleasant weather. Restowed the after Hold & got ready to discharge the Salt. Carpenter sick.

TUES DEC. 8th. 1840. Discharging Salt & assisting the *California's* crew in curing hides. Carpenter quite sick.

WED. 9th. Discharging Salt & various other work. Killed a Bullock for Ships use.

THURS. 10th. Discharged the last of 150 Hhds. [hogsheads] Salt, & Commenced taking in Ballast. Carpenter better.

At 10 AM Started with the Pinnace & 4 Men & Boys for the Corronadas [Coronados] Islands which lie about 20 miles to the South of St. Diego in pursuit of Sea Elephant.[33] At 5 PM arrived at the Northernmost

---

[33] Sea elephant, or elephant seal, were valuable for their blubber, which could be tried out (melted by boiling) into quite pure oil for cooking or,

of the three Islands and found that there was but one
place where a landing could be affected, there being no
beach or any shelter for boats, and the surf breaking on
the rough rock shore making it difficult to get the boat
near enough to jump out. I however got on shore with
one of the men and killed seven Hair Seal, of which
there were about 50 at this place. It now being sunset,
we bore away for the largest Island which was about
2 miles to the leeward. Here I had been informed I
should find a good beach & convenient place for landing but after running about two thirds round the island
& examining every point except the SW I was convinced that there was no place on which we could land
with safety, it being a steep rock-bound shore and no
kind of beach. It was now dark & having no prospect
of making a lee [i.e., of an island] for the night, we
ran the boat into a field of kelp which was at about
½ a mile from the land and attached to the rocks in
ten fathoms water. Here we secured the boat by letting
go the grapnell, and fastening the kelp to her. The
weather looking unfavorable, we reefed the Mainsail
& got ready to cut & run if compelled to. We now took
a cold supper and disposed of ourselves in as comfortable a manner as our circumstances admitted in an
open boat, and beguiled the evening in telling of past
perils. The poor boys did not like the prospect before
them, but after listening to a relation of some of my
former hardships and the long rough nights I had

more likely, illumination. Phelps' motive is clear from a letter to Abel
Stearns of 1842, offering a barrel of good oil: "In the passage up I procured
some from Sta. Barbara Island and tryed it out with a great deal of care
. . . It is a first rate article, and I shall put it to you cheap say 6 Rials
(Hides)." (3 October 1842, Stearns Papers, Huntington Library, San Marino,
Box 49.)

weathered in boats they became satisfied that they were
now in a very comfortable situation and so it proved
to be for about midnight a bright moon shone on a
calm sea and we enjoyed a good night's rest.

FRIDAY 11th.   Fresh Breezes from the Nd. At daylight
got under weigh & proceeded through a large field of
kelp south of the Island in search of Otter, but we saw
none. We then beat up to a small Island (the center of
the group) and on it discovered 7 or 8 Elephant with
a number of pups. They were all laying on some rocks
under a steep bank against which the surf frequently
broke with such force that the poor creatures were
hardly able to hold on.

We anchored the Boat as near the surf as possible
and shot three of them from the boat, two of which
we succeeded in getting lines fast to by swimming
through the surf and hauling them off; stripping off
their blubber alongside, the other drifted in the breakers where we lost him. We also captured three of the
pups & at 2 PM started for the Ship, and after passing
another night in the boat, beating across the passage
with a strong headwind we arrived.

SAT. 12th.   at 6 AM having made a pretty good trip
procuring about three barrels of oil and nine Seal Skins.

SUNDAY 13th.   Pleasant & Warm throughout the day.
All Hands at rest.

MONDAY 14th.   Continuation of fine weather. Crew
employed in ballasting the Ship & various other work.

TUES 15th.   Employed in Ballasting the Ship & in
curing hides on shore. Sent a gang of men to assist
in loading the *California*. Pleasant weather continues.

WED. 16th. Calm and warm weather. Employed variously. Arrived Ship *Monsoon* & Brig *Juan Hosea* [*Juan José*]. Killed a Bullock. Carpenter convalescent.

THURS 17. Pleasant weather throughout. All Hands variously employed in Ships duty. Got up a new Main Topmast.

FRIDAY 18th. Continuation of Fine weather. Wind west. Went with a number of Masters & Supercargoes to attend a party and Fandango at the Presidio, given by Don Miguel Pedroannea [Pedrorena] & Don Henrique Fitch.[34]

SAT. DEC 19th. The weather continues fine & pleasant. The Crew employed in curing Hides & assisting to load the *California*.

SUN 20th. Weather as yesterday. Transshipped some goods from the *California*. Part of the crew on liberty.

MONDAY & TUES. 21st & 22d: Cloudy & Calm, got ready for sea.

---

[34] Miguel F. de Pedrorena was supercargo for several South American vessels on the California coast in the 1830's, and agent for McCall & Co. of Lima. In the 1840's he settled at San Diego, married into the Estudillo family and, until his death in 1850, was a popular figure – perhaps the most popular salesman on the coast. Dorothy Blakey Smith, ed., *James Douglas in California, 1841: being the Journal of a Voyage from the Columbia to California* (Vancouver, 1965), p. 21.

Henry Delano Fitch, born in New Bedford in 1799, arrived in California in 1825 as a supercargo. He became a Mexican citizen, and after a romantic elopement episode (Bancroft III, 140-41), lived in San Diego until his death in 1849. Tall, large, and genial, Fitch was generally well liked as a trader, landholder, and ship captain (he was master of the *Morse,* renamed *Nymph* or *Ninfa,* in which vessel he had a one-third interest). Fitch's account book for 1838-47 lists many transactions with the *Alert* (Bancroft Library, C-B 357, vol. 5).

Following the entry for Friday the 18th, Phelps left a blank page, perhaps intending to write up a description of the celebrations at a later date.

WEDNES 23rd. Pleasant & Warm. Morning calm. Afternoon fresh Trade winds. Carpenter finished the new boat.

THURSDAY 24th. Begins with Strong breezes from NE and clear weather. Assisting the *California* to load.

FRIDAY 25th. Christmass [sic] Day. Pleasant & warm. Crew variously employed. Afternoon crew at rest.

SAT. 26th. Pleasant throughout the day. The crew cutting brooms & various other work. Received on board Old Capt Smith & his baggage. The poor old man says he has been 62 years at sea, and now has not a dollar. I asked what he had done with all his money. His reply was, that he had spent it all for play things.

SUNDAY 27th. Weather Pleasant and warm. People at rest.

MONDAY 28th. Morning Calm & pleasant. At daylight unmoored and hove short, but it coming on to blow from the SE, let go the Best Bower again. Afternoon Mr's Robinson and Mellus started to go up the coast by land. I shall remain to sail in company with the *California*. Ends Cloudy. Wind S.S. East.

TUES DEC. 29th. Moderate & pleasant. Unmoored Ship & hauled the Ship outside the fleet, ready for sea. Killed two bullocks. Left a Man & 2 boys in charge of the Hide House, and left stores & provisions sufficient for three months & arms to protect themselves.

WED. 30th. Begins with strong breezes from SE with squally appearances. Latter Part pleasant.

THURSDAY 31st. Fine Breezes from NW & pleasant weather. At 1 PM Got under weigh and stood out of the harbour in company with the *California*. Passed ahead of her about a mile, backed the Mn Topsail, and waited for her to come up, when after exchanging adieus, we parted with three hearty good cheers – she for *HOME,* & we – *from it*. May Heaven speed the homebound Ship, and bless the gallant hearts that are in her. May they be returned in safety to their families & friends, deeply impressed with their obligations to God for his goodness to them, through their long and weary voyage. With the good Ship *California* also goes many fragile messengers of our hopes and fears to that dear distant home across four mighty oceans where our cherished ones reside, and Oh may she return to us in due time, bringing the glad news that our praying for their health & happiness have found acceptance at a throne of Grace.

At 6 PM Strong breezes. Took in the Top Gallant Sails and reefed the Topsails. Midnight Pleasant & Moderate. Ship between the Islands of Clemente & Catalina.

FRIDAY JANY 1, 1841. Moderate & Pleasant. Ship near Catalina. After breakfast went on shore with the boat to fish. Returned at Noon with a large quantity of fish, and two seal. Afternoon made sail for St Pedro.

SAT 2d. Anchored at St Pedro in 8 faths. (winter anchorage) about 2 miles from the land. Afternoon took a couple of Horses & an Indian boy and went to shoot geese. At dark returned with a horse load.

SUN 3d. Pleasant & warm throughout the day. All hands at rest.

MON 4th. Begins with clear & pleasant & the weather warm. People variously employed in Ship's duty. So ends.

TUES 5th.   Continuation of the same weather as above. Filled some water & landed some freight.

WEDNES 6th.   Weather as yesterday. Transhipped 2 Boats of Tallow to Brig *Catalina*. At midnight light breezes from NE. Got under weigh for Santa Barbara.

THURS 7th.   Beating up the coast, with westerly winds.

FRIDAY 8th.   At 10 PM came to anchor in 9 fathoms water at Santa Barbara. Single Reeft the Topsails and furled sails. The weather continues mild & pleasant and without Rain.

SAT 9th.   Calm & pleasant throughout the day. Thermom. at 65° in the shade. Landed some freight and filled some water. In the afternoon went to shoot Ducks and was very successful.

SUNDAY JAN 10th.   Light variable winds & fine pleasant weather. Thermom. 66° Barom 30:00. The Catholic festivals are now at their height. This afternoon (of the Holy Sabbath) a *Bullfight* takes place in the square of Santa Barbara, which is in sight from the ship. The house tops and terraces are crowded with men women and children. Priests and Indians, who were probably most of them engaged in religious services in the morning, and are now carousing, betting, and swearing around the Bull ring. Such is the Catholic manner of remembering the Sabbath Day to keep it holy unto the Lord. A few sabbaths ago there was a Horse Race, at which the bets were made by families related to each other some ten or twelve families against as many of another name, some families betting Horses, Cows, Cattle of various descriptions, Money, Aguardente, or even the very houses they lived in, the whole stake amounting to 500 head of Cattle, 300 Horses, 200

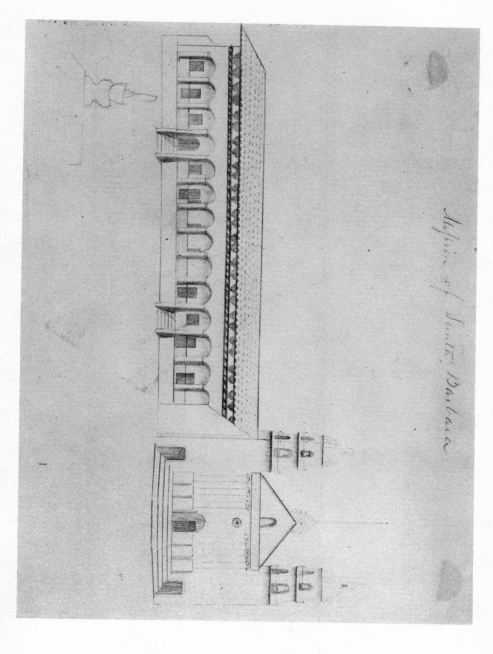

Mission of Santa Barbara

CAPTAIN PHELPS' DRAWING OF THE MISSION OF SANTA BARBARA
By permission of the Houghton Library, Harvard University.

Sat Dec 19th The weather continues fine & pleasant.
The Crew employed in curing Hides, & assisting to load
the California

Sun 20th Weather as yesterday. Transhipped some
goods, from the California. Part of the Crew on
liberty.

Monday & Tues}
20th & 22' } Cloudy & Calm. got ready for Sea.

Wednes 23' Pleasant & Warm. Morning Calm afternoon
full Trade winds. Carpenter finished the new Boat

Thursday 24th Begins with Strong breezes from N E.
and clear weather. Assisting the California to load

Friday 25th Christmass Day. Pleasant & warm
Crew variously employed. Afternoon Crew at rest.

Sat 26th Pleasant throughout the day. the crew
cutting brooms & various other work. Received on board
Old Capt Smith & his baggage the poor old man says
he has been 62 years at sea, and now has not a dollar. I asked
what he had done with all his money. his reply was, that
he had spent it all for play things.

Sunday 27th Weather Pleasant and warm. Pleasant rest

Monday 28th Morning Calm & pleasant. at daylight unmoored
and hove short. but it coming on to blow from the S.E,
let go the Best Bower again. Afternoon Messs Robinson
and Mellus started to go up the coast by land.
I shall remain to sail in company with the Cali-
-fornia, Ends Cloudy. Wind S.S.East.

THE PAGE OF PHELPS' JOURNAL FOR DECEMBER 19-28, 1840
By permission of the Houghton Library, Harvard University. (See text pages 93-94.)

Mares, a number of Farms, Houses, Money, & 100 barrels of Rum. The distance run ¼ of a mile. So Ends the Day. All Hands at rest on board the *Alert*.

MONDAY 11th. Continuation of light winds & warm pleasant weather. Employed in landing goods, taking off Hides & watering. Dined with the Padre President of the Missions (a jolly old man with a good open countenance), an Irish Doctor and a Yankee, who has adopted California for his country, and at the same time exchanged universalism for the Catholic creed and of course is bigoted in the extreme. The conversation ran upon religious subjects, but as I knew that I was considered a Heretic, and that it would avail nothing to argue with such a trio, I succeeded in turning the conversation by enquiring of the Good Father the history of the Missions and he in turn was desirous of knowing what parts of the world I had visited; and when on telling him that I had been in Egypt & visited some of the scenes of Scripture history, he put questions faster than I could answer them. I was much better pleased with the appearance & manners of the Padre President than with any other priest I have seen on the coast. I observed that at dinner he used a knife, fork & spoon which he took from a greasy old pouch which he pulled from his pocket, while the rest of us were accomodated with silver spoons and clean knives & forks. His knife, which had been a common table knife in its better days, was now reduced to about two inches of blade, and the fork was minus a handle, which with a spoon of iron, and all of them black & rusty, seemed to have been his travelling companions for many years. I inquired respecting them, and was told that on the departure of each Missionary from the

College of San Fernando (the Mother of all the Missions of California) they are presented with these articles, at the expense of the establishment, thus furnishing their labourers with tools and trusting to providence & the Indians to supply the materials to operate upon.

Received an invitation to a wedding (while at dinner), which takes place tomorrow and also to a feast which is to be given on the occasion.

TUES. 12th.   Light breezes from the Eastern board, with a heavy swell. Sighted the anchor & came too further to sea-ward in 12 fathoms. Took off two boat loads of Hides. Ends pleasant wind West.

WEDNES. 13th.   Pleasant & light winds. The *Bolivar* arrived from Monterey bringing news that foreign vessels are to be prohibited from trading coastwise. Duty on board prevented me from attending the wedding yesterday, but I accepted an invitation today to dine with the new-married folks, the Groom an American & the Lady a Californian, a schoolmistress (by trade) and said to be the only *Lady* of the country that can write, found a snug little party to dinner, and had a pleasing set down. In the afternoon saw what is called a Bullfight (in the square). The Priests were so much gratified by the spectacle last Sunday, that it was repeated today for their amusement, and consisted of a number of wild bulls being driven into the inclosure, when they were "lassed" [lassoed] and thrown down, their horns sawed off, & then turned loose pursued by 30 or 40 horsemen who would incite the animal by shaking their mantles at him and when he would chase his tormenters, they would follow him & catching his long tail taking a turn with it at their saddle head capsize him head over heels in a most dexterous manner. Others would goad him to madness with nails or spears fastened to poles. When the poor animal was so much exhausted as to not wish to rise after being frequently thrown, they stuck knives into him causing the blood to flow in many streams down his smoking hide, untill finding their exertions useless to incite him to further opposition they dragged him out to make room for a fresh one. Sometimes the bull would turn unexpectedly on them and knock horse & rider to the ground, the man escaped each time but the poor horse was frequently lifted on the horns which were too blunt to penetrate. The *Good Padres* were present and doubtless enjoyed the agonizing bellowings of the poor animals, but I felt that the amusement was cruel and cowardly, and soon quit the arena in disgust.

THURSDAY 14th. Light winds & variable, with pleasant weather throughout the day. Employed in watering & killing Bullock for ships use.

FRIDAY 15th. Moderate & Pleasant throughout the day with a smooth beach. People variously employed.

SAT 16th. Strong breezes in the morning from WSW. Afternoon moderate. 6 PM Light breezes from the NE. Got under weigh for Monterey. 3 Passangers on board. Latter Part breeze freshening & hauling to SE.

SUNDAY 17. Strong breezes & Rainy. Wind SE. Ship under all sail. 9 AM passed Point Conception 2 miles distant. Midnight Squally with much sea. Reeft the Topsails.

MONDAY 19th. Continuation of strong breezes. Course NW at daylight hauled in for the land & made all sail. At noon Ship off Point Pinos becalmed. 2 PM Light

airs from West. 3 PM anchored at Monterey. Found
lying here the Hudson Bay Co's Ship *Columbia*. Ends
Calm.

MONTEREY JAN 19th 1841.[35] Light winds & Rainy. All
Hands cleaning Ship. Went a Ducking in the afternoon up the Lagoon with the gunning float, but met
with poor luck. The birds are more harrassed here than
at other ports on the coast & are shy.

WEDNES. 20th.   Westerly winds with clear weather
& much surf on the beach. Employed in taking off
Hides & landing goods.

THURS 21st. Winds & weather as yesterday. Employment ditto.

FRIDAY 22nd. Continuation of fine weather. Winds
Light & Variable. Employed in Trading, &c., &c.

SAT. 23d. Winds & weather as yesterday. Taking on
board Hides. Took a stroll in the afternoon with my
gun towards Pt Pinos. Shot some quail & a few other
birds. Stopped at a log house in the edge of the woods.
The old couple who inhabited it were complaining
bitterly of the havock which the wolves had made the
night previous among the calves in the inclosure front-
ing the house, a number of which they had killed, and
one poor creature I saw nearly dead, which had been
much torn by the ravenous beasts, and shortly after, I
had the satisfaction of shooting at two of the rascals
who were hovering around the premises waiting no
doubt for the darkness, under cover of which to re-
commence their piratical operations. One of them
hobbled off with a charge of shot in him & the blood

---

[35] On Tuesday January 19, Phelps realized he had the wrong day of the
week in the previous entry.

trickling down his side, and will probably dispense with the veal supper which he had doubtless promised himself. A species of fox (called kioti) [coyote] and also jackalls are very tame & although very destructive to poultry, appear to live on very friendly terms with the cattle, and in company with the calves follow the cows about as if they were equally their children.

SUNDAY 24th. Fresh breezes from NW & pleasant. Watch on shore.

MON 25th. Strong Breezes & clear weather. All hands employed in various duties.

TUESDAY 26th. Moderate and pleasant. Received an invitation from an English Gentleman resident here, to accompany him on a ride to the Mission of San Carlos situated in a valley near the River Carmel, about 2 Miles from Monterey, to the south. At this establishment there were about 300 converted Indians when the Missions were in a prosperous state; now there are but a few & the Church & buildings of the Mission are in a ruinous state. The ride to the Mission from Monterey was extremely pleasant. We were mounted on spirited horses. The day was pleasantly warm, and the scenery sufficiently picturesque to be interesting, while the hills are not so abrupt as to inconvenience a horseman. The road lay through fine pasture lands occasionally wooded with gigantic pines, oak and birch trees, but without underwood the presence of which gives it a beautiful park-like appearance. We galloped past the church without stopping, intending to call on our return, and pursued our game up the banks of the river, occasionally crossing and recrossing. At noon we partook of a cold dinner under the shade of a large oak and again mounted, retraced our way down stream shooting Duck, Geese, & Quail, &c. untill sunset when finding we were late to stop at the Mission, we made the best of our way back to Monterey, for my own part highly pleased with the excursion & promising myself to pay San Carlos another visit.

WED. JAN 27th 1841. Pleasant weather with light winds from NW. The Crew employed in cutting fire wood on the hills & various other work. Yesterday a vessel arrived from the Sandwich Islands bringing Papers & Letters from the U. States up to June 11, *but none for me.* If friends at home knew how acceptable letters are to us poor exiles in this distant region, they would – but I won't scold – perhaps the opportunity was not known, and I must live in hopes untill the next arrival.

THURS 28th. Pleasant weather & light winds. Employed in taking in Hides & wooding. Killed a Bullock.

FRIDAY 29. Continuation of fine weather. Got ready for sea.

SAT. 30th. Got under weigh for St. Francisco at daylight with a light breeze from East in company with the *Fly, Claritta* [*Clarita*] & *Maryland* bound to leeward. Ends with variable winds & a heavy swell. Ship off Pt. Anno Nueva [Año Nuevo].

SUNDAY 31st. Beating to windward with the wind NW.

MONDAY FEB 1st. Fresh breezes & clear weather, wind NW with much swell. Latter Part strong Gales

from NNE. Ship under close reeft Mn. [main] Topsail
& FT [foretopmast] Staysail. Heavy Squalls.

TUES 2d. Strong Breezes and moderating. Made Sail.
Wind hauling to NW. Passed the Farallones and at
6 PM anchored at Yerba Buena. Moored Ship & unbent all the Sails. Found lying here a large Russian
ship from Sitka.

WED 3d. Pleasant & warm. Got out the Launch &
hauled her ashore to repair. Part of the crew watering, the rest variously employed. The tem. at Noon
62° in the Cabin.

THURS. FEB 4th. Fresh Westerly winds & pleasant
weather through the day. The Carpenter at work on
the Launch. Hired two large Launches to bring down
Hides from Sta. Hosea [José] about 30 miles up
the bay. The Crew at work cleaning & rigging them.
Last night Capt. Suter [Sutter] a Swiss gentleman spent
with us. He has a tract of land up the River Sacramento, containing "30 Leagues Square" [36] and had
formed a settlement there with about 20 white men &
250 Indians, with which he traps Beaver & Otter &
is also engaged in agricultural pursuits. Speaks in very
glowing terms of the country but as I intend visiting
him this winter, I will not relate his narrative of crossing the Rocky Mountains and founding his little colony
untill I have seen it.

FRIDAY 5th. Moderate & Pleasant throughout the day.
Mr. Robinson & Mr. Mellus went with 4 men in the
Pinnace to St Leandry. Also despatched the 1st & 2nd
officers with 2 launches & 6 men to St Hosea. The Carpenter repairing the monkey rail.[37]

---

[36] Phelps originally wrote, and then struck out, the phrase "14 acres."

SAT 6th.   Fresh Westerly Winds & clear weather Fore
part of the day. Afternoon calm. Pinnace returned from
St. Leandry bringing 63 Hides; reports there being
a plenty of Salmon in the neck of St. L. One fine fellow
was caught with the boat-hook and brought on board.
The flavour of it I think was equal to any that I ever
eat [sic]. I am told there is an abundance of them up
the Sacramento in March April & May. I asked an
Indian how numerous they were. Taking up both his
hands filled with sand, he asked me in return, if I
could count that?

SUNDAY 7th FEB.   Morning Pleasant & Calm. Afternoon cloudy, wind westerly.

MONDAY 8th.   Pleasant & moderate & continues the
same throughout the day. Sent the Pinnace with 4 men
across the bay for hides. Went up the Mission creek
with my gunning float, and quarter Boat to shoot Ducks.
Returned in the afternoon with a dozen. The weather
is now mild & pleasant. There was considerable rain
fell at this place while we were absent from it, and the
green grass has started high enough to afford tolerable
food for cattle. The hills & valleys have a most beautiful appearance, "A green carpet, with flowers of various hues," corresponding to *May* with us, and *this* is
called *Winter here*. And it is a fact that winter in and
about the neighborhood of San Francisco is warmer
and much pleasanter than it is in *summer,* as during
the latter season the strong Westerly winds constantly
blow and thus the sky is clear & without rain or fog.
The air is very cool. In winter heavy rains are com-

---

[37] The monkey rail is a light rail fixed above the bulwarks of the quarter-
deck.

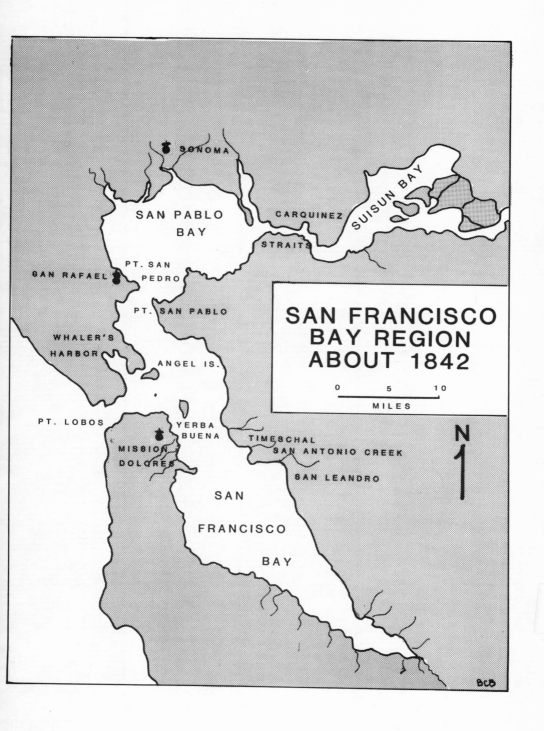

SAN FRANCISCO
BAY REGION
ABOUT 1842

0   5   10
MILES

N

mon and sometimes last for weeks, but the intervals are bright & mild. This winter the rains have kept off unusually late. There has been but little here, while to the south of Monterey, there has been no rain for 10 months, and it is feared the cattle will suffer for feed and the farmers will grow but short crops of wheat. But notwithstanding the unfavourable appearance of things, some of the farms around the bay have commenced sowing, and one man I am told has sown 300 bushels of wheat. Heard to day of the murder of one our best customers at St. Pedro, an Italian by the name of Leandry.

Tues Feb 9th. Continuation of fine weather; winds light & variable. Went up the Mission creek a ducking after breakfast and returned about 3 PM with 35 ducks. Ducks of many varieties and a number of kinds of geese are very abundant in some places about here. The wild Geese are so numerous as to cover large tracts of ground with their efuvia emitting a very offensive odour. The grey ones we find to be very good eating, but white geese are very strong & fishy. The ducks & teal however are excellent and we procure as many as we wish. The feathered tribe in San Francisco are very numerous and have as yet been but little molested. But there are but few that are of beautiful plumage, or of melodious notes. The black vultures (some of them are very large) kites & falcons & hawks are the principal birds of prey. A species of owl of doleful howl flies about in the evening and it is an object of terror to the superstitious Indians. Blackbirds of various species are also abundant, of which there is one kind called by the natives "chenattees" which in its first year is said to be of a greyish slate-colour, during the second changes to deep black, and afterwards black with red shoulders. *Crows* are very numerous and (their tameness is shocking to me) and feed round the houses and door ways in the most familiar manner, and are in fact the most useful bird in the country, they performing the office of scavenger and removing the offal which otherwise would accumulate round the houses in great quantities. Magpies & Blue Jays are found in the woods, and wood pigeons with bronzed imbricated feathers on the back of the neck. To this list of birds may be added the golden winged woodpecker, goat-sucker, – a gold crested wren, ground sparrows, and the hummingbird. The *California Quail* or as they are called by some *Tufted Partridges* are plentiful in the plains. They keep together in large flocks of 3 & 400 are very pretty and are excellent eating. The male and female are distinguished by the former having two handsome black feathers standing erect on the top of the head like the plumes in a soldiers cap, the female having but one. The Indians use these feathers in ornamenting the baskets they make, one basket sometimes containing the plumes of a number of hundred birds. Among the sea fowl there are also Penguins,[38] Pelicans, Shags, Curlews, Divers, &c.

WED 10th. Pleasant weather & light variable winds. Therm. 68° in the shade. The Launches returned from St. Hosea with cargoes of hides, bringing also a deer, a wildcat, & a Gruiya [Grulla, or Sandhill Crane], together with a lot [of] Geese which they shot. At Dark the Pinnace arrived from St. Leandry with Mr

[38] By "penguin" Phelps presumably means some variety of Murre, Guillemot, or Puffin, all large members of the Auk (Alcidae) family; penguins as such are not found in the Northern Hemisphere.

Robinson, Mr. Mellus & other passengers. The crew of the Pinnace were likewise successful in catching some fine Salmon in the creek.

THURS 11th. Weather & winds as yesterday. Employed in trading & packing goods. Dispatched the two launches to Sta. Clara with goods, in charge of the 1st & 2nd officers. Ther. 67° Barom. 30°25.

FRIDAY 12th. Light winds & variable with pleasant weather. Pinnace returned from St. Antonio with Hides.

SAT. 13th. Weather as yesterday. Carpenter caulking between decks.

SUN FEB 14th. Continuation of moderate & pleasant weather. Mr. Leese [39] an Amer. resident at Yerba Buena dined on board to day and reports that one of his Indian boys of about 8 years of age is missing from his house and supposes he was carried off by a Panther that has been prowling round his premises for a number of days. Afternoon took a stroll over the hills and gathered a number of boquets of wild flowers.

MONDAY 15th. Morning foggy & calm. Pinnace returned with a few Hides. Afternoon pleasant. Attended a Pic Nic [sic] on shore given by the Russian officers & in the evening a dance at the house of Mr. Leese.

TUES 16th. Fresh breezes & cloudy in the morning; wind SE at Noon & latter part clear & pleasant. A number of traders on board from different parts of the bay, among them the Mayor-domo of the Mission of

[39] Jacob Primer Leese, born in 1809, emigrated in 1833 to California and soon became a prominent merchant and public figure, first in Los Angeles and then in the San Francisco area. See Bancroft, IV, 710-11 for a summary of his interesting career.

Santa Clara. This mission is now the most considerable
of any [of] the California missions, having about 20,000
head of cattle. The Mayor-domo states that when the
Missions were at their zenith, Horses were so numerous
in the country as to be a nuisance and had known 3000
killed off at one time to get rid of them and leave more
feed for the cattle. The best horses were then to be had
for 50 cents a piece. But there is now a scarcity, as the
Indians on the frontiers for a number of years back
have stole all the horses they could lay hands on. Their
hunting grounds have failed them and they now eat
horses when they can get them, & we have just heard
that Dr. March [Marsh][40] an Am. settler on the
Sacramento has lost every horse (except one which he
was on) which he had on his place amounting to a
number of hundred. The Indians are very ingenious
thieves, and frequently succeed in driving off animals
from the pens or "korrals" where they are confined
at night and even while under the charge of a watch.
An instance of this occurred while we were last at
Monterey. Don David Spence,[41] a Scotch merchant has
a farm about 15 miles from Monterey, and having a
fine drove of tame horses about 40 in number, he built
a "korral" to secure them from the Indians, with a
stout door securely locked and to make doubly sure
a watch house inside of the door in which slept his
Mayor-domo well armed with muskets. During a dark
night the fellow heard a noise as of Indians whispering

---

[40] John Marsh, Harvard '23, arrived in California in 1836, and became
a rancher and some-time doctor (there is some dispute whether he was
licensed to practice). See Bancroft, IV, 730-31; Davis, *Seventy-Five Years,*
317; and George D. Lyman, *John Marsh, Pioneer* (New York, 1930).

[41] David Spence (1798-1875), a Scot by birth, businessman, and public
official of Monterey.

on the outside of the walls. Taking a gun he sallied forth and found the korral door wide open, but could see no Indians, but found that all the horses were yet safe at the back part of the yard, but the animals seemed alarmed and it was evident to the Mayor-domo that all was not right, and he soon found that some Indians were behind the horses trying to drive them out of the door by shaking a dry bladder with gravel in it to alarm them. The Mayor-domo had neglected to shut the door which he found open in his anxiety to see if the horses were gone, and seeing the form of an Indian gliding among the horses he fired his musket at him over their backs. The poor beasts still more alarmed made a rush for the door knocking down their keeper and trampling on him and were received by the rest of the band who were waiting on horseback at a short distance off, and the vagabonds succeeded in getting off with all the horses and were rejoined by the one from within that picked the lock of the door. And when the poor Mayor-domo picked himself up, he heard the rascals whooping & hallooing and hurrying off with their booty untill the sounds of hoofs and the echoes of their shrill voices died in the distance.

The M. domo of Sta. Clara told us a little bear story which I thought worthy of being recorded at the Mission above mentioned. About a year since some of the Indians belonging to the establishment caught a young bear in the woods and carried it home with them to their huts, when one of the women who had just lost her infant and wanting to draw her breasts, took the cub to her bosom, and after a while becoming attached to it, continued her care of [it] untill it grew large and began to exhibit his bear-like propensities by hug-

ging and biting his kind nurse, throwing her down
tearing open her gown and making free with her
breasts in spite of her struggles, and in short treating
his foster-mother with so much ingratitude that the
priest gave orders to shoot him.

WEDNES. 17th.   Morning foggy & calm. At noon wind
West and clear weather. Sent the pinnace to St. Raffel
[Rafael] for hides. At 4 PM the two Launches returned from Santa Clara with 600 Hides. Among the
visitors of to-day was Padre Quijas of Sta. Clara.[42]
This good Father is said to be fond of tempting the
fickle goddess, but has lately experienced her frowns
inasmuch as report saith that he lost $1000 a few days
since at play. Launch reurned from St. Jose.

THURS 18th.   Pleasant & moderate.

FRIDAY 19th.   Weather fine.

SAT. 20th.   Weather as yesterday. At 2 PM went with
the Pinnace to visit the north part of the Bay.

SUNDAY FEB 21st 1841.   Pleasant & Warm. Passed
the forenoon on board the Hudson Bay Compy. Ship
Columbia where we also had passed the night previous.
Capt. Humphrey [Humphreys] was absent, but we
were very hospitably received and entertained by Mr.
Douglass [Douglas], the chief factor of the company
& Mr Forbes, the Supercargo of the ship.[43] About noon

---

[42] Padre José Lorenzo de la Concepción Quijas was a Zacatecano, that is,
a graduate of the Franciscan college in Zacatecas, which in 1833 sent a
contingent to assume charge of the California missions in the San Francisco
area. These padres were generally viewed as less effective or able than
their predecessors (Fernandinos from the college of San Fernando). Quijas,
who took charge of Mission Dolores at San Francisco, but was soon transferred to Solano until his retirement in 1844, was particularly notable for
his fondness for alcohol. Bancroft, III, pp. 318-31, and IV, pp. 224, 785
("yet a good man when sober"); *California Pastoral,* 219-20.

went up the creek to the Mission of St. Raphel [Rafael] and met Capt. H. at the mission. This establishment is in a most beautiful situation, situated in a lovely valley with wood crowned hills on each side. The soil appears rich but is not cultivated and at present only affords pasturing to large herds of cattle. The Mission itself is fast going to decay and the residents are too indolent to raise the most common vegetables. Their whole dependence is on Beef which they can raise without trouble and a few Beans called frijoles which they are enterprising enough to plant and give themselves no further trouble about untill they gather them. The grass is as high here now as it is with us in June. Wild flowers of great variety abound. Peach trees are in blossom. The air is impregnated with their balmy fragrance, and with the singing of numerous birds. There is much to delight the senses.

Took refreshments with the administrador of the Mission and returned to the *Columbia* where we supped and spent the night. The Company has a camp of Beaver hunters at the entrance of the River Sacramento about 20 miles from here, and Mr. Douglass informs me that they contemplate forming a settlement of 150 families on a branch of the above River

---

43 Sir James Douglas, like Capt. Humphreys, was only a temporary visitor. James Alexander Forbes, on the other hand, was a naturalized Mexican citizen, arriving from Scotland in 1831 after some years in South America. From 1836 onwards, he was a local agent for the Hudson's Bay Company in San Jose, and, after 1843, British Vice-Consul for California. After the death of Glen Rae (see below, page 255, n. 35), Forbes, as resident agent, was in charge of the Company's property and agency in San Francisco (1845-46). There is some question whether he was involved in pro-British plots concerning California's future. See Bancroft, III, 743, and Russell M. Posner, "British Consular Agent in California: James A. Forbes, 1843-46," *Southern Calif. Qt.* LIII (1971), 101-12. Forbes died in Oakland in 1881, aged 77.

in June, the preparation for which being the object of his present visit here.

Mon 22d. Started for Yerba Buena at daylight with a light breeze from NE. Shortly after sunrise the wind died away then a thick fog came, upon which, being unable to return to the *Columbia* on acct. of the tide, we landed on Pt. Quentin, made a fire & having shot some wild geese, very soon produced a very good hunters breakfast and to which we did ample justice. While here we observed the Indians catching ducks between the point and a little Island which lies near it. Their method of taking ducks and other wild fowl is rather ingenious. They construct large nets of strips of hide or of flags and repair to such places are the resort of their game which is usually rivers or headlands off which there is an island or mud bank. They fix a long upright pole in each bank and secure one end of the net to the pole opposite to where they hide themselves. A dozen or two of artificial ducks to serve as a decoy (made of bullrushes in a very ingenious manner) are then set afloat under the net and between the poles and the Indians, having a line fast to the other end of the net and passed through a hole in the upper [part] of the pole near them, wait in concealment for their game. When the birds approach they suddenly extend the net across the river by pulling the lines and entercept [sic] them in their flight when they fall stunned into the bag of the net and thus are easily taken.

At 9 AM the weather cleared with a breeze from NE Made sail and arrived on board at noon.

Tuesday 23d. Pleasant with variable winds. Despatched the large launch to Santa Clara with goods in charge of the 2d. Officer and sent a party of 4 men to cut wood.

The few Am. residents who are at Yerba Buena are now busy with their gardens, planting and transplanting, but some who commenced earlier have radishes, salad, & some other vegetables already out of the ground, but the season is unusually dry and unless they receive some rain soon, there will be neither wheat, vegetables, or even feed for cattle. Discharged one of the seamen for repeated drunkenness & disorderly conduct. Sent the Pinnace to St. Leandry with goods, and the Yawl to get shell fish.

WEDNES. 24th. Cloudy, wind South. People cutting wood & various other work. Pinnace returned, bringing some fine salmon. Mr. Robinson & myself went with the cutter and 5 men went to *Borri Borri* (the farm of Don Antonio Sanchez),[44] partly on business and partly to hunt. Anchored there at 2 PM. The old gentleman had heard of our intended visit and provided a dinner for us which was served up in his best style (and poor enough was that). He is possessor of a fine farm 15 miles in length by 4 wide has about 8000 head of cattle, a large house, with but very few of the comforts of life in it, save & excepting a great many children & grandchildren (he is himself a widower) and although his farm is excellently adapted for the raising of large crops – he has not a single acre under cultivation, consequently he [has] nothing to eat but Beef & Beans

---

[44] On Don José Antonio Sánchez, see page 84, note 29; Borri-bori or Buri-buri, formerly part of Mission Dolores, was a few miles south of San Francisco, roughly at modern day San Mateo (the name comes from an Indian tribe formerly resident in the area). Davis, *Seventy-Five Years,* pp. 5 and 171, discusses the rancho; Phelps, above, page 84, gives a somewhat different estimate of the size of the same holding.

and bread made from wheat which he raised 3 years
since and which wheat he would not sell for the reason
that he would not get over 1:50 *cts* per bushel, and he
will raise no more untill that supply fails. It is aggra-
vating to see such a fine country lying unimproved in
the possession of these miserable drones. A Yankee or
English farmer would make it a paradise. However,
we partook of his fare, and being supplied with a
couple of tame horses that would stand fire, we sallied
forth over the plains in pursuit of game, and found
Ducks & Geese by the acre. The plains were alive with
them and upon firing at them, which we did sitting
on horseback, they would rise in immense bodies with
a clang that could be heard at a long distance. Wild
Turkies [sic] were also found in considerable numbers,
and long before sunset we returned to where the cutter's crew had hitched the tent and a noble supper was
prepared from our game and the store chest of the
boat, to which we invited Don Sanchos and his lazy
sons and right glad were they of the chance. To avoid
giving offence Mr. R. & myself accepted a bed at the
house tho we would have preferred passing the night
in our tent, and after a second supper which the old
gentleman forced us to partake of at his house, we
retired to our bed which was a large double bed in
a dark room without a window and as destitute of
furniture as the cell of [a] recluse. The bed was placed
in the corner, and although we were not as much annoyed by fleas as we expected to have been we were
somewhat incommoded (at least I was) when, as I
happened to be the first to turn in, I rolled over to the
wall side of the bed "to make stowage" I encountered
in my way a nest of eggs which some motherly old hen

had deposited on the sheets and as the bed had not been occupied for weeks probably had escaped the notice of the *tidy chambermaid,* who by the way I believe was an Indian boy. However the eggs were all squashed, and as we said nothing of the affair next morning I presume it will be a number of weeks before the disaster will be discovered.

At daylight we again went for more game and were successful. Returned to the tent to breakfast and at noon returned to the ship with lots of game, on

THURS, 25th with strong breezes from WNW and found that the *Bolivar* from Monterey, the *Leonidas* from Sta. Barbara and the *Columbia* had arrived in our absence. The *Leonidas* brought up letters from a vessel which had arrived at the leeward ports from the Islands for Mr. R., Mr. Mellus and others from home, but alas for me I am again disappointed – no tidings for me of my far distant home – but I am sure it could not have been from neglect and will hope soon to hear that my beloved ones are in health.

Today we have had a few hours of rain, which is the first we have experienced for eight months. There is now hopes of vegetation doing well.

FRIDAY 26th. Southerly winds with light rains. Sent the small Launch with 5 men to Sanchez's farm for Hides. Part of the crew filling water. Ends pleasant.

SAT. 27th. Pleasant throughout the day. Launch returned from Sanchez's farm with a load of Hides and was sent for a load of fire wood in the afternoon. Firewood is easily obtained not far from the ship. We have only to send men with axes to the nearest wood and cut what we choose which generally consists of young oak.

Following the example of the people of the country our men instead of cutting down the large oaks at the foot ascend the tree and lop off the large branches that being more convenient than working up the whole tree would be. Ends with fresh NW winds.

SUNDAY 28th. Light winds & cloudy. The large Launch returned from Santa Clara with Hides & Tallow. The political aspect of California is again becoming dark and unsettled. The signs of the times strongly indicate Revolution. The miserable policy pursued by the local government causes strong dissatisfaction among the people and there is evidently a storm brewing that will soon burst upon the heads of the "powers that be" who now rule and misgovern the country. To increase the bad feelings of the people or rather to awaken them still more to see they are sadly imposed upon, the Governor of Monterey has issued an "officio" prohibiting foreign vessels from trading on the coast, which measure is extremely obnoxious to all parties in the country except a few petty merchants at Monterey & some of the Gov*t*. minions. This regulation if carried into effect will exclude our ships from the trade and even now our factor has received an intimation from his Excellency that he must set a time when he will settle his business & depart. But as the cargo of our ship was entered and the duties amounting to about $25,000 were paid with the understanding that we were to trade on the coast untill our cargo was complete for home, nothing but force of arms will turn us from our purpose.[45]

---

[45] The regulation referred to was issued by Governor Alvarado in January 1841 (following a warning of a year earlier), ordering all foreign vessels to discharge and pay duties on cargoes in Monterey only, the coasting

MY DEAR WIFE. As I have now concluded that instead of writing a package of letters to send you by the *Monsoon* (who will probably depart for home in April) I will send you this journal as you may gather more knowledge of our state of affairs and how I am situated and occupied here than perhaps you will glean from my letters. Therefore as it is intended for your eyes alone I shall expect that you will not loan it to any person. If any of the family wish to look over it I have no objection, but I do request that you will not permit it to go the rounds as some of my former hieroglyphics [sic] have. As I have not said anything respecting California yet from which you can judge of its character, population, &c., I will in the next chapter give you some outline of its history. *California.* The extensive tract of country comprises under the general name of California (or the Californias) constitutes at present a part of the Republic of Mexico & was formerly included in the Viceroyalty of New Spain. It extends along the border of the great Pacific Ocean which bounds it on the west. The northern limit of the country actually settled by the Spaniards is the Bay of St. Francisco, the entrance to which lies in the Lat. of 37°19 N. The Southerly boundary is Cape St. Lucas which is also the extremity of the Peninsula of Lower California in Lat. 22°48 N & Long. 109° 47 West; consequently the direction of the coast is about NW. [It is] Bounded on the East by the Gulf of California, the Rio Colorado, and the Indian territory which also limits it on the North.

---

trade being strictly prohibited. The regulation seems to have been enforced only once. When the *Tasso* arrived from Boston, her master simply threatened to depart, paying no duties at all. Faced with the loss of some $20,000 in duties, the authorities quickly gave in (Bancroft, IV, pp. 206-7).

When spoken of conjointly, the two countries have
been, and still are, frequently designated as the Californias, although constituting but one province or
territory in a political sense. They are considered as
two distinct countries, both from their natural differ-
ences as well as their civil history, the Peninsula being
termed Lower as being in a lower latitude and 'vice
versa'. Upper California was settled and civilized by
Father Junipero Serra, a Franciscan Friar, in 1768,
who with sixteen Brothers of his own order were all
taken from the convent of San Fernando in Mexico
to plant the cross on these shores, which they had failed
in conquering by force of arms. *San Diego* was the first
Mission founded by them, afterwards Monterey and
St. Buenaventura and before his death in 1782 he with
his spiritual associates had succeeded in forming eight
Missions, in the accomplishment of which, these pious
and indefatigable men maintained an almost constant
warfare against hordes of wild and cruel natives, but
in all cases exhibited a pious humble and meek de-
meanour, and were always averse to shedding the blood
of the Indians, and it was only in defence of their lives
that they would permit the few soldiers which Mexico
had sent to protect them to resist the aggressions of
the Indians. Pursuing the same plan of colonization
and management commenced by the first Missionaries,
with little or no variation, their successors, persevered
in their labours untill the whole of California, with
most of the natives, came under the temporal & spiritual dominion of the Missionaries. Since the first
foundation of the missions, many large donations have
been bestowed, and numerous estates in lands and
houses left for their benefit, which were consolidated

into a fund called the "California Pious Fund." This
fund was managed by the Convent of San Fernando and
other settlers in Mexico. The proceeds were remitted
annually to California. The King of Spain also in
addition to paying salaries to the Missionaries of about
400 dollars per year, sent a small body of soldiers to
protect them from the Indians and foreign enemies.
Under this state of things, the missions greatly pros-
pered. They went on augmenting their possessions,
increasing their stock of domestic animals, and convert-
ing the Indians untill they had absorbed nearly all the
valuable lands to the almost total exclusion of the free
white settlers. No one could possess land except by a
grant from the Missionaries, who on all occasions were
very reserved in making such grants. The Missionary
establishments were acknowledged to be the great ob-
jects for which the country was settled and maintained
and the spiritual conquest of the Fathers made them
possessors of the land and owners of all its produce.

Upper California is divided into four military dis-
tricts, the head quarters of which are denominated
Presidios. At each of these Presidios (or Presidencies)
are stationed some few soldiers under the command
of a military commandant. These Presidios are San
Francisco, Monterey, Santa Barbara and St. Diego.
The buildings at these different stations are nearly
all of the same class. They consist of a square of about
200 yards on each side, inclosed by a wall of unburnt
bricks called 'dobys' of about 12 feet high and 4 feet
thick, within which are the residence of the commandant, barracks for the troops, warehouses, &c.

The Missions of which there were about 20 were
also all formed on one plan, and consequently resemble

each other. Each mission is governed by one or more
missionaries, all Friars of the order of San Francisco.
One of them is styled "Padre President" and through
him is (or was) carried on all the public correspondence with Mexico, but he has no power superior to the
others, and each is absolute in his own Mission. Each
mission had allotted to it in the first instance a tract
of land 15 miles square, and of course advantageously
chosen. Part of the land was cultivated, and the rest
appropriated to grazing and the rearing of cattle. The
buildings are built in the form of a square, the Church
forming the most elevated and conspicuous part. The
apartments of the Fathers were some of them spacious.
The storerooms and workshops compose the remainder.
The converted Indians lived in huts at about 150 yards
from the prinicpal buildings. The huts are made of
dobys and all the buildings constructed by the Indians
under the direction of the Fathers. The storehouses of
the larger Missions were of great extent & variety.
There were places for making soap, melting Tallow,
Blacksmith's and Carpenter's shops, Sadlers, Tailors,
& Shoemakers establishments, storehouses for the articles manufactured, and the produce of the lands, such
as Tallow, Butter, Soap, Wool, Hides, dried Beef,
beans, Peas, Wheat &c. The Church is of course the
main object of attraction in all the Missions, and is
often, and especially during the festivals, gaudily
decorated with the pictures and paphenalia [sic] that
is generally found in catholic churches. In several there
are pictures, the subjects of them representations of
Heaven and Hell glaringly coloured to strike the rude
senses of the Indians. The Priests all take care to be
well provided with rich dresses for the purpose of

inspiring awe. The whole object of the California Missionary system being the conversion of the Indians and the training of them up to a civilized life, the constant care of the Fathers was directed to these ends, and all who have visited California and has seen what has been accomplished by them, must feel convinced that the *original* founders were men of singular humanity & benevolence and Christianlike motives. To each Missionary, the entire and exclusive management of his Mission is allotted. He is the absolute Lord & Master of all his Indians, and of the soil – he directed all the operations and economy of the establishment, agricultural, mechanical, manufacturing and commercial – and all the produce was disposed of at his will and pleasure. He alloted his lands, distributed his cattle, ordered his seed time and harvest, encouraged, chastised and commanded all the human beings under his charge, and all this without being accountable to any power on earth, and there are but few instances upon record where men have enjoyed such unlimited confidence and power and have not abused them, and yet it is said of none of the original missionaries of California (or of those who ruled during the greatest prosperity of the Missions and while they were left free and untrammelled in their operation) that they have not acted with the most perfect fidelity, or that they ever betrayed their trust, or exercised inhumanity, and the united testimony of all travellers Protestant or Catholic who have visited California certifies the same. Strangers have found at the Missions the most generous and disinterested hospitality, protection and kindness, whatever may have been their country or mode of faith. The best and most unequivocal proof of the good

conduct of the Fathers is to be found in the unbounded
affection and devotion invariably shown towards them
by their Indian subjects. They venerate them not merely as friends and fathers, but with a degree of devoted-
ness to adoration. On the occasion of removals that
have taken place of late years from political and other
causes their distress in parting with their pastors has
been extreme, and they have entreated to be permitted
to follow them in their exile with tears and lamenta-
tions. But revolutions and party measures have given
the death blow to the Missions. In the present unsettled
state of California in its internal and external political
relations, and more particularly in the state of anarchy
which has resulted from the many changes that have
taken place of late years, the Missions have been suffered to decay. Mexico instead of remitting the moneys
which have heretofore been sent annually to pay the
offices and soldiers and for the support of the laws
have left the colony to its own resources. Instead of
money, military officers and placemen have been sent,
increasing its debts by their salaries and California is
left to bear the deficiency as she best may, leaving the
soldiers in rags and the employees without pay. The
result of the whole, is, that all parties have to recur
to the Missions and Friars for their daily maintenance
to prevent them from starvation. Consequently the
cattle of the Missions have been "divided amongst them,
and for the lands they cast lots" and they are now quar-
reling for the largest slices. The poor Indians being
no longer able to procure a living at the Missions, and
not finding the protection they have been accustomed
to find while penned up in the missionary folds, have
most of them returned to again "wander free in their

native wilds." And here you will ask, what have been the actual benefits conferred by these Catholic Missionaries (good men though they doubtless were); what have the natives of California gained by their labours; what service have those Friars rendered to the Spanish nation, or to the world in general? All that we can allow, is, that the Catholic Fathers were honest men, that they pursued with assiiduity [sic] what they believed to be their duty, that they laboured in their vocation with zeal. But we must entirely condemn their system, and lament its results, and California presents another picture of the withering, blighting effects of Catholicism. Under other management it might now have been the abode of millions of the human family, employing all the advantages and comforts of civilization and wealth which some other states of America not so favourably situated are so fully possessed of. The mind of man can hardly conceive a contrast more complete than that between the present state of California, and the United States of America. But there are some hopes of a better state of things for California not very far distant. As the Missions decrease and are broken up, individual property is increasing. The tide of emigration is flowing from the eastward of the Rocky Mountains to these shores, and as we hear that the U. States Govt. is in treaty with Mexico for the California territory, it is not improbable that a few years will see this beautiful country in the possession of a people who can appreciate its natural advantages. As yet there are but few people from the States here (about St. F.) but there about twenty five or thirty at the ports of Sta. Barb., Monterey &c. most of them mercantile adventurers, but few of them however are of decent habits, and I must say this fact, that it reflects disgrace on the U.S. to see so many of its citizens established here, and especially so many as there are from the moral & religious states of the North, without infusing among the degenerate inhabitants of this country somewhat of the correct and sterling principles which they had imbibed or at least been taught at home. I regret to say, that it appears to me, that these mercantile adventurers shook off their principles as they shook off the dust from their feet on leaving their native soil of New England and that on arriving here instead of trying to check by precept & example the progress of dissolute practices, they jumped at once headlong into the vortex, and willingly whirled round in utter recklessness of their better feelings and more enlightened education.

MONDAY MARCH 1st.   Pleasant weather & Westerly winds. Sent the 1st officer with 4 men in the cutter to kill & salt Beef at *Borri Borri*. The launch with Mr. Mellus and 4 men to procure Hides at *San Pablo,* and in the afternoon started myself in company of an English Capt. and a young man (clerk of the *Bolivar*) in the Pinnace for St. Leandry, partly on business and partly for pleasure. Arrived at the landing place at dark, and spent the night at the house of Don Estedillo. Were entertained after their best manner, and passed a very comfortable night in the same room where I was so tormented with fleas the last time I was over here, and now I was aggreeably disappointed at their total absence.

TUES 2d.   At daylight dispatched the Pinnace to St. Antonio for Hides, to return for us on the next tide, and in the mean time we passed the hours pleasantly enough in riding over the plains, shooting Geese, Ducks, and chasing foxes. At high water we stretched an old net (which we found on [a] fence) across the creek and after several attempts we finally caught 19 Salmon. The Salmon here are as large as those that are sold in Boston Market, but their flavour is not so good – but this is early for them, and we are assured that [in] May & June they are better & more abundant. The Boat returned during the night – and –

WED. 5th. [3d] The Morning pleasant. We left the Creek after partaking of an excellent breakfast with our host & his family who I'm sure did all in their power to render our stay as aggreeable as possible. The good Donna and her daughter pride themselves on their skill in the culinary department, and we were fully satisfied that their pretentions were not vain ones. In fact we were enabled while here with the Ducks, Geese, Salmon &c. which we obtained ourselves and which were served up to us in excellent order together with the good things the house afforded such as milk, eggs, good fresh butter &c., &c., to live on the fat of the land & sea. You would be amused at their manner of milking their cows in this country. I noted them several times while at St. Leandry. In the morning they send a boy with a horse and lasso in search of the animals (that are left to roam at pleasure over the plains except when they want milk). Their cows and oxen are all what we should call wild with us, but the tamest of their cows have to be caught with the never failing 'lasso' and dragged to a tree, where they are firmly secured by a rope round the horns. Their legs are tied together, and an Indian sitting down on each side succeeds in extracting the milk while the poor creature is nearly strangled. The method of rigging their ox carts is after about the same fashion. The beast is dragged with horses to the cart, thrown down and his legs tied. Another is brought and placed in the same condition parallel with the first. The spear of the cart is then thrust between them and secured to the yoke which is placed on top of the head and lashed to the horns. Their legs are then untied and they are suffered to get up and as may be expected after such rude treatment are quite unruly, but they manage to get them along after much trouble by having one Indian go ahead of the cattle to show them the way and two others, one on each side, to beat them with long sticks and when the sticks fail they urge them on by pricking them with knives. As I have frequently spoken of the 'Lasso' I will give you a farther [sic] account of their manner of using it when I am less tired than I am now. *So good night* (but I should have said that we arrived on board ship about sunset). All the boats returned to-day.

THURS 4th.   Continuation of warm, pleasant, delightful weather. Bent the Sails.

FRIDAY 5th.   Weather as yesterday. The Crew filling water, repacking beef, &c. Dined on board the Hon. Hudson Bay Co. Ship *Columbia*. I will not trouble you with an account of the dinner – you know I'm no epicure – and will only say that I partook of part of a Beaver which was the first I had ever seen. Mr. Douglass brought it from his hunting camp on the Sacramento a few days before. Mr. D., who is the chief Factor of the Company, has been in the service

27 years and has not been home for the last 20, is still a young man for such a service (about 45), a very gentlemanly man, is a professor of Religion, and possessed of extensive information. I was much gratified with his conversation, and passed a very agreeable afternoon on board.

The H.H.B. Compy [Hon. Hudson's Bay Co.] have their most considerable establishment (west of the Rocky Mountains) at Fort Vancouver on the Columbia River at about 100 miles from the Sea. At that place they have their principal depot, dwelling houses, stores, workshops, &c., containing a population of about 800 souls, all of whom are the Company's servants. They have several hundred acres of land under cultivation near the Fort, but the climate and soil is inferior to California. Mr. Douglass speaks of the Am. Methodist missionaries in the highest terms. He represents them as being in a very prosperous condition, industrious and of ineprocahable [sic] character. He is on terms of intimacy with most of the families and appears to have found much gratification in their society. They nearly support themselves but are in great want of cattle, to supply which band for the purpose of introducing cattle into the Oregon he brought with him to this place 60 men to drive up some thousands of cattle & sheep which he has purchased and which are now on their way to the Columbia. The situation occupied by the Missionaries is on a stream called the *Wallamet* [Willamette] which empties into the Columbia about 20 miles below Vancouver. The Hudson Bay people and ours seem to be on good terms, and gladly welcome any respectable, industrious settlers who come among them.

SAT 6th MARCH. The weather continues delightfully pleasant in the day & the evenings are quite cloudless. Some considerable rain has fallen the last week in other parts of the country and when it was most needed, and there is not much to fear now on acct. of feed for cattle.

Employed in repacking Beef & various other work.

SUN. 7th. Begins with strong gales from N.W. with clear and pleasant weather. All Hands at rest. Oh that it was permitted me to join with my ships' company in the public performance of religious duties on board, but situated as we are, it is impossible. The crew are away in the boats or hard at work during the week, and the sabbath is the only day, during the present state of our work, which they can be allowed to mend & wash their clothes. These voyages are very unfavourable to the cultivation of religion. There are such bad examples from high places as counteract all that I have endeavoured to do for the moral & religious improvement of my crew.

The Church of England service is observed on board of the *Columbia*. On the Sabbath at 11 AM and I intended and wished to have attended, but am prevented by the blowing a gale of wind (Mr. Douglass officiates). My heart longs for the events of the Lord, and while absent from the privilege and blessings which I have been accustomed to enjoy with beloved friends, May the Holy Spirit stir up my heart & raise my desires & affections towards Heaven. Separated by oceans from each other, may we be united in spirit.

The Lasso. I believe I have before mentioned that the Lasso is a rope of hide about 6 fathoms in length, with a slip noose at one end. From the circumstances of the cattle being seldom folded [i.e., closely confined], they are very shy and in a half wild state, for which reason it is necessary in catching them to use the lasso. This is so wonderfully managed by the Californians that it can never be seen practiced without admiration. A time is set apart at certain seasons of the year at all the Missions and Farms for the purpose of overlooking, counting, and marking the cattle by branding them on the flank with the owner's mark (that is, the calves, the increase of the past year) and perform other operations to accustom them to herd together and prevent them from running wild. This is called a *'Rodea'* [Rodeo] and is an occasion at which all the male inhabitants of the estate and its vicinity are present. Great numbers come from distant villages to assist gratuitously at the fete.

The cattle are driven into a large 'corral' or fold, at a wide opening on one side. This is afterwards closed up, except a small gateway, left for one to pass out at a time. Those that are to be operated upon are made to escape at this door singly, and when a bull finds himself in the open fields he makes off with the utmost speed pursued by a score of horsemen swinging their lassos in the air and while in full chase and when they get within point blank [range] those foremost throw their lassos, some round the horns, others round the neck, some entrap a hind leg, others a fore one. They then stop short their well trained horses, bringing taut the lasso, one end being made fast to the truck [horn] of the saddle, and the bull falls as if shot, tumbling heels over head. In this state the wildest bull lies perfectly motionless and suffers any operation to be performed upon him almost without making any effort at resistance. I am never tired with looking on and wondering at the dexterity with which this feat of the lasso is performed, nor can I comprehend by what act a man at full gallop can throw a noose with such precision as to catch a bull by the hind leg while he is in full flight from his pursuers. Early and constant practice can only enable them to accomplish this, and indeed the practice of the Lasous [sic] begins with their earliest childhood. The first plaything you see in a boy's hand is a lasso of thread or twine with which he essays to ensnare his mother's kittens or chickens and perhaps from their elemental essays the theory of the lasso can only be comprehended, for the rapidity and magical like effect with which the real lasso is thrown leaves no time or opportunity to see how it acts. It appears that to secure the hind leg, the large noose of the lasso, which by swinging it around the head is formed into a circle, is thrown so as to pass under the leg at the very moment when this is elevated in making the spring while the bull is galloping, and placed exactly where the leg must fall on coming to the ground. When the lasso is then thrown and the leg is placed within the circle of its noose, the thrower immediately checks his horse and gives the lasso a jerk in the very instant of time when the bulls [46] foot touches the ground and thus draws the noose up and tightens it round the leg. All this must be done in a moment of time and although it appears almost impossible yet I think this is the mode of operating. To catch the animal by the horns or neck is easily understood, yet even to do this

---

[46] In his passage, Phelps has added at a later date the word "bullock" after "bull," bullock meaning in this case "steer," the point being that Phelps is discussing the treatment of ordinary cattle, not full-grown uncastrated bulls.

with certainty to a bullock at full speed, and on a horse in chase, requires much practice and dexterity. *The Saddles* used are well fitted for the purpose. They rise high before and behind and have a knob on the fore part on which the rider can lay hold and secure himself and on which they can make fast or wind up their lasso. The horses are taught to lean over when checked against the direction in which the bullock draws and thereby secure themselves from being capsized by the sudden tug occasioned by the impetus of the animal when it is brought up by the lasso.

The Bridle used is equally well adapted to the purpose, being most powerful in its structure, and calculated for suddenly checking a horse. It is a single curb of peculiar construction, having the bit doubled up high in the mouth without a joint, and instead of a curb chain, it has a solid ring of iron which passes through the upper part of the doubled up bit within the mouth and then passes behind the lower jaw, thus forming a tremendous lever sufficient to break the jaw if powerfully applied. The use of this rendering the horse's mouth so sensible and gives the rider such power over him, that he is checked at full speed in the most extraordinary manner. It is a common practice with the Californians when exercising their horses, to ride up full speed at a wall and when the horse's head is within a few inches of it to check them all at once. This masterly mode of managing their horses can alone enable them to use the lasso with such dexterity as they do.

MONDAY MARCH 8th. Strong Gales from North with clear weather. The Crew repairing sails. Ends the same.

TUES. 9th. Moderate & Pleasant. Sent the Pinnace to St. Leandry. 2d Officer & 5 Men gone to cut fire wood. At 11 A M. Went in company with Capt. Humphrey of the *Columbia* up the creek of the Mission (Dolores) on a shooting excursion. Were supplied with horses at the Mission. Found game very abundant such as Geese, Wild Turkies, Ducks & Teal, and enjoyed an excellent ride on good horses. Returned to the ship at dark. Heard this morning that a vessel from the U. States has arrived at Monterey. Hope in a few days to receive letters from Home. Pleasant & warm weather continues.

WEDNES 10th. Moderate and pleasant weather throughout the day. Crew wooding & watering. At 3 PM the *Columbia* sailed, saluting the shipping with 5 guns which we returned. Mr. Douglass the chief Factor, Capt. Humphrey & Messrs Forbes & Wood we were much pleased with, and we were sorry to part with them after our short but very pleasant acquaintance. "May the shadows never be less."

THURS. MARCH 11th. Cloudy & Moderate. Went in Pinnace to fish, and returned at noon unsuccessful. Part of the crew watering. Sent the Pinnace to San Pablo for Hides. Evening Wind SE with indications of rain. Rain is much wanted to save the grass and wheat. The wheat that is sown in this neighborhood is now about 5 inches high. All garden vegetables are making their appearance also, and hopes are entertained of there being good crops notwithstanding the lateness of the rains.

To give some idea of the richness of the lands in this country and of how favourable the climate is for agriculturists I will mention a fact made known to us by the Major-Domo of San Jose Mission. In 1838 he caused eight fanegas (a fanega is 2 bushels & 1 peck) [47] of wheat to be sowed at the above place, and harvested from that seed the same year 1200 fanegas. The following year they gathered 500 fanegas on the same land of what grew from the seed wasted in the gathering, and last year, 1839, 200 fanegas, from the same seed and without any sowing or cultivating except the first year and it is also expected that there will be another crop from the same this year of perhaps 75 fanegas. But this is not a fair sample of the lands of California. The average yield is computed to be 112 for one, or 112 bushels for one bushel planted. Broad and fair are the plains, and beautiful & rich its Vallies, and may the time come when a busy and intelligent people shall possess them to the exclusion of the lazy drones who now inhabit it.

FRIDAY MARCH 12th. Strong SE winds. Cloudy & some slight sprinkling of rain. Got the launch in, and got ready for sea. Latter part Squally wind SE with Rain.

SAT. 13th. Strong Gales from SE with Rain, and continued throughout the 24 hours.

SUNDAY 14th. Morning moderate breezes from S East and Showery. Pinnace returned [from] San Pablo with Hides. Afternoon Pleasant winds variable. Capt. Suter's boat arrived from his settlement on the Sacramento (which he has named New Helvetia) bringing us a large quantity of Beaver Skins.

---

[47] In California the *fanega* seems to have been two and a half English bushels, as Phelps remarks (See Bancroft, *California Pastoral,* 350) ; more commonly, however, it was one and a half bushels – as noted by Robinson, *Life in California,* 61, who tells the same story from the same majordomo (and see Davis, *Seventy-Five Years,* 103).

MON 15th.   Begins with Fresh breezes from SE with clear weather. People employed in drying Furs & Hides. Unmoored Ship. The sea on the bar breaking heavily rendering it impossible for a ship to get to sea until a change of winds takes place. Ends Squally.

TUES. 16th.   Southerly Winds with Rain. Crew employed in filling water. Ends Pleasant.

WEDNESDAY 17th.   Wind prevailing in the Southern quarter with frequent showers. Received 400 hides from the brig *Leonidas*. Latter part heavy rains.

THURS. 18th.   Pleasant and warm throughout the day. The wind from N to W. The Bar is too rough to pass over it with safety. By the arrival at Monterey before mentioned, Mr. Robinson has received letters dated August but none for me. It is now 14 m*s* [months] that I have not heard a syllable from my family (God grant they are well & happy).

FRIDAY MARCH 19th.   Light westerly winds & pleasant weather at 9 A M. Hove short & made sail on the Ship, but the breeze failing, clewed up & furled the sails again at 12 N. Went up the Mission creek after game. Returned with three Geese & ten Ducks; wounded a Deer but he escaped. The Indians at this season of the year live mostly by the chase and avail themselves of devices to ensnare and decoy their game. In their method deceiving the deer by placing a head of the animal on their own shoulders they are very expert and most always successful. To do this, they fit the head and horns of a deer upon the head of a huntsman, the rest of his body being painted to resemble the colour of a deer. Disguised in this manner he proceeds to the haunts of the deer, armed with his bow & arrows and on approaching them endeavors to imitate their actions, secreting as much of his body as possible for which purpose he selects places where the grass is high. This stragem seldom fails to draw the deer around him, and when one of the herd approaches near enough the arrow is sent with unerring aim (generally) to the heart of the animal who falls without alarming his companions in which case a number is frequently killed before they find out the deception, but if the animal is only wounded, the whole herd immediately put to flight.

The Third Passage

San Francisco to San Diego and
Return to San Luis Obispo

SAT. MAR. 20th [1841]. Begins with a strong gale from the North. At daylight reeft the Topsails & hove short the cable. At 9 AM got under weigh with the ebb tide and worked out of the Bay. At 1 PM Ship clear of the entrance, turned the Reefs out of the Topsails & made all sail for Monterey. Major Warren of Boston (passanger)*. Latter Part pleasant & moderate.

SUNDAY 21st. Morning light variable winds & pleasant. Ship off the Mission of Santa Cruz. Saw a Brig steering to the North. 10 AM moderate breezes from NW. At 1 PM anchored at Monterey with the best bower in 7 fathoms water. Received visits from the port Capt. and custom house officer.

The hills and plains around Monterey have the appearance of dryness. There appears to have been no rain here as yet. The prospect for crops of wheat &c and food for cattle looks unfavourable in this neighbourhood, but at the rate Indians are relieving the colonists of their cattle there may not be many left for them to feed. The boarding officers inform us that four days since [i.e., ago] a body of Indians came within 6 miles of Monterey and stole and drove off two hundred horses belonging to different individuals in the

---

* William ("Major") R. Warren arrived from Honolulu with his wife in 1836; he also worked for Spear at Monterey. Bancroft, V, p. 768.

town. These predatory bands consist of Christian Indians who formerly belonged to the Missions but since they could no longer be provided for there, returned and again mixed with their wild brethren of the forest with whom they sally forth, or rather head and direct their uncivilized companions in their plundering excursions. The horses are eaten by them, and it [is] said they prefer their flesh to that of bullocks. The *Indian* tribes of California are said to be about 25 or 30, so that one Mission (that of Santa Clara) has had natives belonging to it of eleven different dialects. The tribes are frequently at war with each other, often in consequence of trespassing upon the hunting grounds of each other, and sometimes the weakest tribe has been nearly exterminated and the remnant obliged to associate with that of their conquerors. But such is their revengeful dispositions that but little humanity is shown to those who fall in their power.

Their weapons are bows & arrows only; no other is ever seen in use among them. Their bows are elegantly and ingeniously constructed, and will discharge an arrow to a considerable distance. The bows are strengthened by a sinew fitted to the bow while it is wet, the sinew being of the rise of the wood, and covering the back. The ends turn back to receive the string. As the sinew dries, it draws the bow back the reverse way to that in which it is intended to be used, the sinew in drying giving the bow such a great curvature that it requires no small skill and strength to string them.[48]

The Indians of this coast, like the Arabs and other wandering tribes, move about the country pitching their

[48] Author's footnote: "I have a number which I intend sending or taking home with me."

tents whereever they find a convenient place for hunting, keeping however within their own district.

The Religion of all the tribes is idolatrous. The Alchone [49] tribe who inhabit the seacoast between Monterey & St. Francisco worship the sun and believe in the existence of a good and an evil spirit whom they occasionally attempt to propitiate. When a person dies they decorate the corpse with flowers, beads & feathers, and placing a bow and arrows beside it on a pile of wood, burn it amidst the wild acclamations of the spectators who wish the soul a pleasant journey to its new abode in another world which they imagine lies beyond the setting sun.

The Indians in their wild state are more healthy than those which have been subject to the Missions, and it may be said with equal truth of the Indians here as of those in our Western States, that "civilization is death to the Indian." Unaccustomed to restraint, their free spirits sicken and die in the presence of a master, and as Washington Irving truely says, "the sound of the white settler's axe, rings the death knell of the Indian." They cultivate no land, and subsist mostly by the chase, and upon the spontaneous produce of the earth. Acorns of which there is a great abundance in this country constitute their principal vegetable food. In the proper season they gather a supply of these, bake them and then bruise them between two stones into a paste which will keep untill the next season.

---

[49] The meaning of Alchone is not clear, as is usually the case with Indian tribal designations used by Phelps. The area of the coast between Monterey and San Francisco was the homeland of the Costanoan Indians, with seven dialect divisions. These people did indeed cremate their dead. A. L. Kroeber, *Handbook of the Indians of California* (N.Y., 1976), Ch. 31.

Tattooing is practiced among them by both sexes by the way of ornament and also to distinguish one tribe from the other. I saw a girl of the Tularios, a servant in Mr. Luce's [Leese] family at San Francisco whose cheeks and chin were marked precisely in the same manner as I have seen the New Zealanders.

The principal business of the men consists in making the weapons used for their defence, and in the chase, and providing for their support. The women attend to the domestic affairs. They also make a great variety of baskets and ornamental parts of their dresses, likewise blankets of feathers, one of which I obtained from the Sacramento which exhibits much ingenuity and I should think a great deal of labour. Their closely wove baskets are not only capable of containing water, but are used for cooking their meals in. A number of scarlet feathers from a bird which produces one under each wing are wove in with the wood, and to the rim are affixed small black quills of the California Partridges of which birds a hundred pair are required to decorate one basket.[50] They are otherwise ornamented with beads, and pieces of mother of pearl shell. They also embroider belts very beautifully [with] wing feathers of different colours, and the work with great neatness, making use of the quills of the porcupine and the bark of trees for caps and dresses of the chiefs, and a great many other feather ornaments, which I cannot now describe.

Mon. March 22d. Westerly Winds & pleasant in the morning. Crew variously employed in mending

---

[50] Author's footnote: "I sent you by the ship *California* some specimens. Others will accompany this, by the *Monsoon*."

sails & refitting rigging. Received one boat load of Hides. Latter part foggy wind from WSW. One man Sick.

Tues 23d.   Morning moderate & pleasant. Received two boat loads of Hides. Latter Strong winds from WNW. Carpenter repairing the Cutter.

Wed. 24th.   Begins with Strong Gales from NW and a high swell rolling into the Bay. At 9 AM let go the small bower Anchor & gave the Ship a long scope on each cable. Sent down Top Gallant Yards & bent the Sheet Cable. 10:30 Gale increasing, let go the sheet anchor. 4 PM Continuance of the gale, with much sea. The Ship riding with three anchors and 135 fathoms of chains. Midnight moderating.

Thurs 25th.   Moderate breezes & pleasant. Hove up the sheet anchor and sent up the Top. G. Yards.

Took on board a lot of timber for use of the hide house at St. Diego. To day is a fiesta day, with which the Virgin Mary has something to do. Therefore the females of the place have made a general turn out and are to be seen in squads sauntering about the hills, and no small number of them have located themselves on the sand beach opposite the Ships. The females of California remind me of those of Greece, who lavish all they can get to decorate their bodies, while their minds are as barren of knowledge and comprehension of what relates to housewifery as the rooms of their mud-built houses are destitute of furniture, or the most simple comforts of life. Something also may be inferred of the habits of the females from the fact that when the ship was lying at Yerba Buena, Mr. Robinson, on going up to the Puebla [Pueblo] (Village) of St. Jose, was very much annoyed on his arrival there by women & girls thronging the door of the house he put up at to ascertain if he had brought any agadente (Rum of the country) to sell. There are however many respectable females on the coast, but the population is very small. There are some of them who are married to foreigners, who to all appearance make good wives, and were it not for their want of education, would pass muster even in the U. States. Most of them prefer having foreigners for husbands to their own countrymen, as they are treated with more kindness by the former, and are enabled to live easier. The Californians not only abuse their women, treating them with harsh language and even blows, but compel them to do the hardest drudgery. But with the foreign husband, their labour is light, and they have much leisure time to waste in their beloved inaction, or in the amusements of the country. These consist chiefly of dances, and certain games of chance of which they are excessively fond, and [they] spend much of their time like children, as they are, in the performance of them. And Catholicism, with its withering, balefull influence, is the root from which springs ignorance and every thing that is *Ante* to the best interests of man. It however seems to accord too well with the native indolence of their character and total defect of all independent spirit. It is a system that tends most powerfully to keep up and aggravate the natural defects in their character, and to frustrate all prospects of true civilization and all rational improvement. Still they do not appear to be discontented; if they lead the life of grovelling animals, they have at least their negative happiness. If they are as ignorant as the stalled ox, like him, they are fed, protected, and housed, and they have hardly more care or fear for the future than he has. Dark as this picture is of the condition of the Californian women, with regard to the men it is worse. But it is no pleasant task to describe such a set of superstitious, ill blooded scoundrels and I will pass over them with merely saying in the words of Shakespear [sic] that they "are fit for treason, stratagems, & spoil", That they are much addicted to gambling, and frequently lose in this way all they can call their own, the clothes off their backs, the favours of their wives, and even their wives themselves. This picture is not softened by the addiction of intoxication, a vice which they indulge in to great excess. From the total subjugation in which they are to the Priests, they grow up and live, never being taught or indeed allowed to act or hardly think for themselves. They indulge freely in all licentiousness & crime, confess to the Priest, receive absolution, and are ready to repeat the same.

FRIDAY 26th MAR. Begins with light & variable winds and fine weather. Hove up the small bower anchor. Received a number of boat loads of Hides. Killed a Bullock for Ship's use. Went a gunning in the afternoon & returned at sunset successful. Ends with fresh NW winds.

SAT. 27th. Moderate and pleasant. Crew employed in taking off Hides. The Carpenter repairing the cutter. Mr Estabrook, U. States Consul, Alfred Thompson, Esq.,[51] of Santa Barbara, & Major Warren dined on board.

---

[51] Alpheus B. Thompson was in California at least by 1825 as a supercargo on various vessels. In the mid-1830's, he settled in Santa Barbara, married into the Carrillo family, and in 1843 became a naturalized Mexican citizen.

SUNDAY 28th.   Light breezes from the SW with clear weather. Crew at rest. 1 man on the Doctor's list having been poisoned at St. Francisco while cutting wood, by a plant called Yedra, something of the nature of dogwood. Latter part strong S. East winds with Rain. Taking a walk on shore this afternoon I was much pained at seeing many Indians both men and women laying or staggering about, drunk. About half of the houses and huts in Monterey are grogshops, all of which are open Sundays, and in fact sell more liquor on that than any week day. The poor Indian who has been enabled to raise a few rials during the week, by working for the rum-sellers, gets drunk on Sunday, and his earnings return again to his employer's till. The respectable & wealthy firm of B. S. & Co. [Bryant, Sturgis, & Co.] who preach up temperance to their Capts. and Crews before leaving home must be responsible for an immense amount of evil they have, and still are, occasioning among this miserable people, by supplying them with ardent spirits. I envy them not their wealth.

MON. MARCH 29th.   SEasterly winds and fair weather. Ship ready for sea, waiting fair wind. Sent the Pinnace to catch fish. Received a boat load of hides, also some military stores from the Fort to take to Sta Barbara. 2 PM the pinnace returned with a fine lot of fish. The Carpenter in the woods cutting timbers & knees for repairing the boats. Ends with strong winds from south.

A well-known merchant and landowner, his name often occurs in commercial records of the era. He died in Los Angeles in 1867, age 74. See Alpheus B. Thompson, *China Trade Days in California: Selected Letters from the Thompson Papers, 1832-1863* (Berkeley, 1947).

TUES 30th.   Begins with light winds from South. At daylight got under weigh and stood out of the Bay.

11 AM Ship off Pt. Pinos. Wind hauling to SE and increasing with Heavy Squalls. Took in Top Gallant sails, Jib and Spanker and double Reeft the Topsails. 8 PM heavy squalls of wind attended with much Hail and Rain. Midnight the wind shifted to the W. & the weather cleared.

WED 31st.   Light westerly winds and pleasant weather. All sails set. Middle part freshening breezes. Midnight strong breezes & pleasant; ship making fine progress.

THURS APRIL 1st.   Strong Westerly winds & pleasant fine weather. The Canal of Sta. Barbara or in that portion of it between Sta. Barbara and 20 miles to the Westward we have always found the surface of the water covered with mineral pitch which issues from a volcano somewhere in the neighbourhood. Immense quantities of it floats [sic] on the water, while the air is so strongly impregnated with it as to be offensive. At Noon anchored at Sta. Barbara.

FRIDAY APRIL 2d.   Begin with Light variable winds & pleasant weather. Landed the freight & took off 400 hides and a quantity of tallow. Latter Part quite warm; Therm. @ 87° shade.

SAT. 3rd.   Weather as yesterday. Employed in taking off Hides. Killed a Bullock for Ship's use. Dined at the Commandant's. Fast day; rather slim fare. Padre President urged the necessity of fasting as a religious duty. I told him I was a seafaring man and had been compelled to fast for months together during my earlier voyages which I hoped might be admitted as an excuse for not fasting for the future when I had the wherewithal to prevent it. He graciously accorded me a dispensation in consideration of my former abstinance, but at the same time strongly insisted upon the necessity of it as a duty. Capt. L. and his lady, who have resided in the family for 7 or 8 months, are obliged to conform to the family regulations and as poor Mrs. L. does not enjoy good health, and does not like to complain, the deprivation of creature comforts to which she has been accustomed is severely felt by her. It is now about the close of Lent (and forty days fasting) and the poor woman stirred my feelings very much with a relation of the short commons that had been inflicted on her. I promised to endeavour to alleviate her sufferings by smuggling some few delicacies to her from the *Alert's* pantry. The inconsistencies and delusions practiced by the Fathers of the Missions is an abomination equalled only by the ignorance & superstition of their dupes.

SUNDAY APRIL 4th. Light winds and warm weather throughout the day. All Hands at rest.

MONDAY 5th. Light variable winds and fine weather. Employed in watering the Ship & taking in Hides.

TUESDAY 6th. Weather as yesterday. Completed watering. Carpenter repairing the cutter. 4 PM Hove short and made sail, but the breeze failing did not trip the anchor. 8 PM light breeze from NE hove up and stood to the SE. Midnight freshening breezes from SW with cloudy weather. Ship near Anacapa Island.

WEDNES 7th. Light breezes & baffling, with fine weather. The Watch employed in overhauling Otter & Beaver Skins, and packing them in casks. Latter part brisk breezes from NW.

THURS. 8th. Begins Calm & Foggy 11 AM light breezes from SW. At noon anchored at Saint Pedro. After dinner went on shore.

Since leaving here a horrid murder was committed at the Pueblo on the person of a German by the name of Fink who kept a small shop at the place and lived alone.[52] He traded with us a considerable [amount] the last time we were here, was always punctual in his payments, and was a very inoffensive and respecable man (with the exception that he retailed spirits). From his industrious habits and economical manner of living it was supposed that he had a considerable money in his house, and to obtain this he was murdered by three brothers of the name of Valencius [Valencio?]. They entered his shop on the evening (leaving a woman of bad character to watch outside the door), called for liquor, and while the poor fellow was stooping down to draw it off, knocked his brains out with a club, the woman also coming in and finding him not quite dead drove a hammer into his skull. They took away part of his property that night and leaving the dead body on the floor fastened the house up and thus it remained for three days without being discovered. The murderers in the mean time were employed in removing the goods at night. The deceased was a man of retired habits, and his neighbors were accustomed to see his doors closed much of the time and therefore no suspicions were awakened untill the fourth day, when they became apprehensive that he was confined by sickness or had met with some accident. The door was forced

---

[52] Nicholas Fink, a German shoemaker who had arrived about 1835, was about 30 at the time of his murder. Bancroft, IV, 629-30, and *California Pastoral*, 589.

and his mangled corpse found on the floor. Suspicions soon rested [on] the murderers as they were seen in the act of selling goods which it was certain that they had not obtained honestly. They were arrested together with the female. Being brought before the Alcalde they were severally asked, did you commit this murder? – No.– Do you know who did? – No. – Well what further can be done about it? says the official. Nothing, says the Californians. But not yet, says the foreigners; there is strong ground for suspicions. We will have them confined for further examination, and as the few foreigners at the Pueblo are a set of determined and resolute men, they investigated the affair thoroughly, or made the authorities do it, and the result was a full and free confession of the deed. This they were persuaded to do from a belief that they would receive but a few days imprisonment even if found guilty, so tardy are the laws of the country especially where a foreigner is the injured party, and in this case although the monsters were found guilty, yet sentence was not passed upon them, untill the foreign residents assured the Governor at Monterey that if they were not punished by the proper authorities, they would take them out and shoot them themselves. Fearful of the consequences of such an assumption of power, sentence was passed that they should be shot. The order was dispatched by a special courier and apprehensive that the courier might be assasinated [sic] on the road to prevent the execution of the sentence, a duplicate of the order was sent by us. But the courier had arrived safe and the day before yesterday the three monsters were taken from the room where the murder was committed (and in which since their apprehension they had been kept prisoners), their arms tied behind them and being secured to stakes driven down under the eves of the murdered man's house, they were shot by nine soldiers, after being confessed and absolved by a priest. The woman is not yet sentenced, and it is supposed will escape, although deeply implicated. By the confession of the murderers, it appears they were urged on to the perpetration of the horrid deed by their own Mother, who accompanied them part way to the house, and when they hesitated about proceeding further, upbraided them with their cowardice, and pulling a bottle of liquor from her pocket, told them to drink that to fix them for service. Rum did accomplish its usual purpose, and in a few minutes poor Fink's brains were scattered over his own floor. The murder took place about three weeks since, and it seems that the poor fellow had a presentment of his fate, for when I was at the Pueblo, I called to see him, and conversed with him respecting the little protection the laws afforded to foreigners. He remarked that he "wished to wind up his business and quit the country, for as the people of the place knew that he had acquired a little property he was afraid that he should be murdered in his bed."

FRIDAY 9th. Light winds and Pleasant. Afternoon strong breezes from SW. The Crew employed at rigging work & mending sails. Carpenter repairing the 1st Cutter.

SATURDAY 10th. Morning moderate and pleasant. Latter Part of the day Strong Gales from WSW with clear weather. There has been but very little rain on this part of the coast, and the ground which is usually at this time well clothed with verdure, is now parched and dry; not the least green to be seen. The cattle are suffering, and many must perish in a few months for food. Below Monterey it looks likely for a season of great scarcity. The cattle in this country are capable of greater endurance of fatigue than in our country. It is quite common for a person here to ride a horse a hundred miles without stopping. As an instance also of their short commons, I will here mention, that two horses which Mr. Robinson started with last Thursday for the Pueblo returned from there this evening, without having had a mouthful of any thing to eat during their absence of two days & a half and travelling about 80 miles. On their return they did not appear to be much fatigued and were turned loose to seek for what scanty fare they can find among the hills.

4 PM the Brig *Catalina* arrived from St. Diego and reports the *Monsoon* ready for sea, and only waiting our arrival at that place when she will sail for the United States. I immediately sent an express to the Pueblo to inform Mr. R. of the fact and as I expect to sail tomorrow and be at St. Diego on the following day I will now lie down my pen leaving my hieroglyphics to find their way in the best and speediest way they can to that indeared and distant shore which is no less the land of my adoption from sentiment and affection, than it is of my nativity, sufficiently happy if the eye for whom my scribbling is intended and for whose gratification I penned this journal feels as little weariness in tracing their characters as the hand by which they have been impressed. And now I have to record, and which I do with the deepest gratitude of my heart, the constantly superintending and merciful

providence of God over all the vicissitudes of time,
of place, of climate, and of circumstances to which I
have been exposed since I first departed from the land
of my forefathers to commence my fearful wanderings
on the mighty deep. His overshadowing goodness and
protection have alone kept my feet from falling and
shielded me from a thousand dangers, have graciously
guided me in safety through many a dark scene where
hovered the shadow of death, and where nothing but
His hand would have upheld me, have delievered me
from the diseases of various climates, from the pesti-
lence that walked in darkness, and the destruction "that
wasteth at noon-day," raging deep, amidst distressing
shipwreck with the shrieks of drowning companions
ringing in my ears and warning me that their sad fate
was but the prelude to my own. His mercy has spared
me and preserved my life to the present moment in
undiminished health, and strength. And what shall
I render to my Maker for all his abounding mercies
to me.

Solomon tells me, "Fear God and keep his com-
mandments, for this is the whole duty of man." "In
all thy ways acknowledge Him, and He shall direct
thy path."

[At this point Phelps concluded the first bound volume of his
journal, intending to forward it to his wife by the ship *Monsoon,* as mentioned in his entry letter of 28 February. The *Monsoon* sailed from San Diego for Boston on 26 April.]

Volume II

On the California Coast
April 15, 1841 to December 30, 1842

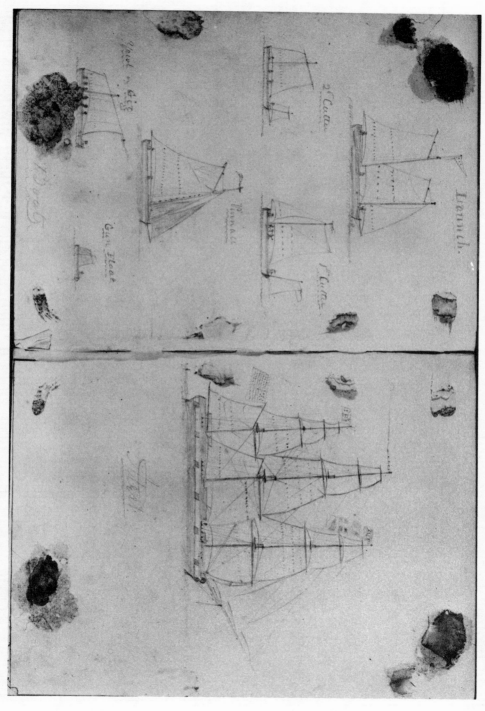

CAPTAIN PHELPS' DRAWING OF THE "ALERT" AND HER SHIP'S BOATS
By permission of the Houghton Library, Harvard University.

Ship Alert on the Coast of California

1841
April 15
Thursday   Port of San Pedro
                        Moderate Breezes from W.S.W with
fine weather.   Crew employed in embarking Hides
At 8 P.M. Got underweigh for S. Diego.   Night Calm.

Friday   Light Breezes from the Westᵈ throughout the day and
16th   clear weather   Crew variously employed in Ships Duty.
At 8 P.M. Hove too under the Topsails, off Pt. Loma head to the
South⁴   At 3 A.M. stood in for St. Diego.   At Noon came
too & moored Ship in 5 fathoms   Found lying here, the Ship
Monsoon nearly loaded for Boston,   Latter part of the day
employed in landing Hides at the House for curing.

Sat 17th   Pleasant weather with variable winds   All Hands
Employed as yesterday

Sun 18th   Weather as yesterday.   All Hands at rest.

Mon 19th   Variable winds with Rain Squalls attended with much
Thunder & Lightning.   Afternoon pleasant.   Landed
1100 Hides

Tues 20th   Clear & Pleasant throughout the day.   Employed in landing
Hides, & transhipping Furs to the Monsoon.

Wed 21st   Forenoon Showers of Rain & Squally.   Afternoon pleas-
-ant   Employed as yesterday

Thurs 22d   Weather Pleasant, Wind N.W.   The crew variously employed in Ships Duty.   Shipped Two Sandwich
Island Natives as seamen.   Ends the Same.

Frid 23   Fresh Breezes from N.N.W. & clear weather.   At 10 A.M. got
under weigh and stood to sea. Mr. Robinson Passenger.
At 11 passed Pt. Loma.   Throughout the day, Light and
baffling winds, with a heavy swell from N.W. found
the Ship to be too light to hold on well — at Sunset a
light breeze springing up from the Wᵗ stood in again
and at 7 P.M. anchored just within Pt. Loma.   Ends Calm.

Sat 24th   Light winds from S.E.   At Daylight hove up the anchor
and proceeded within the inner Point and came too
with the Small Bower.   Got the Launch out and
commenced taking in Ballast —

Sun 25th   Fresh Breezes from W.   Crew at Rest.

THE FIRST PAGE OF THE SECOND VOLUME OF PHELPS' JOURNAL
By permission of the Houghton Library, Harvard University.

Continuation of the Third Passage

1841. APRIL 15th, THURSDAY. PORT OF SAN PEDRO. Moderate Breezes from WSW with fine weather. Crew employed in embarking Hides. At 4 PM Got underweigh for St. Diego. Night Calm.

FRIDAY 16th. Light Breezes from the West'd throughout the day and clear weather. Crew variously employed in Ships Duty. At 8 PM Hove too [sic] under the Topsails off Pt. Loma head to the South'd. At 3 AM stood in for St. Diego. At noon came too & Moored Ship in 5 fathoms. Found lying here the Ship *Monsoon,* nearly loaded for Boston. Latter part of the day employed in landing Hides at the House for curing.

SAT. 17th. Pleasant weather with variable winds. All Hands Employed as yesterday.

SUN 18th. Weather as yesterday. All hands at rest.

MON 19th. Variable winds with Rain Squalls attended with much Thunder & Lightening. Afternoon pleasant. Landed 1100 Hides.

TUES. 20th. Clear & Pleasant throughout the day. Employed in landing Hides & transhipping Furs to the *Monsoon.*

WED. 21st. Forenoon Showers of Rain & Squally. Afternoon pleasant. Employed as yesterday.

THURS 22d. Weather Pleasant, Wind NW. The Crew variously employed in Ships Duty. Shipped two Sandwich Island Natives as Seamen. Ends the Same.

FRID. 23.   Fresh Breezes from WNW & clear weather. At 10 AM got under weigh and stood to sea. Mr. A. Robinson, Passanger. At 11 passed Pt Loma. Throughout the day, light and baffling winds with a heavy swell from NW. Found the Ship to be too light to hold on well. At Sunset a light breeze springing up from the W'd. Stood in again and at 7 PM anchored just within Pt Loma. Ends Calm.

SAT 24th.   Light winds from SE. At Daylight hove up he anchor and proceeded within the inner point and came too with the small Bower. Got the Launch out and commenced taking in Ballast.

SUN 25th.   Fresh Breezes from NW Crew at rest.

MON APRIL 26th 1841.   Morning pleasant with fresh breezes from NW. The Crew employed in boating off ballast. At 1 PM the *Monsoon* sailed for Home. As the ship passed us we saluted her and were returned with three hearty cheers. Ends Calm.

TUES 27th.   Moderate Breezes & variable with foggy weather. Ship ready and waiting an opportunity to get out. Mr. R. left us to go up the coast by land. Crew repairing sails. Ends calm.

WED. 28th.   Fresh Breezes from NNW & clear weather. At 10 AM sailed the Schr. *Nymph* (Capt Fitch) for Ensenada. At 1 PM weighted anchor and stood to sea. At sunset, Pt. Loma NNE pr compass 15 miles dist. Ends calm.

THURS 29th.   Light winds and pleasant weather. Wind from West to NW. Ship beating to windward under all possible sail. At Dark near the Island of Clementia [San Clemente].

Frid. 30th. Weather and winds as yesterday. Ship between the Islands of Clementia & Catalina. The Watch employed as usual. Carpenter repairing the 2d Cutter. The Sailmaker making a new mizzen topsail.

Sat May 1st. Fresh westerly winds and fine weather. Ship beating to windward against a heavy swell. At 5 PM came to anchor under Point St. Pedro in 5 fathoms.

Sun 2d. Strong breezes from West and clear weather. A heavy swell continues in the Canal. Crew at rest.

Mon 3rd. Light winds from West. Killed a Bullock for Ships use, and took on board 120 hides. At 1 PM got under weigh for Santa Barbara.

Sund. [Tues.] 4th. Continuation of light westerly winds & a heavy swell. Ship off Pt. Dume at sunset, working to windward.

Wed. 5th. Forenoon, a continuation of the winds and weather of yesterday. Ship rolling heavily in the swell. At 5 PM a sudden and strong gale from NW which brought the ship under double reeft topsails spanker & F.T. Staysail. Stood to the South to keep clear of the Islands. At Midnight moderating. Turned out the Reefs and tacked Ship to N.W. Wind WSW.

Thurs 6th. Gentle breezes from WNW and fine weather. All sail set. At 9 AM passed between the islands Anacapa & Santa Cruz. Latter part calm with much swell.

Fri 7th. Morning light breezes from NE. At 7 PM anchored off Sta. Barbara in 4½ fathoms (in the summer anchorage inside of the kelp). Latter part all hands employed in repairing the sails & setting up the topmast backstays. Spent the day on shore myself, and dined with the old comma'd't. Ends pleasant.

SAT 8th. Light winds and pleasant. All hands repairing sails. Killed a bullock. 4 PM got under weigh for St. Luis. Ends calm.

SUN 9th. Light variable winds with considerable swell. At 2 AM the ship near the shore and drifting towards it. Lowered the quarter & stern boats and towed her off. At daylight not having steerage way and drifting towards the land. Came to anchor in 7 fathoms. Ends calm.

MON 10th. Light breezes from WSW at daylight got under sail again. Not making any progress at 5 PM came too in 9 fathoms. Pt Conception W1/2S 10 miles dist. So ends.

TUES 11th. Under weigh with moderate breezes from SNW beating to windward. 4 PM exchanged signals with Brig *Juan Josea* [José] bound into Sta. Barbara. Latter part strong breezes. Ship under double reefs outside the canal.

WED 12th. Continuation of full gales. Ship beating up the coast.

THURS 13. Winds and weather as yesterday. Ship off Pt Sal at sunset. Midnight off Pt St Luis. Shortened sail and lay by.

FRID. 14th. Strong breezes & foggy. At 4 PM made sail and stood in. At 8 AM came to anchor in the anchorage of St. Luis Obispo [Bay] in 5 fathoms, sandy bottom. Later part, employed in embarking hides. Ends calm.

SAT. 15th. Begins with strong gales from the NW with clear weather. A bad surf on the beach; we succeeded in getting off about 500 hides and 10 bags of tallow. At 11 AM the British Schr. *Fly* came in to anchor. After breakfast took my gun and walked a few miles up a beautiful valley enclosed by lofty hills, the valley of about from ½ to ¾ of a mile in width, with a fine run of water in the middle of it. Large trees of the button wood, and holly leaved oak, were scattered about the hill sides and wild mustard and oats covered the ground. The mustard was in blossom, which together with an abundance of wild roses, and numerous other flowers filled the air with a most gratiful ([sic] perfume.

I stopped at the Rancho (farm house) of Don Abelard,[1] a miserly and indolent old fellow, the owner of the pleasant and fertile valley in which he *stays*. He has about 1200 head of cattle, and which constitute all his property, besides the farm of 15 square miles. Although to all appearance the soil is capable of yielding great crops, *not one foot* of it is under cultivation. It is astonishing that these people can content themselves with the spontaneous production around them (and they are but few) when by a very little labour they could obtain immense quantities of fruit & vegetables. But in the present instance I was soon furnished with the reason of it. I observed on Old Indian a work near the Korrail [sic] (cattle pens) and ascertained that he was employed by Abelard to supply him with fish (with which the bay abounds). He said he was hired by the

---

[1] Don Abelard, though clearly a ranchero in the San Luis Obispo area, has not been further identified.

month at the rate of $4 per mh and was paid in *rum at $3 per bottle.* Sometimes he made out to get a shirt from his employer in lieu of the rum but that could only be obtained when he was reduced to nakedness. A poor apology for a coarse cotton shirt being the only article of clothing which now adorned his hurculean frame. The poor fellow could not understand how it was he had steady employment, and was economical of his wages (a least so far as his tailors bill was concerned), and yet was always in debt. "There was always a bottle of Rum scored against him." May the day be not far distant when this fertile country shall be possessed by a temperate, industrious and enlightened people. Ardent spirits here as well as in all other countries is the greatest curse of society, hostile to the best interests of man, and productive of the worst evils. Yet here there is probably more liquor consumed than in any other country on the globe and to that source we may trace the cause, why California with its fertile land, and salubrious climate, contains the most ignorant indolent and vicious population of any country I have ever visited. A bag of tallow which we received on board yesterday (with some others) was bought by the man who sold it to my supercargo for a *Bot. of Rum.* The said Tallow was received on board the ship for $8 in goods. A gentleman informed one that he has also seen a good horse sold for a glass of grog. Such are the majority of the people of the country.

The Fourth Passage

San Luis Obispo to San Diego and Return to San Francisco

SUN. 16th [MAY 1841]. Begins with strong gales from WNW. At 10 AM got under weigh and proceeded towards the Canal of Sta. Barb. Passengers Mr. H. Mellus & Capt. Wilson.[2] At ¼ past 3 PM passed Pt Conception. ½ past 3 shortened sail and came to anchor with the small bower in 7 fathoms. Paid out 75 fathoms of chain & furled sails. The distance from St Luis to Pt. Conception is nearly 60 miles, therefore we run at the rate of over 4 knots all the way. At 5 PM the Gale increasing with heavy squalls. The ship adrift. Let go the best bower anchor and gave her long scope on each cable which brought her up. Midnight moderating.

MON 17th. Morning moderate. At daylight hove up the anchors and got the Ship nearer the shore. Came too with 90 fathoms of the small bower. Middle and Latter part, Strong gales which prevented our embarking any hides. Wind NW. So ends.

TUES. 18th. Moderate and pleasant. Employed in boating off Hides & Tallow. Ends Calm.

---

[2] John Wilson was a Scots shipmaster and trader in California in the 1830's and 1840's; married to a Californian, he settled permanently in Santa Barbara as a land grantee and otter hunter until his death in 1860.

WED 19th. Morning pleasant with a breeze from the North. Up Anchor at daylight and proceeded down the canal keeping near the shore. At 7 PM anchored at Sta Barbara. Ends Calm.

THURS. 20th. Moderate & pleasant. Crew employed in watering the ship. Spent the day on shore. Dined with and at the house of Mr. Thompson an American Gen*t* (resident here). While on shore today, and passing through the square where a large number of Indians were playing at their different games (it being a festive day) I saw some more of the beautiful results of intoxication. I turned aside to avoid a drunken Indian who was in the act of throwing a stone at another who appeared to be sober. The latter caught up the same stone and returned it with all his force at the head of his opponent. The stone struck the fellow on the heart. I stepped up to bleed him with my pocket-knife, but the bystanders prevented me, why I know not. He was dragged to the side of a house and left there, and his companions resumed their games, while the sober savage who killed his fellow walked off quite coolly with his hands behind him and no person noticed him any more than if he had killed a dog. Had this poor fellow (who in self defense unfortunately killed his comrade) dared to have raised his arm in defense of his life against a Californian, he would have been stabbed by a dozen knives on the spot and no questions asked, but an Indian is another affair, and they are called "los gentiles", beasts [gentil: pagan, heathen], the Californians, "gente de razon", reasonable beings.

FRID. MAY 21st. Begins with calm and pleasant

weather, a heavy surf on the beach. Another specimen of the beautiful effects of the *rum system* had just been exhibited on board the ship. On my returning on board last evening, I found that a part of the crew who had been employed in filling water on shore had returned on board in the afternoon very much intoxicated and had behaved in a most insolent manner to the 2d officer, who was at that time the only officer on board. Two of them in particular threatened him with violence. As something of this sort had taken place before this, and I had overlooked it on a promise of better conduct being given by the offender, I felt determined now to resort to other measures. And that I might do nothing while under the influence of excited feelings, I waited till this morning, and having consulted with my officers resolved that punishment was necessary. At the usual time the "hands were turned up" and after hearing all sides of the question I ordered the two ringleaders to be put in irons and gave two of the Boys (who had also been insolent) a suitable whipping. The majority of the crew were then ordered to their duty, which they refused untill the prisoners should be let out of irons. Such a manifestation of mutinous feelings calling for prompt measures to restore order and preserve discipline, I sent a note to the Commandant requesting a guard of soldiers which was complyed with and the two rebellious spirits were escorted to the Calaboose (Prison). The crew still refusing to return to their duty, I calmly reasoned with them and pointed out the unpleasant consequences that would result to themselves if they persisted in a disobedience of lawful orders. I then allowed them ½ an hour to reflect upon it, assuring them that at the expiration of that time they *should* go to work or go to prison. Before the time expired they wisely decided upon the right course & returned to duty. Thus ended the first and only trouble with the crew which has taken place since we left home (17 mos.) and which I hope may be the last. And this was caused by a scoundrel of a rum seller who decoyed the crew to his den & got them drunk.

During the fracas a rather ludicrous scene occurred which afforded much amusement and satisfaction to *'Jack.'* On the arrival of the guard alongside the ship I observed that the crew on board —

> Looked upon them with as favourable eyes
> As Gabriel on the devil in paradise.

But when one of the red coated gentlemen in getting up the side missed his hold and fell overboard their joy was great and they no doubt would have permitted him to have gone to the bottom and fish up his musket which he had lost if the officers had not seized hold of his regimentals and drew him out after the poor fellow had got well drenched and described as many figures in the water as his brother lobster could have done.

The Corporal and his guard I did not think were a very safe escort for the prisoners, although the odds were 5 to 2. On shore, they looked "Big Guns & Battle axes" but they got wet coming through the surf which took the starch out of their ruffles and cooled their courage, and the mishap to their comrade alongside completed their discomfiture insomuch that the officer requested me to let the irons remain on the prisoners untill they were safely lodged in the Calaboose, and no doubt had the Tars been able to have got their hands clear and had been pugnaciously disposed on their way to prison, they would [have] knocked the guard into a "cocked hat."

Latter part of the day employed in taking hides on board and filling water.

SAT. 22d. Calm and foggy throughout the day. Employed in boating off Hides.

SUN. 23d. Weather as yesterday. Crew at rest.

MON 24th. Weather the same as yesterday. Employed in watering the Ship. At night released the prisoners from the calaboose and received them on board again on promise of good conduct for the future.

TUES. 25th. Light winds from SW. Killed a bullock for ships use. Got under weigh at 4 PM for St. Pedro (Mr. Robinson and Mr. A. B. Thompson passangers). Ends hazy & calm.

WED. 26th. Light Easterly winds and thick weather. At noon near the Island of St Nicholas. Latter part light breezes from SW.

THURS 27. At Daylight, becalmed near the little Island of Santa Barbara. At 4 AM lowered a quarter boat and landed to kill elephant. Found many of them, but as it is the pupping season they were very poor. We however killed six and loaded the boat with their blubber. We brought on board six of their pups alive. The crew being out of shoes and none to be had on the coast, now obtained a timely supply of material to make moccasins. There were also many hundreds of hair seal on the island which did not appear to be disturbed by our visit. At ½ past 6 returned on board, promising to call again when the Elephant are in better order.

A pleasant breeze springing up from W. Made all sail and at 4 PM Anchored at St. Pedro in 5 fathoms.

FRIDAY MAY 28th 1841. Light variable winds and hazy weather. Mr. Robinson and Mr. Thompson started for Puebla las Angelos. Employed in boating off hides. Carpenter making new Brace Blocks.[3]

SAT 29. Continuation of the weather of yesterday. Crew variously employed in ships duty. The Boys trying out the Elephant blubber on shore. At the landing place of St. Pedro there is but one house, which is occupied by a Mr. Foster [Forster] and family and is kept for the purpose of receiving and depositing goods for shipment and for the accommodation of passengers, the nearest village being the town of the angels above mentioned which is over 30 miles dist. There are a number of Ranchos situated between, the nearest of which is about 4 miles from the beach.

At Fosters there is an old Indian and as he is the last of his race, [he] is an object of interest. He was one of a tribe that formerly inhabited the Islands which form one side of the canal of Santa Barbara, all of which give evidence of having once been populated. In 1825 the Island of St. Nicholas was the only one that had not become depopulated (how they became so is not known). At this time there were on St. Nicholas about 30 men and 23 women. During that year a party of Russians and Kodiacks from the Russian settlements on the NW of about 25 men were left at these islands to hunt otter and after having many quarrels with the Indians of St. Nicholas respecting the women, the Russians at length killed all the men

---

[3] Brace blocks are simply blocks used on the braces, the lines by which the yards are swung at different angles.

with the exception of this old fellow who was badly wounded having his head split open and a number of charges of buck shot fired into him. He however managed to escape. The Russians then became possessed of the women and lived with them about a year, when having an opportunity to gratify the revenge, which may sleep in an Indian but never dies, they destroyed every one of the Russians and Kodiacks in their sleep. About 4 or 5 years since there was but three women and (Black Hawk as my Boys have named him) the Indian above mentioned left, and Capt. Robbins[4] (from whom I have the account) calling there with his vessel persuaded two of the females to go to St. Pedro; the other ran away to the mountains and it is said is sometimes seen by the hunters who still visit the island, but is too wild to be approached. Black Hawk seems to be noncompass [non compos mentis] and the wounds on his head are the probable cause.

While trying out the blubber today on the beach the old fellow smelt out what was going on (he is also blind) and after eating at least 5 lbs of the raw stinking material to begin with, he continued to gorge himself with the scraps as they were tried out, till he could contain no more, when he stretched himself out on the rocks, with a hot sun shining in his face, and after chattering and laughing in his idiotic manner for three hours, he again resumed his station at the trying pot, where he made a sumptous dinner, and before dark he was enabled to partake of a supper, which was

---

[4] Thomas M. Robbins was mate and master of several vessels in California in the 1820's and 1830's; in particular, he was master of the government schooner *California* in the service of several governors. He held an honorary commission as a captain in the Mexican navy. He died in 1857, in Santa Barbara where he had settled.

in proportion to his dinner & breakfast. The blubber yielded about 75 gals of oil.

SUN 30th.   Moderate Breezes from NW and pleasant weather. Crew as rest.

MON 31st.   Pleasant throughout the day. Took on board 10 packages of Beaver skins, & a quantity of Hides. Killed a Bullock & got ready for sea.

TUES. JUNE 1st.   Morning light winds from SE. At 9 AM got under weigh for St. Diego. Middle & Latter Parts Calm & Cloudy.

WED 2d.   Moderate breezes from Eastward. Ship beating to windward. At Midnight near the Island of St. Clementia.

THURS 3d.   Pleasant breezes from NW. At daylight Ship of [off] Puerto Falso [False Port, modern Mission Bay]. Noon Calm. 4 PM breeze from NW. Passed Puenta Loma and anchored about 2 Miles below the Hide House at ½ past 6 in 6 fathoms water. Ends calm.

FRID. 4th.   At Daylight hove up, and ran up, and anchored abreast of the Hide House and moored ship. Landed 2041 hides & other articles of freight. Set the carpenter to work new roofing the Hide House. Found that our live stock at the house had increased finely since we left here. We have now about 30 Hogs & Pigs running about, a large quantity of poultry, and about 20 dogs, which last are very useful to watch the hides at night, otherwise the Indians would steal them. There is an unusual number of the wild Indians about St. Diego at present, and although they are apprehensive that they are meditating an attack on the place, still they do not take the least precaution, and so improvident are they that at the present time there is not 2 lb of powder in St. Diego. The season has been without rain consequently the fruits and spontaneous productions which the Indians have mostly subsisted on have failed them. There is therefore the more fear of their being troublesome this year.

SAT. 5th. Weather fine. The Crew on board fitting new Fore rigging. The Carpenter and gang shingling the new roof of the House.

SUN 6th. Pleasant throughout. Crew at rest.

JUNE 7th. Moderate Breezes from WSW and pleasant weather. All hands employed as yesterday.[5]

TUES 8th. Weather fine. Wind variable. People employed as usual at various work. The Sandwich Islanders (or Kanackers as they are usually called) are very successful in fishing. In the evening they take the boat and a torch to decoy the fish to the light and then spear them. Last evening they caught a good sized Halibut, about 20 or 30 other fish of different kinds, and over 50 lobsters.

WED. 9th. Wind and weather as yesterday. The different gangs of workmen employed as usual.

THURS. 10th. Fresh Breezes from the Westward. Employed in setting up the Fore Rigging and staying the Masts, shingling the house, and curing hides.

FRID 11th. Pleasant. All hands at work on the Rigging and painting the Masts & ship outside. Rode up to the Presidio to get the Ships Roll. The Post Capt

---

[5] In this entry Phelps has omitted the day of the week (Monday); presumably since the hands were usually given Sunday off, he means all hands employed as on Saturday.

demanded two dollars for signing. Knowing it was not customary I refused paying it. He then very modestly asked me to give him two rials (25 cts) but as he had attempted to impose upon me I would give him nothing. A little powder was then requested to defend his family against the Indians. I replied that none could be spared from the Ship but when the foe made their appearance he might send his family on board the ship where they would be protected. He said he would certainly avail himself of the offer and come himself, but he was disappointed when I told him I would receive none but women & children, as the men ought to remain and defend their property.

SAT. 12th.   Pleasant. Wind West. Employed in painting Ship. Got the launch in. Ends calm.

SUN 13th.   Weather fine. Winds light and variable. Crew at rest.

MON 14th., TUES. 15th., WED 16th. Light southerly winds and foggy. Ship ready for sea & waiting a wind to get out.

THURS 17th.   Gentle breezes from SSW at 9 AM got under weigh with the ebb tide & beat the Ship out of the Port at sunset ship off Puerto Falso, wind SSW.

FRID. 18th.   Begins with light airs from SW & hazy. Ship under all sail beating to the Wd. The watch variously employed.

SAT 19th.   Morning cloudy with light variable winds. At noon a fine breeze from ESE. Anchored at St. Pedro.

SUN 20th.   Pleasant weather, wind WSW. All hands at rest. Received a request to visit a sick woman at the

Rancho. Accordingly mounted a horse which was sent for me and started after breakfast. Found my patient suffering from nervous head ache and fever. Spent the day with her, & at sunset left her in a fair way. These people have not the slightest knowledge of medicine, and in fact but little sickness and when any thing ails them they are very much frightened of which I had evidence to-day. Ends calm.

MON 21st. Moderate breezes from SE with hazy weather. Crew boating off hides. Had a little dinner party on board, consisting of Mr. Forster & Family and Mr. Warner. Arrived Brig *Leonidas* from Sta Barbara.

TUES 22d. Morning pleasant & calm. Boating off hides. Killed a bullock. At 1 PM strong breezes from WNWd. Got under weigh for Sta. Barb. Ends calm, ship near Catalina.

WED. 23d. Light winds & variable. Ship near the Island Catalina. 11 AM lowered a quarter boat & went to fish but returned at 2 PM with a very few. Afternoon strong breezes from West. Ship beating in the canal.

THURS. 24th. Light breezes from West with hazy weather. Ship off Pt. Dume. at daylight in 12 fathoms water. Latter part pleasant breezes. Ship off Pt. Conversion.

FRID. 25th. Morning Light variable winds & foggy. Ship working to the westward. Noon & Latter part calm. Ship off the Mission of St. Buenaventura. At 10 PM light breeze from SE. At ½ past 11 anchored off Sta. Barbara.

SAT. 26th. Light breezes from the southern quarter & hazy. Crew employed variously in ships duty. Found laying here the Brig *Lama* which left Boston last August. By her I received neither letters, papers, or any tidings from home. The only articles of news by here are that a Whig Gov. is chosen in Mass. and rumors of war between Great Britain & the U. States. The first item is good, but the latter may the Lord in Mercy avert.

JUNE 27th. Moderate Breezes from the SW & hazy weather. Part of the Crew on liberty, the remainder at rest. Yesterday, I spent on shore and passed the night at the hospitable house of the Commandant. This old Gen*t*. Don Jose Noriega, is the principal man of the place. His family is very large. His numerous children and grandchildren reside with him in a very extensive house of but one story, but covering a large extent of ground. At his table are generally seated about 20 persons, while on the floor, on mats, in different part of the large dining hall, are groups of grandchildren setting or lying down to their meals, with an Indian girl appointed to the care of each one. Table is waited upon by Indian men servants, who have no other *livery* but a cotton shirt and the extremity of which in some cases appear to have been "curtailed of their fair proportions" to repair breaches elsewhere. The scantiness of their clothing would doubtless be considered against the notions of propriety entertained at home and I confess it was at first offensive to me to see young ladies waited upon by a man almost in a state of nudity. But it is the custom of the country, and habit soon accustoms us to look upon such matters with the indifference of natives. When the guests are seated, the old Gent. asks a blessing and in order to save time cuts and distributes the bread during the while. The dinner consists of many courses of which meat is the chief. The plates are always changed but not the *knives* & *forks*. Whether this was owing to a scarcity of the article, or being the custom, I have not yet ascertained. After the meal ended and before rising from table, thanks are returned and the Old Patriach wishes "bien provenchia" (much good may it do you) and is answered with "muchas gracias" (many thanks) by each person. The family & guests are then assembled to prayers. A picture of a saint supporting and exhibiting our crucified Saviour is placed at the end of the hall before which all prostrate themselves and repeat the prayers offered up by the head of the family. I always kneel with them but not to adore "the likeness of any thing" and I do not understand the import of the prayers that are offered. I mingle my prayers with theirs in "the way in which I have learnt Christ."

This morning (Sunday) I was awakened early by a summons to the family to prepare to attend mass at the Mission church about 2 miles distant. I was invited to attend, but not feeling that I could receive any satisfaction from bowing before images made by men's hands, or listening to prayers which I could not understand, I declined, and returned on board to spend the day in a manner more congenial to my feelings, and I hope acceptable to my Maker.

MON. 28th. Morning moderate breezes from the South with fog. All hands boating off hides & repairing sails. Latter part of the day variable winds & squally with spots of rain & some T. [thunder] & Lightening.

TUES 29th. Wind from SE to SW. Foggy weather.

Crew employed in boating and repairing sails. Ends pleasant, wind West.

WED 30th. Pleasant weather and calm throughout the day. Crew employed in repairing sails and filling water. So ends.

THURS JULY 1st.   Begins with moderate breezes from SE with fine weather. Got the ship ready for sea. Took on board a lot of fowl & vegetables, such as green peas, onions, &c. After noon fresh breezes from WSW. At 5 PM got under weigh for 'Refugio'. Passenger, Mr. F. G. Stevens of Gloucester, Mass. Strong breezes throughout the night. Ship working to windward.

FRID 2d.   Light breezes & Pleasant, wind WSW. At 4 PM anchored at Refugio in 7 fathoms. Refugio is the landing place of one or two ranchos in the neighbourhood and also of the Missions of La Perissima [Purísima] & St Eynes [Inéz] and is at the end of a deep and pleasant valley. Ends calm.

SAT 3rd.   Weather as yesterday. Employed in boating off Hides and Tallow. In the afternoon accepted an invitation to visit the farm of Daniel Hill, an native of Haverhill, Mass.[6] Horses being sent for us, Mr. Stevens and myself started and after a pleasant ride of about three miles arrived at the house which we found situated in a deep, pleasant and fertile valley, a fine stream of water flowing through it and affording a plentiful supply for his field, garden, and domestic purposes. Mr. Hill has been in the country about 16

----

[6] Daniel Antonio Hill reached California in 1823. Converted to Catholicism, naturalized and married into a California family, Hill was a leading citizen of Santa Barbara as carpenter, mason, land grantee, and general factotum until his death in 1865.

or 17 years, is an old sailor, and is a poor farmer. He has been engaged in agriculture but about two or three years, however, and there is hopes, as there is also room for great improvement on his farm, which now consists of a respectable vineyard of about 1000 plants, a decently large cornfield, potato & bean patches, & a better variety of garden sauce than I have seen in the country. Also apple, pear, & peach trees. A large grazing district of 12 miles in extent and 300 head of cattle. A fruitful wife and 9 hearty looking children. The afternoon was extremely warm, but we found it very agreeable & pleasant under the apple trees. Found at work here on old tailor by the name of Swift formerly of Plymouth, Mass. Has been in these seas 40 years. He appears intelligent & I was much interested in his stories. Returned at sunset to the ship.

SUN JULY 4th. Pleasant and warm throughout the day. All hands at rest.

MON 5th. Continuation of the weather of yesterday. Celebrated this anniversary of the Independence of the U. States of Amer. by giving a dinner and entertainment on board ship to the young people of the neighbouring ranches, among whom were two daughters of Mr. Hill, Madame Madeline Flores,[7] a fine old widow lady, and four charming daughters. They came on board early in the forenoon and were delighted with the ship, but it being the first time they were afloat they soon felt themselves upon "ground of uncertainty" and as I foresaw their enjoyment on board would speedily terminate, I proposed that we should dine on shore under the fine shady trees in the valley

---

[7] Doña Madeline Flores has not been further identified.

opposite the ship. To this arrangement they gladly consented. Therefore having gratified their curiosity on board, and one of the gentlemen (an Irish doctor)[8] desirous of showing off, having ascended the mizen rigging to the astonishment of the ladies, he was to his own astonishment grabbed by two brawny sailors (to whom I tipped a wink for the purpose) and made fast to the shrouds, untill upon promise of paying them ½ a doz of wine he was released much to his own mortification & the no small amusement of every one else. We now proceeded to the valley and spreading a sail under the ample shade of two noble oaks, where we amused ourselves with chatting, and swinging, &c., untill the steward & boys made their appearance with the dinner, consisting in part of a fine roasted pig, fowls, apple pie, cake & fruit, and to which all hands seemed to do ample justice. The remainder of the day was spent in various amusements, and at sunset the company proceeded with us to the beach and bade us "buenos noches," with many thanks for the entertainment.

In the evening got under weigh for Monterey, Mr. R. and Mrs. S. passangers. Through the night variable winds.

TUES. 6th. Strong gales from WNW. Ship under double reeft Topsails standing to the SW., with a bad sea.

WED. 7th. Strong gales from NW, and much sea. Ship under double reefs, and courses furled. Midnight split the Fore Topsail. Wind WNW.

---

[8] The physician was Dr. Nicholas Den, who settled in Santa Barbara in 1836, became naturalized, and married a daughter of Daniel Hill. Den was a successful land grantee, and sometimes alcalde. (Bancroft, III, 779.)

THURS 8th.   Continuation of strong gales. At daylight unbent the F. Topsail & bent another. Latter part moderate. Let out 1 reef from the Topsails & set the Courses. Passengers very sick.

FRID. 9th.   Strong breezes from WNW. Ship beating to windward under double reeft Topsails. Afternoon, Gale increasing. Run into S. Luis for a harbour and came to anchor with the best bower in 7 fathoms. Went on shore with the passangers to take a walk. Returned at sunset, Mr. R. having ordered horses to be sent in the morning, intending to proceed to Monterey by land.

SAT 10th.   The wind still blowing heavy from the westward outside of the bay, while at the anchorage it is quite calm. Crew employed in repairing sails. Mr. R. started at 9 AM for Monterey. At 10 AM started with the quarter boat and 4 boys for a little excursion, to gun & fish, up the bay. Mrs. Stevens, wishing for a change of scene, also took her work basket and a seat in the boat. We were not very successful in fishing or shooting, but enjoyed a pleasant sail in smooth water along a picturesque coast. At noon we landed on a beach in a snug cove and partook of luncheon, and about 1 PM turned our prow towards the Ship, but were shortly after met by a strong breeze which compelled us to seek shelter, which we found in a beautiful cove where there was not a breath of wind, being protected by high cliffs, and at the same time rendering the place extremely warm. But at a short distance from the boat, we found a spacious cave in the limestone cliffs facing the water, which afforded us as convenient and comfortable a retreat as could be desired. The floor, side & top were of limestone, the floor with a gentle descent to the entrance and quite smooth and clean. Here we spread the boat cloak, and Mrs. S. and myself found amusement in reading, & at length waking up from a comfortable siesta into [which] Mrs. S. had read me, I found her busily engaged with her needlework. Towards sunset the wind lulled and we returned on board.

At 9 PM a breeze springing up from the eastward, we got under weigh and proceeded out of the bay. 11 PM the wind changed to the NW and blew a gale. The ship under close reefs.

SUN. 11.   Continuation of strong gales. At 7 PM split the Mn. [Main] Topsail. Unbent it & bent another.

The Gale continuing throughout the day with a large sea. At 8 PM the ship made a heavy lee lurch which drew the fastenings of the galley and capsized the house & coppers over to leeward. "The Doctor" [9] fortuitously was not at home. Later part moderating.

MONDAY JULY 12th.   Continuation of strong westerly winds. Ship beating to windward against much sea & squally weather.

TUES. 13th.   Weather moderating. The wind continuing at WNW. Crew variously employed in repairing sails & refitting rigging.

WED 14th.   Moderate breezes from WNW and pleasant weather. All sail set on a wind. Tacking ship as occasion requires. Sent up the Mn. Royal yard. Ends pleasant. Ship off the highlands of Saint Antonio.

THURS 15th.   Light breezes from WNW & foggy. Ship making small progress. Ends the same.

FRID. 16th.   Calm & foggy, with much swell from the

---

9 "Doctor" was a sailing-ship term for the cook.

NW. Latter part light breezes from WSW. Lat. Obs. at Nn. 36°33 N.

At 3 PM saw a large barque coming out of Monterey, whom we soon made out to be a stranger. We ran up the Stars & Stripes and were rejoyced [sic] to see the same glorious flag floating at her Mizen. Who can this be, was asked by a dozen voices? She may be a vessel from the Islands, or she may be one of the exploring squadron put in for supplies, and our hopes told us she might be a vessel direct from the U. States. In hopes of the latter being the case I bore away to speak to her and sure enough she proved to be the Barque *Tasso,* Capt. Hastings, from Boston direct. Anxious to hear from home and all hoping for letters every face on board brightened with joy. I ordered a quarter boat to be lowered & manned, and never was a boat in readiness at a shorter notice. I was soon on board, and found they were but six months from Boston which seemed but as yesterday to us who had not heard a word from there for 18 months. The *Tasso* has come with a cargo for the purpose of trading & procuring a cargo of hides so that we shall have more company on this dreary coast which of course is pleasant to us. The *Letters* which they brought out for the *Alert* are left at Monterey & we shall probably get them tomorrow. The wind was light & the weather foggy, and as I could not reach the anchorage to night, I ordered the *Alert* to be kept near the bark & passed most of the evening on board of her. Capt Hastings gave me much interesting news but none so agreeable as that he had heard from a friend of mine just before sailing that my family were well. I obtained a good lot of newspapers which will afford a rich treat and returned on board & hove too for the night. I eagerly conned the papers over untill my eyes could bear no more, and retired to rest but sleep I could not. It was 18 mos. since I had heard from my family and oh what changes might have taken place in that time. My hopes, fears, and joy that I should tomorrow have tidings of my beloved ones kept me awake the livelong night.

SAT JULY 17. Morning calm & foggy. At 11 AM a gentle breeze from WSW sprang up. Made all sail & at noon anchored at Monterey. Mr Robinson came on board, and handed me the much looked for package which contained about a dozen letters from various friends, and they were as welcome as a spring in the desert is to the thirsty traveller. The various custom & other officers who also came on board at our anchoring and who are always in the habit of spending a number of hours on board, I wished at Jericho, but as I could not get rid of them, I ordered refreshments to be placed and inviting them to make themselves at home, I retreated to my room to feast my eyes upon the well remembered hands in which my letters were written. Changes indeed have taken place. Friends and connexions [sic] whom I left in perfect health have been taken away, but thanks to a merciful & overruling Providence those who are nearest and dearest to my heart have been spared.

SUN. 18th. Moderate & pleasant throughout the day. Crew at rest.

MON 19th. Weather as yesterday. Crew employed in boating off hides. Others repairing sails; the carpenter caulking the forecastle.

Since our last leaving Monterey, another murder has

been committed on the person of a poor Irishman, commonly called Dan. He had been in the country many years, married a California woman, and had just built him a snug little hut near the landing place and worked hard to support his family. The last time I was here I employed him a number of days to cut wood for me. About a week since he went out on horseback to hunt up his cattle & did not return at night. The next day the dog which accompanied him came back alone, and entered the house whining and endeavouring by fawning and howling and pulling at the womans duds to make her follow him, but he was not heeded, and [she] said nothing of her husbands absence untill the third day, when the actions of the dog were noticed by the neighbours which led to enquiries. They suspected Dan was murdered, and informed the Alcade [alcalde, local governor] of their suspicions and as the dog continued his importunities with the woman, the alcaidi compelled her to follow the poor creature, and followed himself to see what would be the result. After following about two miles and reaching the edge of a wood, the dog left them & run for a while, and at length got a scent and was off out of sight, but soon his loud yelping was heard not far from them, and there they found him lying on the body of his master, which was cold & stiff and pierced with 7 deep stabs. And what seemed very strange, he ever after avoided the woman. There is a fellow arrested & now in prison who is supposed to be the murderer. Having been to [too] intimate with the woman in her husbands absence, it is thought she was accessory.

JULY 20th.   Moderate winds & foggy in the morning. Crew variously employed embarking hides &c. This

day arrived a Mexican vessel bringing back the foreigners English Americans (or at least 14 out of the
46) who were sent away prisoners from California
about a year since, in an illegal & arbitraly [sic] manner by the government on some frivolous pretext, but
the matter was immediately looked into by the consuls
of the respective nations to which they belonged who
procured their immediate release and the imprisonment of the officer who went to Mexico in charge of
them, and they are now sent back at the expense of the
Mex. Govt. after having been paid some hundred
dollars on account of their sufferings and with the assurance that any claims they may have for loss of property, time, or health in consequence of the unlawful
treatment received from this govt. will be allowed &
paid them. Circulars have been addressed to merchants
here by the British Consul at St. Blas desiring them to
assist these men in collecting their scattered property &
in making out their claims, also informing them that
one of H.B.M. Ships of war will be here in [the] next
month to look after the interests of British subjects to
redress their wrongs. The return of these prisoners has
filled the measure of this Governor's unpopularity,
completely cowed the haughty & ignorant advisers of
his excellency, & will result in the greater security of
the foreign residents in California.[10]

WED. 21st. Weather as Yesterday. Crew employed as
usual. Got the ship ready for sea.

THURS. 22nd. Morning calm & pleasant. At noon a
light breeze from the West'rd. Got under weigh for

10 Phelps is referring to the Graham Affair; see above, page 50, n. 1.
The Mexican vessel mentioned was the schooner *Colombina,* called *"Bolina."*

St. Francisco. Midnight ship becalmed off Pt. Anno Nuevo.

FRIDAY 23rd.   Morning light breezes from E & foggy. Hauled in to make the land. The breeze freshening; all possible sail set. At 11 AM saw Point St. Pedro; blowing strong and the water smooth. Double reeft the topsails & set the spencer & F.T. staysail. At 1 PM passed the Fort at the entrance. Wind moderating, and all reefs & set T. G. Sails & M. Royal. At 2 PM anchored at Yerba Buena. Latter part strong gales from WNW.

SAT 24th.   Moderate & pleasant in the morning. Got the boats all out & rigged them for service, & moored ship with the mooring swivel. Later part all hands cleaning ship.

SUN 25th.   Pleasant throughout. All hands at rest.

MON 26th.   Morning moderate. Latter part strong breezes, the weather clear throughout the day. Received a lighter load of hides from *Santa Clara*. Sent the 2nd officer with the launch to Borri Borri for hides. Myself getting ready for an excursion up *the River El Sacramento* tomorrow in the pinnace. This morning at 8 AM hoisted the colours half mast & fired a salute of minute guns from the ship, having received the sad intelligence of the death of the President of the U. States [Harrison]. I sent a request to the other vessels to hoist their colours half mast, which was complied with. At sunset repeated the salute.

Up the Sacramento to Sutter's New Helvetia

TUES 27th. [JULY 1841]. Morning pleasant. At 11 AM started from the ship in the pinnace with 4 hands & a pilot for the River Sacramento on the banks of which at the distance of about 100 miles from its mouth a settlement has been commenced by Capt. J. A. Sutter (A Swiss gentleman) to which he has given the name of New Helvetia after the land of his birth. To visit this gentleman with whom I had formed an acquaintance previously to see what his improvements & prospects were & to satisfy myself respecting the beauty & superiority of the region about the Sacramento of which Capt. S. had spoken to me in glowing terms was the object of my present excursion. And as I was assured that no ships boat had ever ascended it, I felt desirous of being the first. When I first proposed the trip a number of gentlemen (supercargoes of other ships) were very desirous of joining me, but I now found that although they had been talking the affair over, and making their arrangements for three months previous, yet now they could not go. It was a bad season of the year. The River was low. The weather was hot. Musquitoes [sic] were ravenous, and the Indians cannibals. But as I had made my preparations I was determined to go alone. With a brisk breeze we crossed the passage. At 2 PM passed St Pablo point & entered the bay of St Pedro with a strong current in our favour and a fine breeze, we ran across this bay at a famous rate, a distance of about 18 miles, the course NE. At ½ past 4 PM we entered the straits of the Carquines [Carquinez] being about one mile in width & 3 in length. The land on either [side is] high & mountainous, destitute of trees, but appearing to be well covered with wild oats. Passing these, we crossed the bay of Sta. Lune [Suisun], and after running about 20 miles further entered the mouth of the Rio El Sacramento. Just without the river we met with Capt Sutter's boat at anchor. They had left the settlement five days before & having met with strong head winds, all their provisions were exhausted. Supplied them, and again pushed on to enter the river & find an encampment before night. About a mile inside of the Sacramento we passed the mouth of the St. Joachin [Joaquin], which empties into the former. It appeared to be wide and navigable but I am informed it abounds with shoals, and is difficult of navigation. The tide & winds still favouring us and a bright moon shining in a cloudless sky above us, we continued on for about 20 miles. All the distance the banks were low and covered with rush flags or Tules as they are called here. At 11 PM having passed all the Tule, we ran along the high banks on which were many high trees, we stopped and encamped for the night under a large sycamore were [where] we kindled a fire, cooked & eat a hearty supper and wrapping our blankets around us composed ourselves to sleep around a huge fire with our Rifles by our sides. Our arms consisted of two rifles, a shot gun & a pair of pistols, but our guide who was in the employ of Capt. Sutter assured us we had nothing to

fear from wild beasts or Indians, and [soon] we were
all sound asleep.

I awakened at daylight, and rousing the boys out to
prepare breakfast. Robert (the guide) & myself amused
ourselves with trying our rifles at a target untill our
meal was ready, and before we had got through it, we
observed a large Panther at about 300 yards distance
and sneaking towards us no doubt his olfactory organs
were regaled by the odors which the breeze wafted
from our frying pan towards him. We caught our rifles
and advanced to meet him but however hungry he
might have been, he declined the contest and wisely
(perhaps) returned to a thick jungle to take it out in
smelling. We were now by the best calculation 95 miles
from the ship. The wind now had failed

WED. 28th. and on the flood tide beginning to make
at 5 AM, we commenced rowing and sailing up river.
Towards noon the breeze was entirely gone, and the
weather very warm. We made a number of stops during
the heat of the day. At 1 PM stopped by the side of a
beautiful wood, and dined under the wide spreading
limbs of a gigantic oak. Though the heat was extreme
in the sun and tho' "there was not a breeze the blue
waves to curl" yet we could not lose the tide therefore
we were on our way again at 2 PM and pulled another
hour when we were again compelled to lay too under
the shade of a lofty sycamore untill the high trees
should cast their shadows across the river & afford us
more protection. Them. [Thermometer] must have
been as high as 100 or over in the shade, and I regretted that I had not brought my them. with me, or
rather, my regret was, that the steward had broken them
all. During our passage up, this day, we saw a deer

drinking at the river side but he was off before we could approach near enough for a shot. One Beaver and a number of otter were also seen but we were not able to shoot them. The scenery of the river most of the distance thus far since the morning has been romantic & interesting. The immense size of the trees, the dense thickness of the unpenetrated forests in some places, and the level plains with here and there a bunch of scrub oaks without underbrush in others, together with a profusion of wild flowers such as roses, sun flowers, holly hocks and many unknown ones which shed abroad their grateful perfume added to the beauty of the scene and was charming to the senses. The forests consist mostly of sycamore, a variety of oak, but mostly the white, ash & some wallnut. The width of the river from 200 yards to a third of a mile. A bright moon and a delightful night enabled [us] to proceed while the tide favoured us, and at 11 PM we camped for the night, cooking and supping occupied us untill after midnight when we stretched ourselves around our huge fire, which would have done honour to any Christmas hearth at home, and were soon lost in forgetfulness.

[THURS. 29th]. With the earliest blink of day, the tea kettle & frying pan were put in requisition, and the sun at rising found us eating breakfast in our boat while she was gliding up stream with a gentle breeze.

The course of the river to the sea is nearly south with occasional deviations to the E & W. The scenery improves as we advance. In the morning we passed three canoes which were moored to the bank opposite an extensive plain. They were recognized as belonging to Capt. Sutter's hunters, who were probably hunting elk on the plain. Shortly after, landed at a deserted camp of the beaver trappers. Found the 'caches' where they had stowed away their stores and peltry, while they were hunting in another direction. This camp I afterwards found had been occupied by a party in the employ of the Hon. Hudson's Bay Co. At 7 passed a deserted Indian "Rancheria" (village). The river here is broader than below, and the banks higher. The country looks fertile and with just trees enough to give it a pleasant appearance. For a number of miles on the west bank we pulled under wild grape vines which ran out on the limbs of trees overhanging the river, and the clusters of grapes which were about half grown hung in great quantities over our heads. At this place I shot an otter, but lost him in the thick grass on the edge of the river. Arrived at 11 PM at a Rancheria where we found about 30 Indians belonging to a tribe under the jurisdicion of Capt. Sutter. They are stationed here to catch & cure fish for the establishment. Their huts were formed of willows planted in the ground, bent over and tied together at the top, and covered with thatch. The natives most of them were in a state of nudity and the females with a narrow strip of cotton tied around the hips. The men & boys [were] employed in drying fish, the females were preparing (by washing, drying and pounding) a seed resembling Timothy seed, of which they make a thick gruel, which as the wheat crop has failed, is now their substitute for bread. This place is about 20 miles below Capt S's by water, but only 10 by land. We reposed under the shade of the trees while an Indian was despatched to Capt. S. to inform him of our arrival and to request horses. In about three hours they arrived. Robert & myself with an Indian boy to show us the way started at ½ past 4 and riding over a beautiful gently undulating country abounding with rich feed and agreeably diversified with trees & wild shrubbery. We came in sight of the settlement situated on a rolling ground. On our near approach, I was unexpectedly received with a military salute of cannon and a display of flags. Capt. S. gave me a most cordial welcome, and we were soon seated to dinner which had been waiting for us and consisted mostly of venison cooked in different ways. Two fat buck deer had been killed in the morning and we made a sumptuous repast thereon. Spent the remainder of the day in inspecting the location of the place and the works that were in operation, and the evening in conversation. Capt. Sutter is a Swiss gentleman of an ancient and high standing family. His great grandfather was one of the Knights of Malta. His father was a commander of note, and he himself was Capt. of the Swiss Guards in the service of Charles the Xth of France. He has held a commission since 18 years of age & has seen much service although he is now not 50. His family resides in Switzerland and consist of a wife, three sons and two daughters. His sons are all of them at the celebrated school of Fellenburgh's at Hoffrogh.[11] He left them about 7 years since to seek and secure for them a home in a land of freedom where, free from the trammels and despotism of the European courts, he could prepare a place where he would sit down with his wife & children "under his own vines & fig trees with none to molest." Passing up the Missisippi [sic]

[11] Sutter was not above doing his best to impress visitors and friends with his past history and present contacts: according to one of Sutter's better biographers, there was nothing paricularly notable about the education of Sutter's children. James Peter Zollinger, *Sutter: the Man and His Empire* (N.Y., 1939), p. 259.

he examined and remained some time in the western country, but after experiencing many reverses of fortune & the climate not proving congenial to his European constitution, he crossed the Rocky Mountains, visited the Columbia River & the Sandwich Islands, and at length fixed upon this country, and this part of it, as being the most suitable for his object.

About 18 months ago he obtained from this Govt. a grant of land on the Sacramento consisting of 35 square miles and he is now creating a colony, building houses, raising cattle, civilizing the Indians, and trapping beaver on the waters of the Sacramento & its tributary streams.

The weather being very warm, and the temporary house in which Capt. S. now lives abounding in fleas, a tent was pitched for me near the house, and being very tired I retired early to bed & was soon asleep. But long before morning I was routed from my camp by an army of fleas who had found me out and were drawing on my being at a merciless rate. Giving my bedding a good shaking and myself a thorough scratching, I returned to my quarters again and slept soundly untill after sunrise [FRI. 30th] when on getting up I found that my body and limbs bore some resemblance to a "current dumpling."

Before breakfast, accompanied Capt. S. around his improvements. Found about 100 Indians at work, some making dobys for building the walls of houses, others spreading them in the sun to bake, & others carrying those that are sufficiently hardened to the builders who were employed on the walls. Dobys [Adobe] are unburnt bricks made of mud and straw, about two feet long, 15 inches wide & 4 thick. These become very hard in the sun and by age become cemented together, and are very durable. Of this material most of the walls of the California houses are built. In a square of about 200 feet Capt. S. had a large three story house nearly finished for his own use. The square is to be enclosed by a doby wall 18 feet high & 4 thick, this wall forming the back part of the houses and shops of his artificers such as Carpenters, Blacksmiths, Coopers &c. Those houses of those immediately connected with his household, & his magazines, & storehouses will all be enclosed, together with a horse & cattle Korral. The enclosure as "Presidio" is to be fortified by two bastions at right angles commanding the wall in all directions with a shifting gun also for which there are two embrasures besides those that rake the walls. Under the bastions are the prisons, and the walls will be surmounted in various directions with swivels. Thus he will in a few weeks be fortified at all points and as experience has shown that neither Californians nor Indians are to be trusted, he has wisely prepared to protect himself and those with him. Capt Sutter now has about 20 white men with him of difft. nations, most of them mechanics, and the others, hunters. He has also at his beck 4 or 5 Indian tribes, whom he has won by acts of kindness, and also intimidated by punishments, but by preserving and ruling them with an even hand and being just to all, they now seem devoted to him. 18 months ago they had not a rag of clothing and existed wholly by the chase. Now they are employed by Capt. S. and are well fed by him. He also has induced many of them to wear shirts and other articles of clothing which he furnishes them with in return for their work. When Capt. Sutter came among them the difft tribes

were all at war with each other, now they are at peace
with all, and all work for him in any number he requires. The Presidio walls are fast rising, and will be
finished in about a month. While Capt. S. was pointing
out to me where the difft. shops and magazines were to
be, I inquired where the church was to be located. He
replied, here is to be my hospital, & there my school.
I shall first heal my Indians of the vile disease which
is so widely spread among them, and then educate
them, before I attempt to instruct them in the principles
of the Christian religion. Diametrically opposite was
the method pursued by the Catholic missionaries.
They pursued the poor natives with unanswered force,
dragged them to the mission amidst much abuse, and
compelling them to master a Latin prayer of which
neither priest or Indian knew the import, pronounced
them to be Christians, and consequently slaves to the
church. The treatment they received was similar to
that received by the cattle in the branding season. The
Ranchero lassos his cattle, drags them to the ranch and
brands them as his own. So with the Padres. They
hunted the poor native, even with the lasso, and having
caught him, branded him with the mark of Holy
Mother church and then employed him to entrap his
fellow. The Indians in this neighbourhood at first
manifested very hostile feelings towards Capt S. and
his people. They stole his horses, and made war upon
one of two tribes whose good will he had gained, but
after he had made a number of excursions against and
subdued them and treating them in a different manner
from what the Spaniards did, they all became friendly
and made treaties with him by which they hold themselves ready to assist and defend him, especially against
the Spaniards for whom they have a mortal hatred.

THURS. 29th. [FRI. 30th]. At breakfast we were joined by Mr. Sinclair, an American hunter who resides on the American Fork about three miles dist. from the Presidio.[12] In company with Capt. S. I rode over to visit Mr. Sinclair's place. Our route lay over a beautiful plain, the soil apparently of a rich black mould, and affording abundant feed for cattle.

Mr. S. who is a very intelligent & respectable man, has his establishment which consists of two neat white cottages, and huts for his Indians, on the right bank of the river, with large oaks in front. The margin of the Am. Fork on each side is shadowed by trees of large growth, the land is high and never overgrown, the soil of the richest kinds, and in fact the country hereabouts is delightful. Nature has done every thing for it. Man as yet has done nothing. Deer and Antelope are abundant at a short distance from the house, and Elk can be shot by going a few miles. Mr. S. untill very recently has been without cattle, and the wheat crop having failed this year, he has been obliged to depend upon the hunt to support himself and from 20 to 30 Indians whom he has kept employed. He takes his rifle and an Indian boy with three pack horses, rides to the hunting ground in the afternoon, kills a number of Elk, camps for the night, loads the pack horses in the morning with the skins and meat, and returns by noon with provisions for a week. In front of his house and at not more than a stone's throw from his door he can obtain any quantity of the richest salmon. On these during the

---

12 John Sinclair, a Scotsman, was for some years in the employ of Hudson's Bay Company in Oregon, was in and about Monterey and New Helvetia in the years 1839-41, after which he was naturalized, and occupied a rancho north of Sutter's holdings. He was alcalde of the Sacramento district from 1846 until his death in 1849.

season for them, which is from April to July, the Indians subsist wholly but never dry any. Mr. S. informed me of a fact respecting these fish of which I had never heard, which is that of all the salmon which ascend the river none ever return to the sea alive, that after spawning in the fresh water, they become spotted all over, their colour changes from red to white, and they begin to rot commencing at the tail, and in the latter part of the season the surface of the river is nearly covered with dead rotten salmon floating to the sea. The Indians eat them as long as they are to be found, even in their putrid state. Captain Sutter & Mr Sinclair undertook to cure a quantity this season, but not being acquainted with the business lost all they salted, but the few which they smoked, to try the experiment, turned out well and as I can testify were equal to the best I ever tasted. Next season they intend preserving a large quantity.

Expressing a desire to go out on a hunting excursion Mr. Sinclair proposed an Elk hunt tomorrow and I gladly avail myself of the opportunity of seeing some specimens of a hunting life. Therefore on our return to Capt. Sutter's we got our rifles in order. In the afternoon the hunters were amusing themselves by shooting at a target. I ventured a shot with them, and to my own surprise came off 2 best shot. Towards sunset horses were saddled and I rode with Capt. S. to visit his premises in another direction. We passed over beautiful plains on which the feed, the growth of last year, was still abundant. The grass, which has been very high, had fallen over and lodged and dried in such a manner that it was to all intents and purposes good hay. There had not been rain or moisture enough during the winter to rot it and it had retained its rich freshness to a great degree. Capt. S.'s establishment is ¾ of a mile from the nearest bank of the Sacramento, but his landing place is 2 miles from the house. A deep gully lies near his house, which is partly filled with water and which by excavating about ¼ of a mile at each end and by a little cleaning out will bring the water from the Am. Fork to run by his door and empty into the Sacramento. This he contemplates doing, and at the same time he will not only be enabled to bring his boats near to his house, but will also have a fine site for mills. We returned home along the edge of a forest where his coal burners were at work felling trees and chopping off the limbs to make charcoal. We also passed by an extensive field enclosed for wheat by a fence. I should think about three miles in length, the longest fence I recollect seeing in any part of the world.

To avoid the torment of fleas, my tent was removed for this night to a pleasant place under the trees at a short distance from the house, & here I thought I should be quite out of their reach and I soon fell asleep on retiring without the least sign of their being on my tail, but about midnight I found them as plentiful as they had been the night previous. I could not account for it, but I was determined to withstand their vigorous attacks and sleep it out untill morning. I partly succeeded and on turning out in the morning found the cause of my torment in the likeness of 4 large dogs who had been lying, two on each side of me, and close to the bed all night, and altho' the dogs no doubt provide an excellent body guard for me against wild beasts & Indians, yet they brought such a host of sappers and miners with them, that I lost more blood by them than

the Indians would have probably taken. [SAT JULY
31]. After an early breakfast we, i.e. Mr Sinclair, and
a hunter named MacVicar,[13] mounted our horses (and
a most excellent one I had), accompanied by an Indian
boy with a pack horse, started for the hunting ground.
It being the custom of the hunters to take no provisions
with them on a hunt, I found that they had provided
themselves with nothing but a little pepper & salt, not
even a bit of bread was tho't of. This not being quite
the thing for me, as I did not like the idea of a hard
ride of 40 or 50 miles with no other creature comforts
than the chase might afford, I contrived to stow away
in my blanket unobserved by my companions a bottle
of wine, a few biscuits, a small box of coccoa paste & a
tin pot to boil it in, which, with a good supply of cigars,
I felt better satisfied with than if we had to depend
wholly upon the precarious nature of the chase. After
crossing the American Fork, our route lay over a beautiful country of plains and gently rising hills all well
covered with oats, with here and there groves of trees,
presenting a fine landscape to the eye and many very
promising sites for farms. Nature has been very bountiful to this region, and there appears to be nothing wanting but an industrious population.

The scene of our operations was in a long strip of
high flags [tule reeds] which commenced near the
mouth of the Feather River and extended itself in a
belt of about 2 or 300 yards in width and 15 or 20 miles
in length running nearly parallel to the Sacramento

13 Henry McVicker occurs in California records between 1837 and 1846.
In 1842 he was in command of Sutter's trappers but quarreled with Sutter.
In 1844, aged 26, he took part in a local political overturn, but then dropped
out of the historical record. (Bancroft, IV, 727.)

River at about ¼ of a mile from the bank, its inner edge at a short distance from the thick woods which border it. This is a favorite resort of the Elk who find rich feed among the flags, and a fine shade to sleep during the heat of the day. Our object was to get to leeward of the Elk, and hunt them to windward. Therefore as the wind consistently blows up River, we proceeded to the farthest end of our hunt at once. On our way we started a number of Antelope, and McVicar shot one, a doe, but it was poor in flesh and we left it. I chased & shot a wild cat among the trees and took the skin. About 4 PM we arrived at the extreme end of the (tule) flags and after a short rest and the refreshment of a glass of wine and a cigar, we again mounted and commenced our elk hunt. My companions, wishing to give me the best chance of killing one, advised me to take the middle of the flags where I should be most likely to find the animals asleep, cautioning me that if a buck should be wounded and turn upon me to ride immediately out of the flags where they would be in readiness to assist me or to kill any thing I should drive out. Accordingly dividing ourselves and moving along at a moderate rate, we swept along the route (which was in fact the bed of a lake impassable in winter, but now dry), occasionally starting a few deer or antelope but as there were now considerable small game, we did not trouble them. We had passed about 8 miles when two Bucks and a doe Elk were started by McVicar and drove into the flags. Mr. Sinclair & myself got shots at a Buck but the distance was too great. Mr. S's ball struck him but mine did not. He however scampered off into the woods. It was about sunset; we had traversed the greater part of the ground without

success. We had seen about a dozen elk but could not
approach near them. I was hungry & fatigued with
no prospect of supper and I was about proposing to
leave the elk ground, enter the woods, and try to get
a deer, when I heard the crack of Mr. Sinclair's rifle
and five large bucks bounded from the edge of the
wood into the flags ahead of me. One of them was evidently hit as he lagged in his gait and dropped a little
astern of the rest. It was blowing a strong breeze. I
was dead to leeward of them and as they stood in the
middle of the flags watching Sinclair's movements, they
did not notice me untill I had approached to within
about 60 yards of them. When they caught sight of me,
and throwing their large horns back & snuffing the air
to windward, they started off in that direction. The one
which appeared to be wounded was the last to start,
and as he moved slower than the rest, and I could see
nothing but his head, I stopped my horse, raised myself
in the sirrups, aimed and fired. I heard the ball crush
his skull and saw his proud antlers fall to the ground.
To skin him and cut out his ribs on one side, occupied
us untill nearly dark. We now repaired to the river
side to prepare supper and look out for a place to camp
for the night. We soon had a large fire under weigh,
and as the large oak limbs burnt out and left a bed of
coals large enough to have roasted the elk whole. I lit
my cigar and lay down in the grass to watch the culinary operations. Mr Sinclair spitted the ribs, which
were very fat, on an oak stake which he drove down
before the fire; soon the rich juices began to trickle
down and as the savory viands were turned before the
fire and gave signs of its soon being ready for our hungry jaws, I appreciate most fully the glowing descrip-

tions which I had heard of a hunters feast. As we cut large morsels and devoured them with a hunters appetite, I felt that I should have been unwilling to have left them to sit at "rich man's tables." After supper we fastened our horses to the bushes, and wrapping our blankets around us, and our saddles for pillows, we laid down around the fire with a bright unclouded sky about us and were soon lost in forgetfulness. The night was cool, and the dew heavy, but I heeded it not, for never did I enjoy a sounder nights rest.

SUNDAY [AUG. 1, 1841]. At Daybreak after a slight breakfast we remounted our horses to return. My companions were desirious of continuing the hunt, but as I was fully satisfied for this time and it being the Sabbath, I was determined to return as we were only 10 or 12 miles from the settlement. Therefore after returning to the carcass of the elk and taking off his antlers which I wished to bring away, we shaped our course homeward. The skin of the elk was thrown across the pack horse which the Indian boy rode, and the antlers were placed on the back part of the saddle with the branches projecting forward with the boy squeezed in between them. We had proceeded about three or four miles, when I heard the boy who was behind me cry out. On returning I saw his horse galloping off, and he lying senseless on the ground. I jumped off and ran to him and was fearful that a branch of the antlers had pierced his body and killed him. But we found that he was only stunned by a blow on the head, and while the hunters went in pursuit of the pack horse, which they soon caught, I assisted the poor boy in recovering himself. I was desirous of having the antlers, but for fear of accident I requested

they should be left, but Mr Sinclair insisted on taking
them in for me himself, which he did much to my
gratification and his own discomfort. On our way back,
passed the remains of indian villages, long since abandoned. These were of the tribe of Omutchammes.[14]
Their villages were on a mound which they had
raised about 18 feet high with the earth taken from
the plain on which they built, and the plain being
overflown with water in the winter, puzzled me to
imagine why they should select such a location. However the inhabitants had long since passed away and
there was none to tell their story. The wild beasts had
disintered the bodies of the dead & their bones were
bleaching in the sun. I got off my horse and selected
a couple of skulls and much to the horror of the poor
indian put them into a bag. When he saw me preparing to bring away the antlers of the elk, he looked
with astonishment, as he had never seen a person take
away such things before, but now to see me overhauling dead men's bones, and those the ones of his ances-
tors, he looked upon me with fear and distrust. But
when I offered him the bones and told him to tie the
bag to his horse, he started back in utter dismay, and
it was not untill Mr. Sinclair told him I was a Medicine Man, and could harm him with my incantations,
could he be persuaded to take them. On our arrival
at Mr. S's house he told his companions of my doings

---

[14] The Indians of the American and Sacramento rivers described in this
section were generally of the Maidu stock, but it is not possible to determine
which village or tribal group is meant in this and the following journal
entry. Phelps' handwriting is very difficult to decipher in the case of these
terms, compounding the problem of locating "tribes," which were often
simply village names, and put down as they sounded to Phelps' untrained
ear. See Kroeber, *op. cit.*

and, about 30 of them collecting together near the house, concluded to send a Kanaka [15] who was then overseer on the premises to ask Mr S. what I was going to do with their father's bones. As it would have been impossible to have made them comprehend any thing on the subject of phrenology, he told them I wanted them to make ornaments of [them] and that I wished to get some with the hair on also. This was quite sufficient for them to know, and afterwards I could not get within speaking distance of them. Just before crossing the American Fork on our return we stopped at a settlement of the Secumnes Indians consisting of about 40 persons. The Old Chief advanced to meet and welcome us. He was sick and appeared feeble, possessed a pleasing countenance and was well made. An old check shirt without sleeves was the only article of clothing he had on. The rest of the tribe were unincumbered by the least article, even women & children. The men were not at work. This tribe being under Mr Sinclair's protection, he will not allow them to work on the sabbath. Some of the females were preparing their food consisting mostly of acorns and roots. I saw a string or stretch of about 500 feet in length into which the feathers of the wild duck were closely worked, part of it white and part black. This was to form a blanket or at least the warp of one. The labour of making one of these blankets is immense. Capt. Sutter presented me with one which he assumed occupied six females four months in the making. We arrived at Capt. Sutter's about 11 AM. I found him employed in paying off the indians who had been em-

---

[15] "Kanaka" was the term generally used among seafarers for Sandwich (Hawaiian) Islanders.

ployed the previous week. He regretted that he was
compelled to do this on Sunday and said that he should
soon establish a better order of things. He pays them at
[the] rate of 25 cts. per day, in goods. The only articles
they now want is cotton to make shirts, and beads to
gamble with. They are not allowed to gamble for anything but beads and it is an amusement of which they
are passionately fond. Those who have distinguished
themselves during the week he rewards with an extra
string of beads, or a few needles and some thread.
He tells the Chief how many hands he wants for the
next week, and at daylight on Monday they are sure
to be there.

MONDAY [AUG. 2]. This morning I despatched the
boat to a landing place about 20 miles down the river
where I intend joining her tomorrow & return to the
ship. Spent most of the day in riding with Capt. Sutter
over various parts of his territory. During the day visited two tribes of indians on the right bank of the
Sacramento. Most of the men were away at work for
Capt. S. Those who were at home with the women
were employed in repairing their houses. The women
were making shirts and preparing food. Most of these
indians were clothed (i.e., had shirts on). Their houses
are made of young willows stuck in the ground in a
circle of about 15 or 18 feet in diameter. The tops are
brought together and secured and the whole covered
with thatch interwoven closely. A small hole is left
for the smoke to escape in the top. The rest of the roof
and the sides are water proof. There is also attached
to each settlement a large house built after the same
manner and situated in the center of the village which
is used for holding their councils and dances. This

being a year of scarcity, many of the indians were employed in collecting a bulbous root called amole, the
coats of which resemble those of an onion. This root
is an excellent substitute for soap and roasted is very
palatable food. They also were making bread of acorns,
but the principal article of their food was of grass
seed. This is collected with much labour on the plains,
by holding a blanket under the heads of the grass with
one hand and beating off the seed with a stick with
the other. It is then winnowed, washed, roasted, and
pounded, and then made into a gruel which they call
atole.[16] They had an abundance of a small fish dried
in the sun, which they take with nets in the river. Some
of the men were busied in making a liquor from a
berry resembling the juniper, which they do by pul-
verizing & steeping it, letting it ferment and then
straining it. A chief gave me some to drink and I
found it very pleasant, without any intoxicating properties, and very similar to sherbet made by the Turks
of Smyrna from dried grapes. Their fishing nets and
lines the indians make from a stalk similar but somewhat higher than hemp. This they break and hackle
[i.e., mangle] with their teeth. The process is consequently very slow, but the line is strong and neatly
made. The indians of the Sacramento are good looking,
more intelligent and warlike than those of the sea
coast, but they are much afflicted by that horrid disease
which Europeans & Americans generally introduce
wherever they go. Capt. S. is doing all in his power
to eradicate this scourge and it is to be hoped that
the benevolent plans and system which he has devel-

16 *Amole,* or "soap plant," was used for bathing; *atole,* a thick gruel of
maize or acorns, was widely used by California Indians.

oped for the moral and intellectual improvement of
the poor indian may be attended with success. The
following are the names of the Indian tribes at *New
Helvetia* (the name Capt. S. has given his settlement)
and its vicinity on the *Rio El Sacramento*. A village
consisting of the remains of what were once very
large powerful and warlike tribes (viz), The Losum-
nes, Omutchamnes, Ochejamnes, Chupumnes, Solo-
lumnes, Walaqumnes, & Lhckcalemnes now very
much reduced and living together. These are all employed by & devoted to Capt. Sutter. Another large
village of Bushummnes reside on the American Fork.
On the Feather River are the Secumnes, Yusuminess,
Vyski & Yalesumnes. Also far to the South are the
Hock, Olesumnes, & Yukee. On the Sacramento also
are a number of large tribes who have never had in-
tercourse with white people. Some of them are represented to Capt. Sutter by his indians who have been
among them as being very warlike, some friendly,
some not, and all very shy. Further to the south of
New Helvetia are the Unkulimnes, a village discharged from the rich Mission of St. Jose, for the
want of food. Still farther south are the Lichimnes,
Loclomnes, Wapumnes, Laygayacumnes, &c., friendly, and labouring people of New Helvetia. Beyond
them are the Horse thieves of whom I have before
spoken as the tribes who occasionally trouble the Californians for their surplus horses.

TUES. [AUG. 3]. After breakfast, I prepared for my
return to the boat. Capt. Sutter had treated me with
hospitality, and the utmost attention. One of his best
horses had been kept at the door saddled for me and
a boy to attend to me at all times, and in every way

that he could contribute to my comfort or amusement, nothing was omitted. Last evening was the grand finale he ordered 15 of his indian boys to get themselves ready for a war dance. After supper one of them came to the door to let him know they were ready. We went out into the court of the Presidio, where we found the little naked savages with bows and arrows in their hands, their faces and naked bodys painted most hideously with white, red and black paint. They were all less than 16 years of age. Three of them were making music by beating reeds together and the others dancing around a fire singing war songs, making gestures of defiance & looking more like demons than human beings. After being sufficiently gratified by the exhibition Capt. [Sutter] ordered them to wash off the paint and come to his door to receive a lump of panocha (Mexican sugar) to reward them for their endeavours to please.[17] Mr. Sinclair returns to the ship with me to get a passage to the Sandwich Islands, where [he] goes upon business for the settlement. Capt. Sutter & Mr. Gyger [Geiger][18] an American accompanies us to the boat. The distance was about ten miles, and the ride pleasant. We bid adieu to our friends and immediately shoved off, the wind being against but the tide in our favour. We pulled about twenty miles down the river and encamped on the left bank to [prepare] dinner. While it was repairing, Mr. Sinclair & myself went out a little ways to hunt. Killed an antelope and followed the fresh tracks of a bear for some

---

[17] Panocha generally means ear of millet or maize, but the word was used in California to mean coarse brown sugar in small cakes, moulded in a wooden mould. Bancroft, *California Pastoral,* p. 364.

[18] William Geiger was a young (24) teacher from New York, who reached New Helvetia in 1841 via Vancouver, Fort Ross, and Honolulu.

distance but found that he had gone into the high flags
where we dare not seek him. At this encampment I
picked up a skull which had been perforated by a
bullet. Mr. S. identified it as belonging to an indian
of the Columbia River, in the employ of the Hudson
Bay Co., who was killed here about a year since. The
account he gave me was this. Two indians were trapping for beaver on the Sacramento. One of them had
a wife with him which the other was desirous of taking from him. While the men were on the river one
morning in their canoe and the woman was preparing
their meal on shore. the unfortunate possessor of the
woman was sitting in the bow of the canoe paddling,
with his back to his companion who was paddling in
the stern, when the latter shot his fellow through the
head with his rifle and took him on shore to his wife.
The poor creature told the murderer that he might
as well kill her also, which he instantly did by shooting her on the spot. He afterwards confessed his crime,
was *flogged* for it by the H.B. Co., but was shortly
after destroyed by a bear while trapping. I looked for
the woman's skull but could not find it. [WED., AUG.
4]. The breeze being strong and the river wide enough
to beat in, we took in a quantity of oak wood for ballast and at the turn of the tide made sail and commenced working down the river. At dark stopped to
cook supper at the last encamping place in the river,
and made sail again at 8 PM with a strong breeze &
a bright moon. About 10 PM we were out of the river.
At midnight blowing hard with a rough sea. Anchored
under the lee of a small low island covered with high
flags, and held on till daylight, when we again got
under weigh with reeft sails and proceeded on our

way. [THURS., AUG. 5]. Before leaving the anchorage
I shot a beaver which came swimming along near the
boat with a limb of a tree in tow, and also a land otter.
The weather this morning was very windy and rough,
and as we had the prospect of a long passage to the
ship, and our fresh meat was getting scarce, I thought
it best to land somewhere and replenish our stock.
Accordingly about 10 AM seeing a good landing place
and a herd of wild bullocks feeding on the plains near
by, we ran in and hauled the boat on shore. While the
crew were preparing breakfast, Mr Sinclair & myself
took our rifles and went to hunt, but as we could not
screen ourselves from their sight while approaching
them, the cattle at the first glimpse of us started off
at full speed. We fired a long shot but without effect.
These cattle are some that have probably strayed away
from the missions in former years, and have become
quite numerous, no person claiming them, but they be
so very wild that it is difficult to shoot or take them.
After breakfast we made another attempt and were
more successful. We observed about twenty coming
down from the hills towards the watering place. We
hid ourselves near to where we thought they would
pass. But, ever on the alert, before they came within
shot we were discovered by them. However Mr. Sinclair by imitating the cries of a calf in distress touched
the feelings of the compassionate cows and enduced
them to approach within about 80 or 90 yards of us,
where they stood gazing at us and pawing up the
ground. We selected a fine young cow from the lot,
and both fired together at her. The herd started off
for the hills, but we were confident of having wounded
our object and soon saw her begin to lag, and at length

she left the herd and took off in another direction alone. By this movement we knew she was badly wounded. We followed and watched her untill she lay down, when we separated and approached her in different directions. She first discovered Mr. Sinclair, and by keeping her eye constantly on him, permitted me to approach her unobserved 'till within about 60 yards, when I fired, putting a ball between her horns which glanced up and only penetrated the skin. This much enraged her and making a run after me I was obliged to retreat untill another shot from Mr. Sinclair brought her to a stand. Quickly reloading I now sent a bullet through her liver and she fell dead. The boats crew had watched the chase and now came up, took off the hide and conveyed the quarters to the boat. The beef was tender and fat, and a monstrous piece of it was soon roasting before the fire. We dined most sumptuously & at 5 PM got under weigh & beat down as long as the ebb tide lasted, anchoring about 10 PM. The wind still blowing strong from the NW. Passed the night in the boat, now very comfortably. The weather was cold and our quarters were so small that I was obliged to enjoy what sleep I did get with my head and knees in close contact, describing something like the figure 8 by my position.

FRIDAY [AUG. 6]. At 4 AM the wind blowing hard, with much sea, we were again under weigh with reeft sails on the turn of tide, with the spray flying fore & aft giving us a thorough drenching. We beat down to the Straits of the Carquines, here meeting the tide of flood. We landed at the foot of a pleasant valley about 9 AM. Building a rousing fire, we were soon busily engaged in roasting, frying, and feasting, topping off with a cup of chocolate and a cigar. The beef we killed yesterday was certainly the best I ever tasted, and Oh the deliciousness of that breakfast will [be] dear to my remembrance in all after times of scarcity & hard fare. Stretching myself under the wide spreading limbs of a holly leaved oak, I partook of two hours' very refreshing sleep, and on waking saw a fine buck & doe deer quietly grazing at about 40 yards from me. It was a most glorious chance, and leveling my rifle at the buck I—snapt. My gun had been loaded over night, was damp and missed fire. The pair of them bounded up the steep hills & were soon out of sight. While waiting for a favourable tide, Mr. S. & myself ascended a considerable mountain to obtain a prospect. The ascent occupied over an hour and was very laborous, but the extent and beauty of the scene presented to our view, amply repaid our toil. I always feel in such a place more in the presence of my creator, and 'tho He is every where, and his presence prevadeth all places, yet in such an elevated situation, Man feels more his own littleness, and consequently the unbounded power, wisdom, and goodness of the Almighty, than he is apt to do in the every day walks of life. I sat down and enjoyed the scene, and my own reflections untill I found it time to return. I wished that I were alone in such a place, or with a friend of congenial feelings. The mountains and hills in this vicinity are barren of trees, but are covered with abundance of wild oats. The soil is apparently very rich and no doubt would yield abundant crops if cultivated. At 2 PM after a slight and hasty dinner, we again started. As we expected to pass the following night in the boat, I ordered the men to have something cooked to take with us. Accordingly on my return to the boat, I found they had roasted a quarter of beef whole, and in such a manner that it would have graced the board at a city feast and been an object which a bevy of aldermen might have regarded with affectionate interest. It was taken to the boat and triced up, where each one could "cut and come again" as he felt disposed and the way that we had walked into its affections by the next morning "was a caution." Passing the Straits we saw a band of 2 or 300 elk feeding on the north side, but we could not spare time to hunt, as it was late and we should lose the tide. With the prospect of a pleasant night we stood across the bay of Sonoma with a light breeze from the SW, and proceeded about 15 miles, when at 8 PM the wind increased to a complete gale. We doused all sail immediately and let go the grapnel, but a strong current running in nearly an opposite direction from which the wind was blowing caused a dangerous cross sea. The current caused the boat to ride with her stern to the sea which frequently combed over it in such a manner that for a few minutes our situation was any thing but agreeable or safe. We however by settling the mainsail double reeft brought her head to the sea and lay comparatively safe until watching a lull we up anchor, set the jib and drove the boat towards the land near to Pt. St. Pablo, where we anchored and remained the night in smooth water. We were all well drenched & the night was cold, but after freeing the boat of water, we made a vigorous attack on the roast beef, and comforting ourselves with a glass of wine, which I had reserved for such an occasion and topping off with a cigar, we willed ourselves away in the bottom of the boat drawing the wet sails over us to keep off the cold wind and slept soundly, while the wind in furious gusts continued till after daylight.

SAT. [AUG. 7]. At 7 AM got under weigh again and with reef sails and a strong breeze crossed over to the western side of the bay, and reached Angel Island about an hour before sundown, when finding that it was blowing heavy in the passage and that we could not reach the ship 'till after dark, I judged it unsafe to proceed any farther. Therefore running into Raccoon Bay, we hauled up the boat, built a fire, cooked supper, dried our clothes, and camped for the night.

SUNDAY [AUG. 8]. After a good night's rest, we again started with a favourable tide and strong wind and arrived at the Ship about 10 AM. Found all right on board. The boats had all returned from their different trips, and all hands at home. Mr Sinclair arrived just in time to secure a passage in the *Lama,* which sails for the Sandwich Islands tomorrow.

MON. AUG. 9th to SAT 14. During the week variously employed, some of the boats bringing Hides & Tallow from diff*t.* parts of the bay, others wooding and watering. A gang employed in killing and salting beef and getting old sails in order.

SAT. 14th. This Afternoon arrived the U.S. Ship *Vincennes,* the flag ship of the Southern Exploring Expedition. Knowing that they were strangers on the coast, I immediately went on board to offer any assistance which I might be able to render them. The officer of the deck conducted me to the cabin and introduced me to Capt. Ringgold of the U.S. Brig *Porpoise,* but now in command of this ship. Capt. R. informed [me] that he left the Columbia River 4 days since; that the *Peacock* had been lost there in going in but all hands and the Chronometer & charts saved; that Comdt. Wilkes & Capt. Hudson remain with the *Porpoise* & *Flying Fish* to complete the survey of the Columbia and would afterwards join him at this place to return homeward by the way of Manilla & Cape of Good Hope. He thanked me for coming aboard and was desirous of information which I was enabled to give him respecting the situation of things in this place. I also gave him much later news from the U. States than they were in possession of. The account of Presdt. Harrison's death affected Capt. R. almost to tears. As he had many questions to ask I remained with him about two hours, and left him with a promise to dine with him tomorrow. Passing into the ward room I was introduced to all the officers & the scientific gentlemen. All were full of questions – what is the news from home, &c., &c. I answered all their enquiries and gave them all the news I could. Nothing seemed to please them so much as the prospect of war with England. The officers and crew of this ship are all a fine looking set of fellows who no doubt have seen very hard service during this cruise, and are ready for more. Took tea in the ward room, after sending a boat for part of a bullock to the *Alert*. As they were entirely out of fresh provisions on board the *Vincennes* this proved quite a treat for them.

SUNDAY 15th. Strong breezes & foggy wind SW. Crew at rest. Went on board the *Vincennes* at 2 PM. Dined and spent the afternoon with Capt. Ringgold in his cabin & part of the evening in the wardroom.

Recommended Capt. R. to go to Whalers Harbour[19] on the Western side of the bay as being the most convenient place to erect their observatory, obtain wood & water and refresh his crew, where they would be away from grog shops. He aproved of my advice and concluded to go there with the ship after calling upon the authorities at Yerba Buena.

The Whaling ship *Orozimbo* of N. Bedford 8 mos out arrived here yesterday, with part of her crew very bad with scurvy. Sent on board all the fruit & vegetables I could find on board the *Alert*.

MON. 16th. Pleasant & calm weather. Dispatched the Launch to Sta. Clara for hides – the Pinnace to St. Leandry. Capt. Ringgold and one of the Lieuts. of the *Vincennes* called on board. I went on shore with them to call upon the Alcaldi & Commandant. Capt. R. wishes me to pilot his ship to Whalers Harbour; [we] shall therefore start with the tide tomorrow. In the afternoon took a ramble with the naturalist of the expedition Dr. Pickering over the hills to get specimens but I think he was not very successful. As this would be an excellent chance to compare my chronometer with the standard one of the expedition I obtained leave to put it on board the *Vincennes*.

TUES. 17th. Pleasant with strong breezes from the Westw*d*. At 1 PM went on board. At 2 PM got under weigh & beat the *Vincennes* over to Whalers Harbour under single reeft topsails. At 4 PM came to anchor in 7 fathoms water. Dined in the ward room, & supped in the Cabin. Capt. R. was much pleased with my

---

[19] Whaler's Harbor: modern day Sausalito in Marin County, on the north side of San Francisco Bay.

account of the Sacramento and intends to explore it as far up as possible, feels much interested in Capt. Sutter's settlement and said that he would certainly visit him even were it a hundred miles out of his way. I felt glad that he determined to explore the river hoping that his expedition up there would be of service to Cap. Sutter, and feeling not a little pleased that I had myself forestalled [i.e., obtained] the honour of mine being the first American boat that ascended this river, which must in after years be alive with navigation.

WED. 18th.   Started early this morning with Mr. Gale the 2 Lieut. & Dr Fox the Fleet Surgeon to hunt deer. We routed a number. I wounded one but we got none. The Dr. had 9 fair shots, but killed none. On his return to the ship he was run pretty hard by his messmates. They insisted that he must have made a mistake and put pills from his dispensary into his gun for buck shot. In the afternoon two of the officers went out & killed a deer each. This put them all in a fever to hunt, and the Dr. says every officer in the ship has the Buck fever. Today being the third anniversary of the Expedition leaving home, was celebrated on board by the ward room officers giving a grand dinner to which Capt. Ringgold was invited. The entertainment was social and pleasant and the evening was spent in pleasant conversation & singing. The boats for the Sacramento have been preparing to start tomorrow.

THURS. 19th.   As the indian I have sent for at St. Raphael to pilot the boats to the river had not arrived the exp. does not go today. Some of the officers & crew have been employed to day in getting up the Observatory & instruments on shore. In the afternoon went on a hunt with a number of the officers on horseback; returned at dark with three deer, of which I shot one.

FRID. AUG. 20th. At 6 AM Capt. Ringgold started with 7 boats and over 60 officers and men well armed and provisioned for six weeks to explore the Rio El Sacramento. I spent most of the day in looking over the charts and drawings of the expedition, which afforded me much satisfaction and amusement. On board the *Vincennes* as a prisoner is a chief of high standing at the Fegee Islands, where the Expedition had two officers murdered. This chief stands charged with the cutting off and murdering the crew of the Brig *Chas. Dagget,* the mate of which vessel he murdered himself. It is unknown what Capt. Wilkes's intention is with respect to him, but he will probably take him to the U. States. He is a noble looking savage and has quite an intellectual head. The officers give many interesting accounts of the natives of the Fegee group but as they will appear in the history of the voyage I will not repeat them now.

SAT. 21st. The Pinnace came for me. Sent her up to the Mission of St. Raphael to get a load of hides to call for me on her return. Spent the forenoon in shooting at a target on shore. In the afternoon rode out. The officers have all purchased horses. They keep them staked out to feed opposite the ship, with an Indian to look after them. There is a great want of saddles among them. Bridles they make of sennet [sennit], spunyarn,[20] &c. but they cannot easily find a sub-

---

[20] Sennit and spunyarn are both forms of braided yarn made from old cordage, with both ornamental and practical use, such as chafing gear.

stitute for saddles, and it is quite amusing to see their fit outs. Returned to the ship at dusk after a pleasant ride and having shot three deer.

SUN. 22d. The pinnace returned during the night from St. Raphael and after breakfast I started for the *Alert,* the boat being very deep with cargo and five Californian passangers. We reached the ship in safety about 10 AM.

MON 23rd. to MON 30th. Weather pleasant. Crew variously employed in boating hides from diff*t.* parts of the Bay. Filling water, cutting wood, repairing sails, &c. &c. The Carpener repairing the Starbd quarter boat. On Friday I piloted the whale ship to Whalers Harbour & returned on Sat. with my Chronomoter. This week arrived the Hon. Hudson Bay Co. Ship *Cowlitz* with a cargo for California trade. By this ship I received a letter from Home by the way of Valpraiso [sic] & Sandwich Islands. Killed two bullocks for ships use.

TUES. 31. Pleasant with fresh breezes from SW. At 11 AM got under weigh to beat out. At noon a thick fog setting in, ran in an anchored in Whalers Harbour in 17 fathoms. A boat from the *Vincennes* was sent with an invitation for Mr. Mellus & myself to dinner, which we accepted and spent the afternoon & evening there.

WED. SEPT. 1st. Strong winds and foggy weather. The crew employed in wooding. Spent much of the day myself at he *Vincennes* Observatory.

THURS 2d. Continuation of yesterday's weather. Crew employed as usual. Afternoon strong gales from west.

The Fifth Passage

San Francisco to San Diego and Return

FRID. 3rd. [SEPT. 1841]. Strong breezes from West & partially clear. 2 PM hove up and made sail beating out of the passage. At 7 PM passed the bar. Light airs & variable with foggy weather through the night.

SAT. 4th. Calm & foggy. Ship drifting into 10 fathoms water. Came too with the small bower.

SUN 5th. Weather as yesterday. Remained at anchor untill 4 PM when we got under weigh with a light breeze from SW. Sent up the royal yards. Moderate & thick through the night.

MON. 16th. Continuation of light variable winds & foggy weather, with a heavy swell setting on shore. At 4 PM anchored near Pt. St. Pedro in 12 fathoms. At 8 PM a light breeze from the land, got under weigh again. Midnight calm.

TUES. 7th. Moderate breezes from NW. Ship off Pt. Anno Nueva. At 9 AM was boarded by a boat from the whaling ship *Sapphire* of Salem, out 19 mos. with 2200 bbs oil, bound into Monterey. Had been off the point a week in a fog and unacquainted with the coast and requested me to keep him in sight & show him the way in. Afternoon & night light variable winds.

WED 8th. Morning light breezes from SW. All sail

set beating into the bay. *Sapphire* in company. Noon
strong breezes. At 1 PM came too in 6 fathoms off
Monterey. Found lying here the *Braganza* of N. Bedford (Whaler).

THURS. 9th.   Pleasant. Employed in landing freight
& taking off hides. The boats of the *Sapphire* killed
two whale this morning in the bay & got them alongside.

FRIDAY 10th.   Moderate & foggy most of the time.
Crew taking off hides & [11th] getting ready for sea.

SUN 12th.   Moderate breezes & hazy. 11 AM got
under weigh for Sta. Cruz. At dark calm & foggy;
anchored on the north side of the bay in 9 fathoms
water.

MON. 13th.   Morning Calm. 11 AM light breeze
from West. Up anchor and beat down to Sta. Cruz and
anchored at 5 PM in 4 fathoms.

TUES. 14th.   Pleasant & clear. Employed in rafting
off & taking in lumber for Sta. Barbara.

WED. 15th.   Took off the last of 18,000 feet of lumber
& hove short the chain but the wind failing remained
for the night.

THURS 16th.   Morning light breezes from North.
11 AM up anchor and made sail for Sta. Luis Obispo.

FRID. 17th.   Arrived at St Luis at 2 PM. Latter part
of the day employed in taking off hides.

SAT. 18th.   Pleasant throughout the day. Employed
as yesterday. Killed a Bullock for ships use.

SUN. 19th.   Fresh breezes & pleasant. At 10 AM got
under weigh for Sta. Barbara. Passangers Messers.

Hartnell, Denn [Den], Robinson, & Mellus. 7 PM
Anchored at the Cojo [21] in 7 fathoms.

MON. 20th.   Pleasant & calm. Waiting for Hides.

TUES 21st.   Weather as yesterday. Employed in boating off hides & repairing sails. At noon got under way
for Refugio.

WED. 22nd.   Calm & very warm. We have experienced a very strong westerdly current the night past
and find ourselves about 15 miles outside of where
we was last night. At noon a light breeze from WNW.
At dark the wind getting light ran in shore and came
too in 9 fathoms, 4 miles from Refugio.

THURS. 23rd.   Under weigh with a light breeze at
10 AM and did not get to anchor at Refugio untill
sunset. Found a very heavy surf on the beach.

FRID. 24th.   A moderate breeze with a heavy swell
from SE & thick weather. The surf high & dangerous
to land in. Landed the passangers, filling the boat &
nearly capsizing her. Afternoon the same.

SAT 25.   Morning pleasant with the surf falling. Succeeded in taking off all the cargo that was ready for
us. While the boat was loading for the last time I rode
up to see Mr. Hill's family, ordering the four boys to
wait with the quarter boat on the beach for my return.
I was absent about two hours, and on returning met
Mr. Everett the 1st Officer on the hill side. I knew
immediately on seeing him coming to meet me that
something was wrong. I imagined that it might be
some damage to the cargo, a boat stove, or perhaps some

---

[21] Cojo or El Cojo was a cove at Point Conception, the embarkation point
for hides and cargo from the Purísima Mission area (modern day Vanden-
berg Air Force Base). Regarding Hartnell, see page 290, fn. 52.

little fracas on board, and O that it had turned out to be either, or all of these, or any other accident (not touching life) rather than the sorrowful tidings which I was to hear, which was, that one of my poor boys was drowned in the surf. They were amusing themselves by swimming inside of the surf and diving through the breakers after the work was done. They were all good swimmers, except Lowell H. Dana and he had been cautioned by myself the day before to not go into the surf without having hold of the boat, and he was now advised by his companions to not go into the water, but he thought there was no danger and went in & sported about inside of the breakers for some time and came out and dressed himself, and shortly after again stripped and went in a second time.[22] This time he was accompanied by Andrew, a German lad who was a good swimmer, but took an oar with him for greater safety and advised Lowell to do the same which he neglected. On attempting to swim where the water was up to his middle he got into a strong underto or refluent water of which he was ignorant which swept him outside of the breakers before he was aware of being out of his depth. He shouted for help and en-

[22] Lowell H. Dana is not mentioned on Phelps' original crew list; nor is it clear how he came aboard. "Andrew," mentioned below, is similarly unidentified. The mystery is probably explained by the fact that young lads, serving either as cabin boys or unpaid apprentices, were often carried on such vessels. In Dana's case, this supposition is fortified by a letter from Phelps to Stearns earlier the same year (3 January 1841; Stearns Papers, Huntington Library, San Marino, box SG 49) introducing Dana, "a lad of respectable family, is of good habits and has some knowledge of store keeping and I think he will be useful to you in your business after a short initiation," but adding that Phelps would keep Dana with the *Alert* until the vessel left the coast, paying him $15 per month in the meantime.

The drowning is related in Robinson's *Life in California,* pp. 193-94, who adds the detail that Phelps flew his flag at half mast.

deavoured to get on shore but was unable. Andrew
turned towards him on hearing his cries and swam
towards him and pushed the oar so that Lowell got
hold of it, and if he had held on A. would have pulled
him on shore, but he let go his hold and sank to rise
no more. Mr. E. & a boat's crew had used every exertion to recover his body but did not succeed. I immediately sent on board for two boats & all hands to
come on shore while I remained watching for his body
on the beach. We spent the quarter part of the afternoon dragging for him and overhauling the kelp, and
made every possible exertion to get the body, but it
was without success as the underto had taken him off
into the regular current which had probably swept
him far away from the place where he was drowned.
All that I could do was to offer a handsome reward
to the people in the neighbourhood if they would recover the body and bring it to me at Santa Barbara
and I also requested Mr. Hill to use his endeavours
to recover and do all that should be necessary to the
poor fellow's remains if they are found at any time,
which he promised to do. We returned on board silent
and sorrowful, and at sunset made sail for Sta. Barbara.
Light winds through the night & foggy.

SUN 26th. Morning light, variable winds & overcast. At 10 AM anchored at Santa Barbara & furled
sails. Latter part of the day crew at rest. About 5 PM
some Rancherios came to the beach abreast the ship
& hailed having found the body and brought it to
me. I went on shore immediately after setting my carpenter to work making a coffin. They had found the
body not far from where he was drowned early this
morning. We washed and laid it out as decently as

possible and in the evening put it in the coffin. There was no bruise, and the corpse with the exception of the face being discoloured by blood was but little changed.

MON. 27th. Pleasant weather throughout the day. After breakfast the crew were ordered to muster in clean clothes, to say the last sad duties to the remains of their deceased shipmate. I went on shore at daylight to obtain permission to bury the remains on shore, it being the custom here, as in other Catholic countries, to refuse burial in a catholic burying ground to a prot- estant (or as they call us Heretics). Permission being had, I employed some Indians to dig the grave in a pleasant spot near the town under the shade of some large oaks, where was buried another American, a gentleman of the name of Pierce [Peirce] who died here about two years ago.[23] At 10 AM I left the ship with one of the officers & nearly all the crew. Firing a gun and hoisting the colors at half mast to give notice to any of the foreigners who wished to join the pro- cession, from the building on the beach where he had been kept the night previous, the poor lad was borne to his grave by four of his messmates, the crew & my- self, with most of the foreign residents in the place following in procession, many of the natives accom- panying us. A rude coffin, plain, unvarnished, and unornamented, contained his remains, the stars and

---

[23] The grave was that of Hardy Peirce, a young mate on a Hawaiian vessel who died suddenly at Santa Barbara about 1838. His older brother, Henry Augustus Peirce, arrived in California in the 1820's, and had a con- siderable role to play in California and Hawaiian affairs; as part owner of the *Maryland,* this Honolulu-based merchant was, at a later time, Ha- waiian Minister of Foreign Affairs and U.S. Minister to the Hawaiian Islands. (See H. A. Peirce, Journals of Voyages, Bancroft Library, p. 177.)

stripes was his pall, and tho' no relative attended the poor relicks of humanity to their last resting place, a simple and kind hearted crew as they lowered the coffin to the earth, mourned him as a brother. I read the funeral service, and offered up a prayer at the grave, and tho' I was surrounded by a large number of people, and felt rather doubtful when I began, as to my ability to go through the performance in a proper manner, but I soon felt that the spirit of prayer was given me, and that the Lord was my helper.

A neat fence encloses the grave of Mr. Pierce, and I have given orders to my carpenter to enclose Lowell's with a similar one.

TUES. 28th. Weather pleasant. All hands variously employed in landing freight and taking off hides.

WED. 29. Calm & pleasant. Employed as yesterday.

THURS. 30th. Morning calm & foggy. Afternoon fresh breezes from NW and clear weather. Employed in filling water.

FRID. 1. Weather as yesterday. Employed in watering & taking off hides. Carpenter employed at the grave putting up a fence.

SAT. OCT 2nd. Morning calm. At noon got under way with a fresh breeze for St. Pedro. Midnight ship off Pt. Dume.

SUN. 3rd. Ship at St. Pedro. All hands at rest.

MON. 4th.[24] Calm & foggy. Employed in landing freight & taking off hides. Mr. Robinson gone to the Pueblo.

---

[24] Phelps seems to have become confused in his dating here; all the dates from the 4th to the 10th are a mixture of erasures and writeovers, most difficult to read.

Mornings calm & foggy. Afternoons pleasant with westerly winds. Received [SAT 9th]. the last of the hides & got ready for sea.

SUN [10th]. Morning pleasant with moderate breezes from NW. 9 AM got under way for St. Diego. Pleasant breezes throughout.

MON. 11th. Anchored at St. Diego. At 10 AM moored ship, furled sails. Got out the launch & commenced discharging hides. Found all well at our hide depot, with the exception of the stock, 7 or 8 of the hogs having died of starvation since we were here.

TUES. OCT. 12th. Moderate & pleasant weather throughout the day. Employed in landing hides & repairing the house (landed 2000 hides).

WED. 13th. Weather as yesterday. People employed as above; landed about 2000 hides. Killed a bullock.

THURS. 14th. Weather fine with light variable winds. Landed the remainder of the hides. We have now at the depot about 16,400 hides.

FRID. 15. Weather delightful. Employed in landing firewood to house for homeward passage & putting on shore freight, &c. Latter part a boats crew cutting broom stuff.[25] Got the launch in.

SAT. 16th. Weather as yesterday. Unmoored ship at high water. In swinging to the small bower, the ship took the flats and the tide falling before we could get her off, she must remain untill tomorrow's tide. In the afternoon the ship having slud [26] 7 feet, set all hands

---

[25] The reading of "broom" is guesswork; the word is not clearly legible.
[26] The meaning of "slud" is "slewed," i.e., the vessel listed enough to expose seven feet of copper bottom plates.

at work cleaning the copper. Got the kedge out, readying for heaving off.

SUND. 17th. Moderate & cloudy. At 10 AM the ship floated. Hove up the small bower warped off to the kedge & moored in 8 fathoms water. Latter part, all hands at rest.

MON. 18th. Moderate breezes from the Nd. At daylight got under way but the flood running strong & the breeze failing came too just within the point at ½ past 7. At 9 breeze freshening hove up & made sail. Passed the Rubicon & set studding sails. At dark, ship off Puerto Falso, becalmed.

TUES. 19th. Morning light & variable winds & very smooth sea. Ship off Las Flores. Latter part fresh breezes from NW. Midnight, wind from SE & overcast.

WED. 20th. Light winds from SE. 2 AM took in light sails & hove too, it being too dark to run for the anchorage. At daylight calm. Ship about 2 miles from St. Pedro Point. 10 Light breeze from NW. 11.30 anchored at the winter anchorage. Furled the topsails with a reef in them, & got the ship buoy on the chain ready for a Southeaster. Found lying here the brigs *Bolivar, Catalina* & Schr. *Fly.*

THURS. 21st. Pleasant throughout. Winds light & variable. Crew variously employed in ships duty. In the afternoon went to a lagoon about 6 miles dist. on horseback in company with Mr. Foster who had informed me that the wild geese were to be found there. They were rather shy & but few of them. I however succeeded in getting six of them. Mr. F. was unsuccessful. These are the first of the season.

FRID. 22nd.   Morning calm & warm. Latter part strong breezes from NW. All hands employed in restowing the hold &c., &c.

SAT. 23rd.   Morning light northerly winds and pleasant weather. Employed on the rigging. Went to fish for mackerel with the pinnace; caught about 60. They are just making their appearance, and are quite fat. Latter part fresh breezes from NW with a light shower of rain in the morning.

SUN. 24th.   Pleasant & warm throughout the day with light Westerly winds. Crew at rest.

MON. 25th.   Morning calm & foggy. Sent the cutter fishing. Received a few hundred hides from the Pueblo & 17 casks of aguadiente. At noon the cutter returned with about 2 bbls large fat mackerel & a halibut.

TUES. 26th.   Morning calm & foggy. Employed in taking off Hides & tallow. Don Tomas Yorba,[27] a full blooded Californian & one of the wealthiest and best men of the country visited the ship today & brought as a present to me three large baskets of delicious grapes. This old gentleman (for he is about 60 years old) is the greatest dandy in the country. His dress is the most fantastic that can be imagined, and highly set off with gold & silver trimmings. With his gala dress on and mounted on his best saddle, his outfit cannot have cost him less than 4 or 500$. He has a young wife of 25 but the best of it is, he is one of our greatest & most punctual customers. Today arrived the bark *Index,* Capt. Wilson, from Sta. Barbara.

---

[27] Don Tomás Yorba; presumably Don Tomás Antonio Yorba (the family was a big and important one), age 57 in 1841, landowner and sometimes alcalde in the Santa Ana area.

WED. 27th.   Morning light breezes from SW & foggy. Afternoon clear & pleasant with fresh westerly winds. No business doing.

THURS. 28th.   Weather as yesterday. Employed in taking off Hides & tallow, and doing various other work. Afternoon loosed the sails to dry.

FRID. 29th.   Morning moderate & pleasant. Took off a boat load of hides. In the afternoon a strong gale with heavy squalls. Wind at NNW and continued until midnight. During the blow such clouds of dust covered the ship that it was impossible to see her length, and at times it was impossible to open the eyes, or to speak on account of dust.

SAT. 30th.   Moderate and pleasant throughout the day. Employed in various duties on board.

SUND. 31.   Moderate & pleasant throughout. At 9 AM got under weigh for Santa Barbara. Made but little progress.

THURS. NOV 4th.   Owing to very light & variable winds we did not arrive at Sta. Barbara untill this afternoon. Anchored in 10 fathoms, and prepared for a *slip*. Yesterday we were becalmed off the Island of Anacapa. Took the boat and went near the Island to fish and met with fine luck. Caught about 30 fine large Rock fish, some of them weighing 12 & 15 lbs.

FRID. 5th.   Light variable winds in the forenoon, and strong westerly winds in the afternoon & evening. Crew employed watering. Today heard of two more murders, one of them at the Refugio. A fellow who has frequently been employed by our agent to travel with him and take care of his horses in a jealous fit shot his

wife dead. He ran to the next house and told the people
that his wife had shot herself, but she was yet alive
when they reached the house and was able to tell the
particulars. The other case is that of a Greek at Monterey with whom I was well acquainted. He was beaten
to death a few weeks since by some of the Californians.
The murdering villian who destroyed his own wife
(who was pregnant at the time) is in prison at this
place, but will probably go unpunished, because he is
extensively connected. The particulars of this affair
and the history of the parties concerned are too disgusting to relate. Sufficient to say, it presents one of
those dark tales of vice, infamy, and degradation which
but seldom occurs. It is indeed lamentable that the laws
of the country are so often violated, and that the su-
pineness of the executive winks at such outrages as are
now frequently committed.

SAT. 6th. Strong westerly winds throughout the day.
Killed a bullock and got ready for sea.

SUN 7th. Weather pleasant throughout the day with
fresh NW winds. Crew at rest.

MON 8th. Morning pleasant with light easterly
winds. Today had a considerable conversation with
J. C. Jones Esq.[28] formerly Amer. Consul at the Sandwich Islands respecting the case of the missionaries
in the affair of the expulsion of the French Catholics
from those islands. Mr. J. was long a resident there
and condemns the missionaries in toto in all their acts

[28] John Coffin Jones, Jr., a Boston man, was long a merchant and American agent in Honolulu, visiting California yearly in the 1830's as supercargo
on his own vessels, including the *Bolivar.* In 1841 he settled in Santa Barbara, paying visits to Honolulu as master and supercargo, returning to
Boston in 1846. William Davis, author of *Seventy-Five Years,* was his
stepson.

and principles. They have endeavoured (as Mr. J. says) to get the reins of Govt. into their own hands, and exercise unlimited power over the Islanders, and persecute those who resisted them. But those acquainted with Mr. J's habits and principles will readily account for his hostility to the true missionaries. I am convinced myself from what I have heard from various sources that they are a body of men who conscientiously and fearlessly perform what they conceive to be their duty and "walk worthy of their vocation."

TUES. NOV. 9th. Moderate winds from NW. At noon got under way for Monterey. Passangers Messrs. Hartnell & Mellus. Moderate & pleasant through the night. Latter part calm.

WED. 10th. Begins calm. 2 PM light breeze from NE with a heavy swell. 3 PM strong breezes & squally. Wind variable. Took in light sails & reeft the topsails. 8 PM split the fore course, unbent it & bent a new one. Tacked ship as occasion required through the night.

THURS. 11th. Weather pleasant with NW winds. Ship off Pt. Arguello. Took the cutter inboard to repair. Ends moderate.

FRID. 12th. Light variable winds & foggy throughout the day. The watch picking oakum. Carpenter repairing the cutter. So ends.

SAT. 13th. Light NW winds & pleasant weather. All useful sail set. Crew variously employed. Lat. Obsn. at noon 33°56′.

SUN 14th. Begins with light NE winds easy. All possible sail set. Middle & latter part squally with much rain. Lat obsn. 35° 42′.

MON. 15th. Weather as yesterday. Run up the Lat. of Point Pinos at 3 AM and hove too for daylight. At 5 AM made sail and stood in for the land, weather foggy, wind SE. At noon made the land about Pt. Anno Nuevo. Found we had experienced a strong northerly current & have set to leeward of the point. Hauled our wind to the south & shortened sail.

TUES. 16th. Strong breezes and cloudy. Took in a reef in the topsails and sent down the royal yds. 5 PM squally with rain. Double reeft the topsails. Midnight wind shifted suddenly to west, with heavy rains and much swell, the current setting strongly to the Nd. Latter part moderate. Wind SE. All sail set on a wind.

WED. 17th. Begins with light winds and rainy. Afternoon pleasant. Made all sail. Sent up Mn [Main] Royal yard. Evening squally. Took in light sails. 10 PM fresh gales and squally. Double reeft the Topsails & furled the M'nsail, jib & spanker. Midnight same. Wore ship to SE, wind SSW.

THURS 18th. Morning weather moderating with squalls of rain & variable winds. Made sail and stood into Monterey Bay. 4 PM strong breezes. Took in light sails. Double reeft the Topsails, took the bonnet off the jib & bent a new mizen topsail. Pt. Anno Nuevo NW ½ N, Pt. Pinos SE by South. At 4 PM tacked ship to the south & we'd [westward]. At 8 PM, the weather looking favorable for a moderate night, tacked in shore. At 10 perceiving a sudden and considerable fall of the barometer, wore ship immediately and stood off shore, carrying all possible sail to make an offing as the signs of a coming gale were now too strong to be neglected, the ship being under double reeft topsails, fore & main courses, topmast staysail & Mn. spencer. At ¼ past 11 the gale was fast increasing, the sea making a breach over fore and aft and the ship straining hard. Took in the mainsail as it was impossible to carry it longer. By [i.e., since] heaving the ship too at this time would cause her to drift dead on a lee shore and her fate (if not that of all hands) would be sealed before morning, therefore the remaining sail must be kept on her untill we had gained sufficient offing to give her a clear drift, or the sails or spars must be allowed to blow away. At ¼ of an hour before midnight the gale was very severe. The squalls of wind and rain were so violent that it was impossible to look to windward. The ship was madly diving and plunging into a frightful sea but still making good progress from the land. All hands were stationed at their posts to act as occasion required and many an inward prayer was breathed that the sails and spars would outlive the violence of the gale, or at least untill they had placed us in a safe situation, but they performed their duty well as we could expect, but not so well as we hoped for. A few minutes before 12, the fore topsail yard broke in the middle and while securing the sail which was also split, a fearfull rent with a noise similar to the report of a gun told us that the main topsail had also taken leave of the yard.

Frid. 19th. After about two hours' severe toil the remnants of the two topsails were secured, and the broken yard lashed aloft. The mizen topsail was safely furled, while the topmast staysail had blown to fragments. At this time 2 AM the gale had increased to such a height that it seemed impossible for it to blow harder. The sea was also tremendous. Still the foresail

and main spencer held on, the ship willing, and plunging and drifting dead to leeward. We had done all
that could be done to ensure safety of the ship, and
now all we could do was to let her drift and anticipate
the fearful result. Part of the officers and crew were
now sent below to secure the casks, boxes &c. which
were in commotion under deck, while the rest were
looking out for the breaking of a lee shore. At his time
I retired to the cabin to determine the position of the
ship with regard to the land, and found that my passangers were silently and with great anxiety no doubt
preparing themselves for the worst. Ungrateful indeed
was the task of setting off the ship's place on the chart,
and painful the discovery that we had not over 20 miles
distn. in the direction we were now drifting. I knew
that the passangers were anxiously watching my every
look. I controlled my feelings as much as possible but
dare not look them in the face lest they might read
something there that would not add to their comfort,
and to their enquiries of our prospects I could only
say that we must hope for a favourable change. We
were heading SW; with the lee way and variation
were making a NW course. In this direction and at
the distance of about 15 or 18 miles lay Pt. St. Pedro,
a high headland with dangerous rocks near it, to the
Wd. of which the barred entrance of Saint Francisco
denied us entrance on account of the tremendous sea
which was now rolling over it, threatening destruction
to any ship that should approach it. WNW of us were
the rocky Isles of the Farrallones, which are dangerous
to approach even in fine weather, and should we fortunately drift clear of these, a few miles further and
we must bring up on the rugged headland of Punto

de los Reyes. I returned to the deck. After recommending ourselves to the protection of *Him* who alone "rides on the Tempest and directs the storm" and making what arrangements which the occasion seemed to require, I as calmly as possible awaited the result expecting to hear the dreadful breakers every moment and untill that appalling event should occur I deferred informing the crew of their situation. But O the intense agony of feeling produced by a dark stormy night and the horrors of a lee shore none can know but him on whom rests the sole responsibility. It is at such a time that a single night will do the work of years in a mans age. At 6 AM the day broke but the gale still raged in all its fury. The land could not be seen, as the gloom was thick & the rain descending in torrents. Our full object was to get down the fragments of the Mn. topsail and bend a new one. This we accomplished and at 8 o'clock a close reeft Mn. topsail brought the ship more head to the sea and relieve her very much. After the refreshment of some hot coffee and a slight breakfast of which I could not partake, we again turned too and sent down the wreck of the F. Topsail Yard and sail and as all this work had to be done in the teeth of a severe gale it occupied us untill noon. I now judged that it was impossible to be more than 2 or 3 miles from the land, and imagined every moment that I could "hear the warning voice of the lee shore, speaking in breakers," when of a sudden we were taken hard aback by the westerly wind blowing off shore and shortly after a clear sky showed us that we were distant from the breakers about 10 miles, but that the direction in which we were drifting would have enabled us to have kept off shore about 12 hours longer had the gale continued. Thanks to a Mercifull and prayer-hearing God we were preserved from wreck. And in the afternoon got up a new topsail yard, bent new sails, and at sunset when the sea had subsided bore away with a fair wind. At midnight hove to to wait for daylight.

SAT. NOV. 20th. Begins with moderate breezes and showers of rain. At 10 AM came to anchor at Monterey. Latter part of the day pleasant. Crew at rest.

SUNDAY 21st. Calm & foggy throughout the day. Part of the crew on liberty on shore, the remainder at rest.

MON. 22nd. Rainy throughout the day. Wind at SW. Sent down the fore topsail yard to refit. Hands employed in repairing sails &c. Latter part wind south, weather foggy.

TUES. 23rd. Commences with strong breezes from NNW, weather pleasant. Crew variously employed on the sails & rigging. 11 AM an American ship of war entered the bay, appearing to be a stranger. I boarded and brought her into the anchorage. Proved to be the US Sloop of War *Yorktown,* Capt. Aulick, 12 Months out, & 16 days from the Sandwich Islands. Dined on board and spent a few hours with Capt. A. This is the ship which had long been expected here, to settle the difficulties of the American residents who were sent prisoner to St. Blas. But Capt. informs me that he had no instructions for that purpose, and has no authority to demand redress for their wrongs. Thus while British and French Men of War have been here and compelled this Govt. to recognize and admit the claims of *their* subjects, nothing has been done for the

American citizens although two of our National vessels have been here during the present year.

A British ship of war sailed from here last week, after having ample satisfaction for the imprisonment and ill treatment of their countrymen. A sum of 3 dollars a day for their time while prisoners and damages for loss of property and personal injury was demand for them, with the assurance that Monterey should be battered to the ground in 12 hours if refused. The terms were accepted before the time expired. I informed Capt. A. of this and assured him that it would be very unfavourable for our people here if something was not done before he left to convince this miserable government that American citizens were as well protected by their govt. as those of France & England.

This afternoon arrived the Amer. Brig *Maryland* from Oahu (S. Islands). The Capt. tells me that he had a large quantity of letters & papers for the *Alert* on board his vessel while at the Islands, but they were transferred to a fast sailing Schr. which was bound here and he expected she would have arrived here before the *Maryland* (they were brought to the Islands by the *Wm. Gray* from Boston). Therefore we most anxiously await the arrival of the Schr. *Julia Ann* – "Hope Deferred". We are informed by letters recd. at the Islands from Boston the Messrs, Bryant & Sturgis our owners have retired from business [and] that the ship *California* is sold, but is on her passage out for a new concern. But we place no confidence in Sandwich Island news.

WED. DEC. [NOV.] 24. Light NW winds and pleasant weather throughout the day. Crew repairing sails and rigging. Accompanied a party of the *Yorktown's* officers to the valley Carmel to shoot ducks & geese. Returned at dark after a fatiguing and not very successful hunt. At Mr. Larkin's house we found refreshments prepared for us and to which ample justice was done.

THURS. 25th. Pleasant throughout the day. Wind light from the NW. Crew employed in taking off hides. Cut out a new foresail, FTMd. Staysail Mn TG Sail & Royals. Breakfasted on board the *Yorktown* by Capt. Aulick's invitation in Co. with Messrs. Larkin & Peirce.[29] Capt. A. has sent for the Americans who have claims against the Californian government and will do what he can to forward their interests. In the afternoon Capt. A. being desirous of obtaining some California shells (the haliotis) I went with him in my boat to Pt. Pinos where at low water we obtained some very good specimens.

FRID. 26th. Weather as yesterday. Crew employed in wooding, watering and taking off hides. Killed a bullock for ship's use. The heavy rains of last week have changed the appearance of the earth wonderfully. The grass has sprung up, and the hills are quite green. This has saved the cattle. If the rains had held off a month longer thousands of them must have died. Many have already perished for the want of food, but it is now expected there will soon be grass enough. The cattle are extremely poor, and there is not a horse to be had in this place, and they must still be farther reduced as the green grass by purging them always produces that effect.

SAT. 27th. Morning pleasant & calm. Unmoored ship

29 On Henry Augustus Peirce, see above n. 23.

at daylight. At 2 PM got under weigh in company with the *Yorktown* and commenced beating out, with a moderate breeze from NW. At 5 PM the wind light and inclining to calm; came too with the small bower in 9 fathoms water 1 mile from the Fort. At 8 PM a gentle breeze came off the land. Hove up & made sail out of the Bay. Capt. Aulick succeeded in effecting the same terms for the Americans which were obtained for the Englishmen but had the authorities refused to have done any thing towards an adjustment the *York-town* would have gone away and left matters in a worse state than they found them in as Capt. A. was not authorized to use force. The *Yorktown* parted co. during the night & bore away for Mazatlan.

SUND. 28th.   First part light Easterly winds. Middle & Latter part of the day light Westerly winds. Ship working to the Northrd. At dark off P. Anno Nuevo, a brig in sight.

MON. 29th.   Morning moderate & variable winds with foggy weather. Afternoon strong breezes from NW. Took in T G. Sails and single reeft the topsails. Night squally. Tacked Ship as occasion required.

TUES. 30.   Continuation of squally weather, Wind NNW. 4 AM took the bonnet off the jib & furled the Spanker. Tacked off Shore, Sn. Pedro point bearing NbW. 8 AM wind increasing; double reefd the top-sails. At noon strong gales; close reeft the topsails & furled the jib & mainsail.

WED. DEC. 1st.   Gale increasing with much sea. 5 AM took in the fore & Mizen topsails and wore ship; 7 moderating set the topsails. Latter part strong winds from NW and thick weather. Ship beating to windward under single reeft topsails. Carried away the weather F. topmast backstays. Wind NNW Ship off Pt. St. Pedro.

THURS. 2nd. Weather as yesterday. Ship making but small progress against a strong Northerly current. 4 PM Pt Lobo [Lobos] NbW 15 miles dist.

FRID. 3rd. Winds variable & squally, with thick fog. Standing off shore. Middle part pleasant, wind north. All sail set on a wind. Ends the same.

SAT. 4th. Morning pleasant with fine breezes from SE. Made all sail and stood in for the land. Wind freshening. At 11 AM ship in the narrow passage, the wind failing us at the time most needed. After being about two hours among strong eddies without any wind, and the ship being frequently much nearer the rocks than was agreeable, we succeeded by the help of light airs in getting past the points, when we held a light SE breeze and assisted by a feeble flood tide. We worked up to the anchorage at Yerba Buena and came too at 4 PM. Found here the *Bolivar, Nymph, Don Quixote,* & *Catalina*. Moored ship & unbent all sails. Through the night strong SE gales, heavy rains.

SUND. 5th. Calm and pleasant throughout the day. All hands at rest.

MOND. 6th. Morning pleasant with strong breezes from SSE. Crew employed in transhipping tallow to the *Nymph*. Afternoon squally with rain. Arrived bark *Index,* Wilson, long passage from Sta. Barbara, experienced heavy gales on the passage. The country now begins to present a more agreeable appearance than it has since we have been on the coast. While at home, the face of the earth is probably hidden from view and the streams are ice bound, here the hills, vallies & plains are clothed in green. Wheat and early vegetables are up and the farmers are preparing to plant corn & potatoes.

DEC. 7th, 1841. [TUES.] Begins with light breezes from SE with rain and continues the same throughout the 24 hours. All hands employed in scrubbing & cleaning ship inside & out.

WED. 8th. Winds light from SSE with frequent showers. Discharged the last of the tallow. Afternoon heavy rains. Crew employed between decks. The Mexican brig *Ayacucho,* which sailed from Monterey (a short time before my arrival there) for this place is cast away on Punto los Reyes, about 25 miles to the North*rd* of this port; crew & part of the cargo saved; cargo valued at 80,000 dollars.

THURS. 9th. Wind continues at SSE with heavy rains. Crew mending sails in between decks; carpenter repairing water casks. Ends with strong squalls

FRID. 10th. Hard gales from SE with heavy rain. Employed as usual. Evening partially clear.

SAT. 11th. Morning squally with light showers. 2d officer & 3 men cutting wood on shore. Sailed bark *Don Quixote* for Monterey. Ends clear with indications of a SEaster.

SUND. 12th. Last night about midnight it commenced a severe gale from SE with heavy rain. At daylight much sea in the bay. A whale boat belonging to Don Vetro Castro,[30] who came to the ship last evening

---

[30] Phelps refers to Don Victor Castro, a land grantee who lived at San Pablo (see Bancroft, II, 755). My thanks to Adele Ogden for this identification.

in her with a boats crew of Indians, swamped alongside and went to pieces. The gale still increasing. A
number of launches struck adrift. One belonging to
the *Bolivar* went on the rocks and soon disappeared.
Our launch was well moored in near the shore to a
heavy kedge anchor with a chain. The pinnace was
moored to the Launch with a small chain & two parts
of a rope. I felt they were safe and would have insured either of them for a trifle. At 11 AM the chain
of the Pinnace broke. Knowing that the rope would
soon part, I lowered a quarter boat & sent the 2d officer
with 4 good men to reach her if possible & secure her
with orders if they could not return to the ship to bear
away for a cove to leeward and haul their boat up.
before they could reach the Pinnace she broke adrift
and went on the rocks. The boats crew then made for
the shore, hauled up their boat, and saved the sails of
the Pinnace, but could not prevent her being stove. The
gale continued till near midnight. With great violence.

MOND. 13th.   Moderate & pleasant. Got the Pinnace
off the rocks and hoisted her inboard to repair. Found
7 of her timbers broke, & most of her bottom plank
gone. Afternoon went with Don Vetro to his farm on
the opposite side of the Bay about 15 miles dist. Started
with the cutter & 5 men at 1 PM, and arrived there
about 3. Poor Vetro has been quite unfortunate the
last week. The wild Indians had stolen about 30 horses
from him last Monday. On Saturday he came over to
the ship and lost his boat, and on returning home with
me today, found one of his houses had been levelled
by the tempest. After supper we all began to make
arrangements for the night, with the prospect of a
stormy night. No one could think of sleeping out of

doors, and as the pitiless storm had spared the poor fellow but one house, and that containing but three rooms which were very small, I felt rather curious to know how we were all to be disposed of. Don Vetro although having a splendid farm of his own and a few thousand head of cattle, was sadly deficient in buildings and possessed but of few articles of furniture, and indeed so few that they could all be enumerated at a glance. They consisted mostly of two bedsteads & one bed, 1 pine table, 5 or 6 chairs, a wooden clock in one corner of the principal room, and an open closet in the other in which on some rough shelves were arranged sundry articles of crockery, odd knives & forks, broken spoons, and a row of empty bottles. However poor a Californian Racherio may be, they always contrive to have one handsome bedstead, and although it may have to stand on a ground floor, it has generally as good a bed, curtains, & the other etc., as can be found in the best chamber of well to do folks at home, and this bed is always given up to a stranger who passes the night with them, even tho the man's wife & children sleep in the open air, as is often the case, for the Californians with all their vices, and failings, are hospitable in the extreme.

My host was but just started for himself, and had an excuse for being so short of the conveniences of life, which most of them have not. His wife also was young and inexperienced in the art of housekeeping and I could not help contrasting our necessities, with our wants which the present opportunity afforded. The boat crew were quartered with the Indians in one room, where with sides of leather, hides & deer skins, they made themselves quite comfortable. Two Frenchmen (Ranchieros) who were here waiting to get a passage over the bay, stretched themselves out on the floor of the room where I was sitting, taking their saddles for pillows and "ponchos" for blankets, and soon gave evidence of sound sleep. The Senorita who had been busy in the mean time in overhauling a number of bags of wool, now gathered it up and spread it over the sacking bottom of the bedless bedstead in the next room, which was just large enough to contain the two bedsteads which were alongside of each other, a few trunks, and two chairs, with scarce room for a person to move between them, spreading a sheet over the wool and tucking under the edges, she completed the arrangement with clean sheets, blankets, &c., and I was told that my bed was ready. But instead of letting me take possession of the temporary one I was desired to occupy the carved *mahogany high poster* with the handsome curtains. Against this I protested inasmuch as this one was much the widest and the other was but a scant pattern for a man, his wife, and two children. On any other ground I should have offended them by saying a word on the subject, and as it was, they insisted and I had to comply. The next difficulty was, who should go to bed first, but a hint from Vetro gave me to understand that it was expected of me. Therefore bidding them "buenas noches", I stepped inside of the curtains and soon disposed of myself. Nor were they long in following my example, but as they seemed to have some trouble in the disposal of the children, I urged to have one of them put in with me, but no, I must keep my bed to myself. And so unpleasant did I feel in dispossessing them in this manner of their accustomed comforts (and Heaven knows they are few enough) that it was a number of long hours before I compose myself to sleep. I was awakened before daylight by my host, rising and mustering his Indians and horses to start off in pursuit of his cattle. My principal object in coming over here was to get a good bullock or two as none were to be had at Yerba Buena. At early daylight I heard Vetro and his Indians depart, and again I fell asleep, hoping that my hostess in the mean time would make her toilet and vacate the room, but at sunrise I ascertained that she was still moored in "blanket harbour," and as there was no signs of her getting under weigh, I found that I must, therefore. Partly dressing myself within the curtains, I emerged from them to behold what would perhaps have shocked my modesty had I not been a family man, a pretty young woman sitting in her bed nursing an infant. But however as she did not seem disconcerted neither did I. So bidding her good morning I took my gun and sallied out in pursuit of game.

TUES. 14th. Shot a few geese, and went to the boat where breakfast was preparing. While eating, Vetro and his Indians drove a herd of about 300 bullocks into an enclosure near his house. From these he selected two of the fattest, threw the lasso over them and run them down to the boat. While the crew was killing and dressing them, I jumped on a horse and went in pursuit of geese, was absent about ½ an hour and returned with 8. Geese and ducks are uncommonly scarce at this season and quite shy. 11 AM started for the ship & arrived on board at 4 PM. Ends calm & pleasant.

WED. 15th. Strong breezes from SSE throughout the day with rain. Sent down the TG Yards.

THURS. 16th.   Wind as yesterday, with squalls of rain. Crew employed between decks.

FRID. 17th.   Continuation of yesterday's weather. Carpenter getting out new timbers for the pinnace. Crew employed on the sails.

SAT. 18th.   Morning squally, wind NW. Sent the 2d officer and five men to cut fire wood. Ends pleasant.

SUND. DEC. 19th.   Weather clear & pleasant throughout the day. Mr Mellus and four men gone across the bay in the cutter. The remainder at rest.

MON. 20th.   Morning strong SE winds with rain. Afternoon wind NW; clear and pleasant. Crew employed variously.

TUES 21st.   Pleasant, wind NW. Cutter returned. 2d officer & 5 men chopping wood at the mission creek.

WED. 22d.   Variable winds with rain throughout the day. Employed as usual.

THURS. 23rd.   Pleasant, with NW winds. Part of the crew cutting fire wood at the mission creek; others employed on board; carpenter repairing the pinnace.

FRID. 24th.   Weather as yesterday. Crew employed the same.

SAT. 25th.   Christmas day; begins with light variable winds & pleasant weather. Set the colours & kept holiday. The amusements of the forenoon were games of ball & shooting at poultry. Dined at the house of Nathan Spear, Esq., in company with about 20 foreigners.[31] The dinner was excellent, and the afternoon

---

[31] Nathan Spear was a well-known storekeeper in the 1820's in Monterey, moving to San Francisco in 1838, where he did well, with interests in several schooners and a grist mill. He died in 1848, aged 47, after several

and evening was spent in a social & pleasant manner.

SUND. 26th. Weather as yesterday. All hands at rest. A fandango was given in the evening by the Alcalda, to which I was invited, but did not attend. Such is the way in which the Lord's day is honoured and kept holy by catholics and I am ashamed to say by many here who call themselves protestants.

MOND. 27th. Morning calm & foggy. This morning I came very near having a ball sent through my brain by my own carelessness, but I escaped by putting a rifle ball through the hand of another person, Mr. Robert Davis, a young gentleman, native of the Sandwich Islands but who has received a good education in the U. States and is a very intelligent and respectable young man.[32] [He] spent the Sabbath on board the *Alert,* and I accompanied him on shore Monday morning. Shortly after breakfast, we were standing at the shop door of Mr. Spear conversing, when a crow lighting on a post in front of us, Mr. D. requested me to take a shot at it with my rifle which was standing behind the door. I took the rifle and wiped it out, and felt sure of there being no charge in it, on blowing into the muzzle I found there was some obstruction and put a cap on the nipple to blow it out. Mr. D. took the gun in his hand to examine it and I turned the muzzle towards my own head to feel if any wind came out, and desired him to pull the trigger. Had he

years of ill health. Spear was married to a Hawaiian; since he was never naturalized as a Mexican citizen, he held no land grant.

[32] Robert Davis arrived in California in 1839 as clerk on the *Monsoon,* returning again in 1841-42. He was later a trader at Honolulu. His brother, the better-known William Heath Davis (see below n. 40), in his memoirs *Seventy-Five Years* (p. 152), puts the shooting incident, which he describes, on the 26th, the day after Christmas festivities.

done so, I should have been killed instantly. As it was, he placed the rifle in my hands saying that he was unacquainted with guns and would hold his hand at the muzzle in order to feel is any wind came out. The first cap broke without any effect, but at the second trial the result was that a bullet passed through the middle of his right hand. But fortunately the bullet was small and passed between the bones and tendons without apparent damage to either. Much as I regretted the accident, I was truely thankful that it was my friend's hand instead of my own head. But still more serious would have been the results had Mrs. Spear occupied her usual seat at the breakfast table this morning, as the ball passed through the room where 5 or 6 persons were breakfasting and in a direct line over Mrs. S's vacant chair, and would no doubt have killed her had she been sitting there. Mr. Davis's hand was immediately dressed, and though he suffered much pain during the day & the following night (which I spent with him) the wound has a very favourable appearance.

TUES. 28th. Winds light & the weather pleasant. Sent the Launch for wood. Carpenter repairing the pinnace. Mr. Davis doing well.

WED. 29th. Wind & weather as yesterday. Sent the cutter across the bay to procure beef. The remainder of the crew wooding. The 2nd officer informed me that while they were cutting wood yesterday, a large she bear with a cub made their appearance near them and obliged them to retreat to the boat, leaving their dinner at the foot of a tree, of which the intruders took possession. I went up the creek this forenoon to have a shot at them, but though I found fresh tracks of the gentry, they did not choose to show themselves nor did they disturb the people during the day.

THURS. 30th. Variable wind & pleasant weather. People employed as yesterday. The cutter returned with two bullocks. Received a launch load of hides from Sta. Clara. The Hon. Hudson's Bay Co. bark *Cowlitz* arrived today from Columbia River in 6 days passage, having on board Sir Geo. Simpson (the Governor), Dr. McLaughlin, and a large number of supernumeries.[33] In the afternoon, waited upon the above gentlemen, and was received with much cordiality. Our accounts from Europe and the States were later by a couple of months than theirs; consequently we were able to tell them some news.

FRID. 31st. Weather calm & pleasant. Crew employed in various duties. Mr. Davis doing finely. Dr. McLaughlin has examined his hand and calls it a very *pretty little wound* and will not be of much consequence.

SAT. JAN. 1st. 1842. Morning strong breezes from North with clear weather. The cutter started for Sonoma but returned again in consequence of too much wind. Crew employed as usual. So ends.

SUND. JAN 2d. 1842. Morning calm & foggy. Middle & Latter part pleasant. Crew at rest.

MOND. 3rd. Wind fresh from the north. Crew employed in wooding. The Carpenter at work on the

---

[33] Sir George Simpson's *Narrative of a Journey Round the World During the Years 1841 and 1842* (London, 2 vols., 1847), records his visits to California. See also Glyndwr Williams, ed., *London Correspondence Inward from Sir George Simpson, 1841-42* (London, 1973). John McLoughlin was Simpson's Chief Factor.

pinnace. When the wooding party returned at night they complained of the visits of the bears, having been driven from their work again. Ends pleasant, Wind NW.

TUES 4th. Fresh northerly winds & clear weather. Sent the launch to St. Antonio for hides and the cutter to Timeschal [Temescal].[34] In the afternoon took 5 hands with me, well armed with guns and axes, and went in pursuit of the bears, but although we saw many fresh tracks we were unable to find the animals. We however got a good mess of ducks & curlew. Ends pleasant.

WED. 5th. Morning fresh breezes from North with clear weather. At 9 PM the launch returned with hides. Afternoon pleasant. Crew employed in various duty. Ends calm & pleasant.

THURS. 6th. Strong east winds with rain. Crew employed in between decks at rigging work & repairing sails. Ends the same.

FRID. 7th. Begins with fresh northerly winds & pleasant. Sent the cutter to St. Leandry for hides. Crew employed in wooding. Ends calm.

SAT. 8th. Moderate & pleasant. Crew employed variously on board. Painted the pinnace. Latter part calm.

SUN 9th. Moderate & pleasant throughout the day. Crew at rest. Cutter returned from St. Leandry. Rec'd.

[34] Temescal means a steaming place, or hot springs; the meaning here, however, is "a place south of the creek of that name about a half mile not far from the depot at Sixteenth St., Oakland" (Davis, *Seventy-Five Years,* p. 59), where hides and tallow were collected after the cattle were slaughtered on the banks of the stream. Little sign of the creek now remains, save Lake Temescal, located at the junction of California state highways 24 and 13 in Oakland.

an invitation to dine with Sir Geo. Simpson & the gentlemen of the Hudson Bay Co., but was indisposed. The company have purchased a large house at Yerba Buena and have established a trading post here, in charge of Mr. Glen Ray [Rae],[35] one of their factors, probably with a view of monopolizing the trade of California. They have said that it cost them $75,000 to drive my owners (Messrs. Bryant, Sturgis & Co.) from the trade of the NW coast, and they will now expend $500,000 if it is necessary to drive the Yankees from the trade of California.

MON 10th. Light winds pleasant weather throughout the day. Got the pinnace out and rigged her. Took on board two launch loads of fire wood. At sunset despatched the launch & pinnace with the 2d officer & six men to St Jose for hides.

TUES. JAN 11th., 1842 Begins moderate and pleasant. Mr. M. & myself went with the cutter to Whaling Harbour. Arrived at Capt. Richardson's [36] Farm at 1 PM. Partook of a good dinner there, after which Mr. M.

---

[35] William Glen Rae, after his arrival in 1841, was placed in charge of the Hudson's Bay Company's business in California. Able, popular, handsome (Davis reports him as tall and attractive, but then most of the people Davis mentions are similarly described) – business problems coupled with domestic problems (his infidelity became public knowledge, according to Davis) caused him to commit suicide in 1845, aged 31 (Bancroft, V, 687; Davis, *Seventy-Five Years*, p. 70).

[36] William Antonio Richardson deserted as mate from the whaler *Orion* in 1822. A talented man in more than navigation, he was allowed to stay, married locally, was naturalized in 1830, and remained in the San Francisco area to practice navigation, carpentry, rude doctoring, and no doubt smuggling. He is credited with founding Sonoma, and with building the first shanty structure in San Francisco. Although Richardson lived in Sausalito, he was for many years captain of the port of San Francisco until 1844, and often in some difficulty for trading illegally with whalers for the wood and water available at his "Whaler's Harbour." He died in 1856, aged 52. See Davis, *Seventy-Five Years*, pp. 6-12.

started on horseback for the Mission of St. Rafael.
I intending riding up there myself but learning that
there was to be a fandango there in the evening and
at such a time there is generally much intoxication
and always a row, I concluded to remain at Capt. R's.
Mrs. Richardson and her daughter, a nice buxom lass
of about 16, were engaged in making butter & cheese.
The cheese is rather inferior to poor skim milk at
home, but the butter is excellent. Consequently I fared
sumptuously while here on bread and milk & fresh
butter. The temporary house afforded but one sleeping room, and I was obliged to turn poor Mariana out
of her bed to accommodate my lubberly carcass, while
she made a fieldbed for herself in the opposite corner
near her father & mother.

WED. 12th. Gentle breezes from NE and pleasant
weather. After breakfast went up the creek with the
boat to Mr. Reed's [Read] farm, in pursuit of hides
and to meet Mr. M. on his return.[37] Mr. Reed is an
Irishman and is a tolerable farmer, has a fine tract
of land, well situated, and will probably be valuable
some few years hence. At noon Mr. M. arrived accompanied by Padre Quijas the priest who presides
over the missions of St. Rafael & St. Solana (and a
great reprobate he is). He was now on his way over
the bay to officiate at the Mission Dolores (near to
Yerba Buena) next Sunday. The old fellow was quite
happy (with liquor) when he entered the boat, and
having a bottle of grog with him, became absolutely

---

[37] John Read was an Irishman who arrived in the 1820's and built a
cabin in Sausalito. He was naturalized in 1834 and became a land grantee.
He is often mentioned in Larkin's books. He died in 1843, having served
as alcalde at San Rafael.

drunk before we were half way across the bay. Understanding a little English he endeavoured to entertain us with stale jokes, interlarded with frequent oaths, and filthy expressions, untill his vocabulary was exhausted, and I reprimanded him so severely that it was some time before he would speak to me. He at last, to make up with me, promised me the prettiest girl for a wife that I could pick out in his district, and insisted on giving the boat's crew a glass of grog from his bottle, but as he was not allowed to do so he watched an opportunity and emptied a part of it on my head, pronouncing me a "buen catholic". I showed my grateful sense of his favours by pulling to the nearest shore and landing his reverence to make the best of his way to Yerba Buena on foot.

Arrived the Ship at sunset. Learnt that Monterey is in an uproar on account of a Bishop having arrived from Mexico to assume the control of the Missions, but as this govt. prefers their spoils themselves, they are determined to expel his Holiness.[38]

THURS. 13th. Light SE winds and overcast weather. Sent the Cutter to Timeschal for hides. Afternoon calm & pleasant. Took tea and spent the evening at the Hudson Bay Co's establishment. Mr. Glen Rae, Esq., their factor at this place, is married to a daughter of Dr. McLaughlin. She is a half breed, her mother being a native of the Columbia. There were present Mr. B., a

---

[38] Francisco García Diego y Moreno, who had been head of the Zacatecan missions of California, was appointed Bishop in April 1840 with San Diego as episcopal see; he preferred living in Santa Barbara. See below, entry for 23 May and 12 June. The episode is described in Maynard Geiger, *Mission Santa Barbara, 1782-1965* (Santa Barbara, 1965), Chapter XXI; Robinson, *Life in California,* pp. 196-97; Bancroft, IV, pp. 332-35.

French Canadian, who is chief of the Blackfeet Indians
and also is their prophet, is held in great reverence
by them, and at the same time he has charge of the
Co's trading post among that nation. He speaks English fluently, and has just returned from a visit to
England. She informs me that he was in Boston last
March. Mr. Ermatinger,[39] the capt. of the Co's hunting & trapping this side of the Rocky mountains, was
also of the company, and is the best specimen of a
hunter I have seen, hardy, vigorous, and active, ex-
travagant in word, thought, & deed, heedless of hardship, daring of danger, prodigal of the present, and
thoughtless of the future. Twenty five years spent as
a trapper, and the chief of trappers, has accustomed
him to continued toil, peril, and excitement, and the
details which I drew from him with regard to life
among the mountains were related to me with so much
simplicity and frankness as contrasted singularly with
the wild and startling nature of his themes. He has
now a band of 70 trappers encamped near the *Strats*
[*Straits*] *of the Carquines* and about 800 traps set, and
is now on a short visit to his old companion and friend
Mr. Rae. I was amused at one observation of his, and
one which shows also the contempt in which these
hardy sons of the wilderness hold the comforts of civilized life. (Captain, says he,) "this is the first house
I have slept in for two years, and last night I did a
thing which I have not done before for 24 years – I
slept in sheets – but I was drunk, and Rae put me into
them, therefore the sin must lay at his door."

<hr>

[39] Francis Ermatinger was, as Phelps notes, in charge of the Company's
trappers in California, 1841-44. His career, however, falls far more into
the history of the Company's efforts outside the confines of California.

During the evening, Padre Quijas came into the room, pretty well corned, and soon began to use familiarities that were disgusting such as hugging and kissing, after the Spanish fashion, & in fact was very annoying. Ermatinger eyed him pretty close, and kept clear of him as being an animal unknown among the Rocky Mountains, but as the priest increased his libations, his fooleries increased in proportion, and at length he attempted to take the trapper in his fraternal embrace, but most unexpectedly found himself lying on his beam ends at the opposite side of the room. "Stranger," said the hunter in a voice resembling something like the growl of an infuriated bear, "when I was in the Rocky Mountains I swore that I would never allow myself to be hugged by a *Bear* or a *Blackfoot Indian,* but I would suffer the embraces of either in preference to those of a *drunken priest."* The poor padre found he was "barking up the wrong tree" and that as his cowl and habit did not protect him in such rude company, he had better make his exit, which he accordingly did very soon after his disaster.

FRIDAY JAN 14. Morning fresh Northerly winds and pleasant weather. At daylight the launch and pinnace arrived from St. Jose with cargoes of hides and 5 Indians passangers. Afternoon, sent the pinnace with the boatkeeper and 4 Indians to Sonoma for hides. Crew on board, employed in bending sails & drying wet hides. So ends.

SAT 15th. Pleasant weather with light variable winds throughout the day. Employed in taking off fire wood & bending sails. The boats returned from St. Jose with 210 hides.

SUN. 16th.   Wind SE with frequent showers throughout the day. All hands at rest.

MON 17th.   Begins cloudy with variable winds. Bent
the courses. Latter part of the day strong northerly
winds with showers of hail & rain. Pinnace returned
from Sonoma.

TUES. 18th.   Begins pleasant & calm. Employed in
watering ship. Afternoon, I took the cutter and went
across the bay to St. Antonio Creek to cut timber for
ships use. Arrived there about 5 PM, pitched the tent,
and while one of the boys got supper ready, the others
assisted the carpenter to cut and bring to the boat the
timber required. I have frequently heard of the vora-
city of the Indians, and this evening had an opportunity of seeing a specimen of what they could do in the
way of feeding. 5 Indians of the Mission of St. Jose
were in the boat. Shortly before entering the creek
they picked up a large dead sturgeon floating on the
water, and which stunk so bad that I would not let
them take it in the boat. They were allowed to tow
it on shore, and they soon had a fire under way, and
the fishing [sic] roasting. It weighed at least 30 lbs.
They took out the entrails and partly broiled them on
the coals devoured them, while the fish, cut into strips,
was also getting ready for their capacious maws, and
before dark nothing but the bones were left, although
they had eaten a reasonable dinner before leaving the
ship. In fact they crammed themselves to such an extent that they were incapable of walking and appeared
to be quite intoxicated, and such I am told is the effect
produced on them when they gratify their appetites
on animal food, and which they always indulge in

when opportunity offers. At other times they are known to do without food for weeks and not complain.

The night was clear and pleasant, but the jackals & wolves kept up such a constant yelling around us that we did not get much sleep.

WED. 19th. Pleasant breezes from NE with fine weather. Took an early breakfast and started for the ship at daylight being favored with a fresh breeze and a strong tide we arrived on board at 9 AM. Got off the remainder of the water, unmoored and got ready for sea.

THURS 20th. Moderate & pleasant. Hove short & made sail, but the breeze failing at 10 AM clewed up & furled the sails. 4 PM the Brig *Bolivar* in coming up the harbour took the ground opposite the Presidio. Sent the 1st & 2nd officers with the cutter, pinnace, & twelve men to her assistance. At 10 PM the boats returned, having got the Brig off and anchored in a place of safety.

This day we are TWO YEARS from BOSTON, and thanks to Almighty God, we have been preserved from dangers seen & unseen, and are at the present time in good health, and the officers, men and boys who constituted the crew of the good Ship *Alert* at the time of her sailing still are the same with the exception of 1 boy drowned, 1 seaman discharged for habitual drunkenness, and one ordinary seaman deserted.

FRIDAY 21st. Winds & weather as yesterday. Crew variously employed.

The Sixth Passage

San Francisco to San Diego and Return

SAT 22nd. [JAN. 1842]. Strong gales from North. At 8 AM got under weigh on the ebb tide under double reeft topsails, and after laying under the lee of Wood Island to secure the anchors stood out of the port. After crossing the bar the wind moderated; [shook] out all reefs and made all possible sail. (Messrs Wm & Robert Davis passangers.)[40] Midnight, ship near Point Anno Nuevo.

SUND. 23rd. Moderate & variable winds, weather pleasant. At noon anchored at Monterey, and were gladdened by the receipt of letters from home, all telling of the health and well being of far distant friends.

MOND. 24th. Weather as yesterday. Landed some freight & recd. on board some hides.

TUES. 25th. Pleasant weather with light easterly winds. Crew variously employed. Killed a bullock.

---

[40] William Heath Davis, Jr., brother of the Robert Davis already referred to (see page 251, n. 32) was born in Honolulu in 1823, and made several trips to California as a boy (his father was in the China trade at Honolulu). Although educated in Boston, he returned to the coast to act as clerk and manager for his uncle Nathan Spear (see page 250, n. 31) at San Francisco until 1842, when he left Spear's service, and became supercargo on the *Don Quixote*. In later years he was a prominent merchant at San Francisco. See his memoirs, *Seventy-Five Years* (San Francisco, 1967).

WED. 26th. Morning, light breezes from East to N East. Hove up the anchor and made sail for Sta Barbara. At 12M. Point Pinos bearing ESE 10 miles distant. There being a bad sea & wind a head, with prospect of a gale, bore away for the anchorage. 4 PM anchored in 10 fathoms water. Night rainy.

THURS. 28th. JAN'Y. Begins with moderate breezes from SE with rain. All hands variously employed. Ends the same.

FRID. 28th. Strong winds with rain. Wind SE.

SAT. 29th. Light winds and variable throughout the day. Crew employed in making a new fore Course & Mn. T. G. Sail.

SUN 30th. Morning moderate with a heavy swell from NW. Latter part calm & cloudy. Crew at rest.

MON 31st. Morning moderate breezes from NW 10 AM made sail and hove up. At noon calm; let go the small bower anchor & furled sails. So ends.

TUES FEB 1st. Morning fresh breezes from NW with a heavy swell setting into the bay. At noon the wind increasing gave the ship 60 fathoms of chain. 3 PM a heavy gale from NNW. Let go the best bower. Midnight moderate.

WED. 2d. At daylight unmoored and hove short on the small bower. At 1 PM moderate breezes from NW with hazy weather. Hove up and made all sail. Beating out of the bay in company with the Bark *Don Quixote*. At midnight ship off Pt. Pinos, wind light & the weather foggy.

THURS. [FRI.] 4th. Light variable winds and pleasant weather through the day. At midnight ship off Mascatpatan [41] becalmed.

SAT 5th.   Morning calm & pleasant. Bark *Tasso* in sight to the south, bound up. Got the boats ahead & towed the ship to the anchorage in 10 fathoms. Ends calm.

SUN 6th.   Winds moderate from SW with fine weather. AM hands at rest.

MON FEB 7th.   Pleasant weather with light SW winds through the day. Employed in landing freight and taking on board hides. Killed a bullock for ship's use.

TUES 8th.   Pleasant and calm throughout the day. Crew employed in boating off hides, horns, & tallow. Ends the same.

WED 9th.   Weather as yesterday. Crew employed on new foresail & F.T. Staysail. Ends with strong breezes from NW.

THURS 10.   Begins with strong breezes from SE and thick fog. Killed a bullock for ship's use. The cattle are now tolerable fat on this part of the coast. The weather being warmer this side of Pt. Conception than it is above, the grass is more forward. Latter part pleasant with light breezes from NW. 3 PM got under way for St. Pedro. Passanger Mr. R. (our agent). Midnight calm.

FRID. 11th.   Morning light easterly breezes & pleas-

---

41 "Mascatpatan" is Phelps rendering of "Mescaltitan," or sometimes "Mescalitan," an Indian settlement or rancheria on an island of the same name in Goleta Slough or Estuary. The island's dirt was used to fill in the slough and now lies under an airport. My thanks to Jack Hunter and Adele Ogden for this reference.

ant. 10 AM ship becalmed near the Island of Santa Cruz. Lowered the boat and went on shore to take a look at it. Found nothing worth noting. The island is very mountainous and barren, but might afford pasturage for some thousands of cattle. It is 25 miles in length & three wide. Tried along the shores for fish but caught none. Afternoon & evening moderate breezes from W.

SAT. 12th. Pleasant weather & fresh breezes from WNW. At 1 PM anchored at St. Pedro.

SUN 13th. Moderate & pleasant throughout the day. Crew at rest. Strong breezes at night from west. Mr. R. gone to the Pueblo.

MON. 14th. Morning calm & foggy. Employed in boating off hides & horns. After breakfast went with one of the boys & two horses to kill geese. Found immense quantities of them on the plains. They were difficult to approach on foot, but on horseback easy. Killed as many as loaded both horses and returned on board at 1 PM. The plains and vallies in this vicinity, now, present a beautiful appearance, the grass in many places being as high as the saddle stirrups, which with an abundance of clover, affords rich feed for the cattle, while numberless wild flowers shed abroad their fragrance, charming the eye with their beautiful appearance and refreshing the senses with their grateful perfume.

TUES. FEBR'Y 15th. Light winds and pleasant weather throughout the day. Crew employed in boating off hides & various other jobs. In the afternoon, took a boy with me & went to hunt ducks & geese. Returned at sunset having been very successful.

WED. 16th. Morning cloudy. Wind light at SE.
Boating off hides & tallow. Dr. Gamble [42] a young
gent. from Philadelphia, who lately crossed the Rocky
Mountains for the purpose of Botanizing and picking
up "nice things" in California, met me on shore this
morning and came on board to dinner. Latter part
squally with rain. Wind west.

THURS 17th. Strong gales from WSW & clear weather. At 9 AM tripped the anchor and made sail for
St. Diego. Strong breezes throughout the day. At
7 PM anchored inside of Pt. Loma (Entrance of St.
Diego). Night calm with a heavy swell.

FRID. 18th. Morning light breezes from East. Hove
up at 9 AM and [43] [rode] up with the flood. Moored
ship abreast the hide house. Furled sails and landed
600 hides & various articles of freight. Ends pleasant.
All well at the house.

SAT 19th. Pleasant through the day. Employed in
landing hides.

SUN 20th. Pleasant with fresh westerly winds. Part
of the crew on liberty, the remainder at rest. So ends.

MON 21st. Weather as yesterday. Crew employed in
landing hides, horns, & fire wood, & taking on board
freight. Took on board the boy Sam and supplied his
place at the hide house with a Sandwich Islander.

WED. 23rd. Weather as yesterday. Crew employed

---

[42] William Gamble, a yound naturalist, was sent out from Philadelphia to
collect specimens. Reaching California by way of New Mexico, he seems to
have been short of cash, so worked for Commander Jones as clerk on the
Cyane. Bancroft, III, p. 752.

[43] The following word is not legible, but the meaning is clearly that he
rode up with the flood tide.

variously. Mr. Robinson and myself rode up to the Presidio and dined at the house of Capt. Fitch.[44] Capt. F. is the person whom *Dana* describes as the "fat, vulgar, yankee trader" who was living on the vitals of the Bandini family. He is now absent at Mexico, but we were hospitably entertained by his Lady. Capt. F., of whom I have seen much during the last 18 months, is fat, & also a trader, but I have never seen or heard of any thing respecting him to induce the belief that he is not fair & honourable in all his dealings, and I know that he is kind hearted, and liberal in the extreme. The only motive Dana could have for using such terms respecting him (it is said) is that he entered Capt. F's house intoxicated & using offensive language, [and] *was kicked out!*

THURS. FEB 24th.   Begins with calm & foggy weather. Unmoored ship. At 9 AM light breezes & clear. Got under way for St. Pedro. 11 passed Pt. Loma. Latter part light variable winds; ship near the Coronadas. (Passanger, Jas. McKinley Esqr.)[45]

FRIDAY 25th.   Light variable winds & pleasant weather throughout the day. The watch employed in cleaning ship outside. Ends with light SW winds.

SAT. 26th.   Morning pleasant with moderate breezes from WNW. All possible sail set. Noon wind strong

---

[44] Fitch is discussed in n. 34, page 93 above; the Juan Bandini family was of considerable prominence in the San Diego area. A sketch of Bandini, a San Diego alcalde, occurs in Dana, *Two Years,* Ch. XXVII.

[45] James McKinlay was a much travelled agent for Captain Cooper, a Monterey merchant, owner, master, and supercargo on a number of vessels trading along the coast (he was also Larkin's half-brother). Apparently without any permanent base, he had commercial interests in San Francisco, Los Angeles, Monterey, San Juan Capistrano and San Luis Obispo. He died in 1875, aged about 72. See Bancroft, IV, p. 725.

from NW. 3 PM took two reefs in the topsails. Latter part squally. Ship off Pt. Falso.

SUN. 27th.   Morning strong breezes & cloudy; wind SE. Made all sail. 5 PM anchored at St Pedro in 10 fathoms. Ends moderate & cloudy with light rain.

MON. 28th.   Fresh westerly winds & pleasant. Landed the passangers & their freight. Latter part, boating off hides.

TUES 29th. [MAR. 1] Pleasant with westerly breezes throughout the day. Crew employed as yesterday. Ends calm. Heard of the arrival of the Ship *California* at Monterey.

WED 30th. [MAR. 2].   Midnight light southerly winds. Hove up & made sail for Sta. Barbara. Middle & latter part, light easterly wind. Ship off Pt. Dume. Passangers Donna [Doña] Eustachio Pico,[46] a widow lady, having with her one of the handsomest Indian girls I ever saw. At night, as the old lady was too corpulent to get into a berth, I ordered beds to be spread for herself & girl on the floor of the trade room, and so jealous was the donna of her beautiful Indian lass, that she requested me to lock them in. Calm at 10 PM.

THURS 3rd.   Light westerly airs & pleasant weather. Crew employed in scraping ship outside & blacking the iron work. Ends with fine weather & calm.

FRID. 4th.   Begin with fresh breezes from west, with a strong easterly current. The ship has not gained 10 miles in the last 48 hours.

[46] Doña Eustachio Pico's identity is uncertain; the Pico family was large and widespread. See Marie E. Northrup, *Spanish-Mexican Families of Early California, 1769-1850* (New Orleans, vol. I, 1976), 295, for several possibilities.

At 7 PM ship in the bight of Buena Ventura. The wind dying & a heavy swell making. Finding the ship setting towards the breakers, let go the small bower anchor in 9 fathoms. Paid out.45 fathoms chain & furled the light sails. Ship pitching heavily.

SAT. MARCH 5th. At ½ past one 1 AM [sic] a light breeze springing up from NE got under way, but the swell prevented our making much progress. At daylight off the Mission of St. Buena Ventura. Middle part of the day, beating up with strong westerly winds. Afternoon squally. Ship under single reeft topsails. About 4 PM while standing in shore with a strong breeze a man was sitting on the lee anchor fixing the buoy rope and while so occupied a squall struck the ship, bringing the anchor under water and washing the poor fellow off. I was standing by the wheel, and hearing the cry of "A man overboard" immediately brought the ship to the wind with all the sails aback, and quickly lowering a quarter boat picked him up, but not untill the poor fellow was most exhausted, and had he not been a good swimmer he would have drowned, as the ship having rapid headway at the time was at some considerable distance from him before she could be checked. At 6 light baffling winds. A boat from the *California* boarded us. ½ past 6 came to anchor. Midnight strong breezes from NW.

SUN. 6th. Light variable winds & pleasant weather. Crew at rest. Spent part of the day on board of the *California, hearing of Home.* So ends.

MON 7th. Morning moderate & pleasant. Spent the forenoon on shore. Afternoon in getting stores from the *California.* At dark there being symptoms of a

S'Easter, got all ready for slipping, but as the wind continued light from the Eastern quarter through the evening and no swell setting in, I tho't it best to hold on. But about 11 PM the wind freshened with much rain & a considerable swell. The night was very dark so that we could not see the land or the other vessels (*Index* & *California*) but as they were lying inside of the *Alert,* I concluded to hold on untill they slipped. At ½ past 11, found that our anchor was dragging and we were fast drifting towards the point. As I should not have room enough to make sail & clear the point I was now compelled to let go the Best Bower, which brought the ship up. As it now was impossible to think of getting off, all necessary preparation was made for riding out a Gale of Wind. All the chains were roused on deck, the yards pointed to the wind &c., and all hands kept on deck. The rain fell in torrents and the wind at midnight was strong at SE. But as the sea did not make, I had strong hopes of a short continuance of the present weather.

TUES 8th. 1 AM weather the same. Gave the ship long scopes on both chains. ½ past 2, light winds & heavy rains. 3 wind off shore (all right). 8 AM strong westerly winds and clear weather. The *California* and *Index* sent assistance to help get our anchors. Ends cloudy; wind light & variable.

WED 9th. Weather clear. Fresh breezes. At daylight hove up and shifted to an anchorage farther east. Killed a bullock. Latter part moderate & pleasant.

THURS 10th. Morning strong; northerly winds with clear cool weather. Middle part moderate. Employed in taking on board corn, on freight. Ends the same.

FRID. 11th. Moderate winds and pleasant weather throughout the day. Employed variously on board. Today had two calls upon me while on shore to visit sick people. In vain I protested I was no Doctor. I had cured others who had applied to me for medicine, and go I must. One case was that of a young woman who was confined to her bed by Rheumatism and had also much fever. The other was a girl of 8 or 9 years of age who was covered with an eruption on the skin. To the first I administered a dose of Peruvian bark, and to the second a thorough dose of sulphur – medicines which if they do not *cure* are pretty sure not to kill.

SAT 12th. Morning moderate and pleasant. Ready for sea. 5 PM got underway for windward coast. Light variable winds through the night. So ends.

SUN. 13th. Winds & weather as yesterday. 3 PM left the ship becalmed and pulled up to Refugio to ascertain if there were any hides ready for us. Met Mr. Hill at the Rancho with a letter from Mr. Robinson at St. Ynnes [Inéz] requesting me to anchor at this place. 5 PM returned on board and brought the ship to anchor. Ends calm.

MON. 14th. Morning calm and pleasant. 9 AM a drove of mules arrived from St Yness [sic] with hides. Embarked them, and at 5 PM got underway with a land breeze, and made sail up the canal. Midnight calm.

TUES. 15th. Morning light breezes from NE. 11 AM sent a boat on shore at the Cojo and took off 40 hides. At noon passed Pt. Conception with fine breezes. Ends pleasant. Ship off Pt. Arguello.

WED. MARCH 16th. Light winds from the southern quarter with smooth water and pleasant weather. All useful sail set. Crew variously employed. At night ship off St. Luis.

THURS 17th. Winds and weather as yesterday. At sunset tacked ship with a fresh NW breeze. Pt. Lobo [Lobos] bearing NNE dist. 6 miles. Moderate breezes through the night. Tacked ship as occasion required.

FRID. 18th. Morning fresh breezes from NE and thick fog. Ship beating into the Bay of Monterey. Noon calm & clear. 4 PM off Carmel Bay, with a light air from South. 7 PM passed Pt. Pinos with light variable airs. ½ past 9 anchored in 11 fathoms; weather thick and rainy.

SAT. 19th. Light winds from WSW with rain. At 5 AM hove up the anchor and run further in. Anchored abreast the fort. Found lying here the Ship *Fama* of Boston from St. Francisco, Capt. Hoyer. Paid business visits on shore during the day, and took tea and spent the evening on board the *Fama*. Capt. Hoyer has his Lady on board (an American) also a sweet little daughter 28 months old, born since they left the U. States. I was much reminded of home, and spent the evening very pleasantly.

SUND. 20th. Begins with strong breezes and rain squalls; wind SW. All hands at rest. Ends the same.

MON. 21st. Continuation of squally weather with frequent rain. 1 PM heavy squalls from SSE. Gave the ship 60 fathoms on the small bower chain. 4 PM struck a drift in a violent squall. Let go the best bower and brought up. Heavy squalls and much rain through the night. The *Fama* has dragged about 3 miles.

TUES 22nd.   Morning moderate with rain. 9 AM hove up the anchors and beat up to the former anchorage. Latter part fine weather. Employed in landing freight and taking off hides. Night heavy squalls with rain from SE. Let go the best bower.

WED 23rd.   Morning moderate with much swell. Loosed sails to dry. Carpenter repairing boats. The *Fama* broke a flake of her Best Bower in the last blow. Supplied her with a stream anchor. Ends calm with much swell.

THURS MARCH 24th.   Winds light & variable with pleasant weather. Employed in taking off hides. Latter part hove up the best Bower & sighted the small bower. 8 PM light breezes from SE. Got underway for St Francisco in company with the *Fama* for Sta. Barb. Passanger Sr Don Pedro Narvisa [Narváez],[47] Capitana la Porta &c. Light breezes through the night and fine weather. All possible sail set.

FRID 25th.   Morning pleasant breezes from NE and fine weather. Ship off Point Anno Nuevo. Latter part the same weather. Pt St Pedro NNE 15 miles.

SAT. 26th.   Begins with moderate breezes from NE. All sail set standing in for the entrance of St. Francisco. A heavy swell from the SW. Noon wind light from SEast. 4 PM ship in 7 fathoms on the Bar, with a heavy swell & prospects of a Gale. Tacked ship & stood off shore. 10 strong gale from SE. Ship under double reeft Topsails, carrying on for an offing. Midnight hove too under close reeft Mn Topsail & Mn.

---

[47] Pedro Narváez was a Mexican naval lieutenant, captain of the Port of Monterey, 1839-1844.

Spencer. Ship outside the Farralonnes (islands). Heavy rains and a high sea.

SUN 27th. At 1 AM heavy rains. Wind moderating with much swell. Set F & Mizen Topsails, Foresail & jib with the Bonnet off. 4 AM weather pleasant out all reefs. Moderate through the day. Sea falling. Midnight winds light from NW. Made sail in shore.

MON 28th. Morning fresh breezes and fine weather. At daylight entered the passage; found the tide strong ebb. Ship making slow progress. 6 AM passed the fort. When the tide slackened we beat up the harbour and anchored at Yerba Buena at 11 AM. Latter part strong SE winds with rain.

TUES. 29th. Weather moderate and pleasant. Employed in getting out the launch, rigging the boats for service, mooring ship, and landing freight. So ends. There are now lying here the Barks *Don Quixote, Roger Williams, Tasso* & Brig *Bolivar*.

A Second Visit to
New Helvetia

WED. MARCH 30th. [1842]. Morning light winds and pleasant. At 9 AM I left the ship with the cutter with a crew of the 2nd officer, 4 stout hands, and an Indian pilot for the Sacramento. With the oars and a light breeze we crossed the Bay and entered the Straits of the Carquinez at 4 PM and at 10 PM encamped on the left bank of the River. Made a fire and cooked supper. Night clear and pleasant.

THURS. 31st. Morning pleasant with gentle breezes from SW. 4 AM commenced sailing and pulling up the River. The current very strong against us, but by keeping close to the shore [we] were enabled to make tolerable progress. 10, commenced raining and continued most of the day. 3 PM raining hard; took shelter under the trees where we made a tent of the Tarpaulings stretched over the oars under which we made a fire and prepared dinner. 5 PM weather clearing, with a fair wind up river. Sailed and rowed untill 11 PM when there being no dry place to encamp we anchored and slept in the boat. The night was clear and beautiful. The moon rose about ½ past 11, and as it shed its bright beams upon the silver surface of the beautiful river, and the lofty sycamores throwing their broad shading along the margin, a picture was presented on which the eye could dwell with much

pleasure. As I sat in the stern sheets of the boat gazing on the lovely scenery around me, I felt no inclina-
tion to sleep. The river at this place was broad; on
either side were spread thick primeval forests, where
the axe never resounded. All is quiet, save the chirping
of the cricket and the gentle ripple of the eddies as the
majestic torrent moves in solitary grandure to mingle
with the sea. "Night's silvery veil hung low upon its
bosom and the eddies curled their glassy rings beneath
it, like the still unbroken beating of the sleepers pulse.
The reeds bent down the stream, the willow leaves
forgot the lifting winds, and the long stems whose
flowers the water (like a gentle nurse) bears on its
bosom, quietly gave way and leaned in graceful atti-
tudes to rest." Majestic solitude! Who supplies thy
unexhausted springs. Wherever hast thou thy begin-
nings? Who ordereth that when thy swollen waters de-
cends into the deeps they rise not to overwhelm the
earth? The Lord openeth his omnipotent hand; He
causeth thy irrestable current to shoot onward like the
wheel of destiny. I see thy never resting waters run,
and I bethink me how the tide of time sweeps on to
– Eternity. So passes man! How applicable are the
lines of "Bryant" to this *neighbour* of the Oregon,
which he has sung of that River, "Where rolls the
Oregon and hears no sound, save his own darkings."
Here its waters are seldom disturbed by the oar, occasionally the solitary hunter paddles his canoe along
its margin to entrap the Beaver, or monthly a boat
from New Helvetia drops down with its rapid current, else all is silent.

FRID. 1 APRIL.   At 11 AM we again were on our way
with pleasant weather, and frequently a favourable

breeze gave the men a resting spell at the oars. At 10 we stopped at a camping place, nearly opposite the forks of the River. Here we staid about two hours during which time we spread our wet clothes to dry, partook of a hearty breakfast, & again put out. The banks are in many places overgrown. The plains which were dry when I was last up here, now are covered so as to resemble a sea while the little hills and detached clumps of trees resemble islands in the distance. At 10 PM we saw a number of Indians on the bank and on questioning them found they belonged to Capt. Sutter and were gathering acorns to make bread. We shortly after made fast to a tree and passed the night in the boat. Here I had a most singular dream and one which made such an impression on me that I shall not forget it while I live.

SAT. APRIL 2nd. Morning pleasant, with fine breezes from West. Scenery at sunrise splendid. We started at early daylight, and after a hard pull arrived at the Fishing Ranchireo at 8 AM. Here we cooked and ate breakfast. I found here about the same number of Indians as on my last visit. The country is so much inundated by the rise of the river that there is no communication with Capt. Sutter from here, except by canoes. Recognized my old friends the Chiefs of the tribe, Antonio & Amalhee, who shook me cordially by the hand. I sat down in the huts and distributed some trinkets among the women and children. Astonished the natives by discharging Cochran's patent many chambered gun at a tree, putting six balls in a small cowpatt, and continued on my way to N. Helvetia. Reached the "embarkadiero" at noon. Found the road to the house impassable; sent the Indian with a note

to Capt. Sutter to request a horse to be sent me. By
wading and swimming the Indian reached the house
in about two hours, and at 4 PM a light skin boat
(called a Bayardaka) [bidarka] managed by two
Sandwich Islanders, arrived with a note from Capt. S.
stating that a horse could not reach me, but that I
might safely trust to the two Kanakas who would
bring me safe. This canoe was about 15 or 16 feet in
length, a light frame of sticks for timbers, and covered
with seal skins, very light and buoyant, and extremely
ticklish. It had one hole in each end just large enough
to contain a person's body, while his legs were coiled
away under him. These were the places for the natives
to sit and manage the craft, while another round hole
amidships was for the passanger's accommodation.
I did not admire this mode of travelling, but lighting
my cigar stowed my self away (a la Turke) and with
his nonchalance resigned myself to fate. The waters
were madly rushing through the forest, the eddies were
whirling around fallen trees, and every instant we
seemed to be on the point of sticking a snag or of being
upset, and through it all we dashed at a fearful velo-
city, and finally came to the broad and open water of
the plains, and in comparative safety. The water was
so high as to permit to approach the very walls of the
Presidio, into which I stepped after ½ an hour's navigation over trees & stumps & was kindly received by
Capt. Sutter.

SUNDAY APR 3rd/42. Weather fine. Passed the day
at the House in reading and conversation. Capt. S.
I was glad to see had discontinued his former practice
of paying his Indians on the Sabbath. I strongly urged
him to prohibit the use of ardent spirits on his premises

and pictured to him the evil which would result to himself and the Indians if he established a distillery at New Helvetia, which he has in contemplation. O that I had the tongue of a *Pierpoint,* or a *Hawkins* to portray the evils of the disgusting and inhuman traffic.[48] Capt. S. acknowledged [that] my views of the matter were correct, and promised that he would abolish the use and manufacture of it, and I have reason to hope that New Helvetia will become the head quarters of Temperance and Morality in this new intemperate and immoral community.

MON 4th.   After breakfast mounted a beautiful horse and rode over to visit Mr. Sinclair and with him rode about 15 or 20 miles to look at the country with which I was much pleased. Nothing can exceed the beauty and richness of the lovely plains covered with luxurient feed and a vast quantity of flowers of every hue and of great variety. The woodlands consist of oak and maple trees of large growth, and so clear of underwood and brush as to resemble an English Park, among which we frequently chased the Deer and Antelope, but as we had no rifles with us, we agreed to start early tomorrow morning for a short hunt. Returned to dinner about 3 PM. It consisted of venison worked in different ways and was excellent, after which we took a look at his wheat fields and garden, and being rather tired laid down to take a nap on a bed of down, the wild flowers waving over our heads and emitting a most grateful perfume. I was soon aroused from my slumbers by a troop of horsemen galloping by me on

---

[48] John Pierpont (1785-1866) was a Boston pastor (grandfather of J. P. Morgan), known for his anti-slavery poems; Hawkins apparently was another abolitionist leader.

the full run, which I found to consist of my boat's crew. I gave them liberty to amuse themselves the best way they would for a few days, and Capt. Sutter had furnished them with horses on which they were taking full swing.

TUES. 5th.   At early dawn Mr. S and myself started to hunt antelope attended by a boy with a pack horse to bring home the game. The morning was clear and pleasant without a breath of wind, and we rode along the banks of the American Fork at a rapid rate to reach the hunting ground of the Antelope before they had done feeding. The scenery during the ride was exceedingly fine, and the purity of the air, and fragrance of the flowers and herbage gave life and buoyance to the spirits. About 7 AM after a ride of 15 miles, we entered the woodlands and at the same time espied a herd of deer, but they saw us first and scampered off like the wings of the winds. Shortly after a number of animals made their appearance grazing under the trees, which Mr. S. with his practised eye could not make out. I thought they were horses. He thought they were Elk but these animals he had never known to frequent these *diggings*. Antelope or Deer they evidently were not. However getting the largest trees in a range we approached near enough to ascertain their character, and found that they consisted of 5 Doe and 2 Buck Elk of 2 year olds. Separating we approached cautiously to within about 100 yards of them, before we were discovered. I was the first to fire. Mr. S's gun snapped. One was badly hurt and separating from the herd, trotted off by himself evidently much disabled. The herd took a hurried turn around us and spreading their ears and expanding their nostrils again came to a stand. We both fired and two others were wounded. While Mr. Sinclair pursued them on horseback, I returned to the one first wounded and found it near a tree much exhausted, but yet capable of giving me a chase. Therefore getting a tree between me & the game. I approached to within about 30 yards, levelled my rifle and brought the animal to the earth, but still the poor animal gave battle and it was not till after I plunged my hunting knife to the hilt in its heart that I felt sure of my prize. It proved to be a Doe, not fat, but in good order. Leaving the Indian Boy to dress and pack up the game, Mr. S. & myself continued on in pursuit of more sport. The boy had orders to return to the house with the spoils and prepare some of it for dinner. Mr. S. had pursued the two wounded Elk untill they took the river and swam across with the rest of the herd. At the river bank we dismounted and partook of a slight breakfast and taking a hearty draught of Nature's beverage we struck away among the edge of the high woodlands. Saw a Doe Antelope feeding under a tree which Mr. S. dismounted and shot. A beautiful creature it was, and I felt that our sport was cruel if not unjustifiable in destroying these beautiful and unoffensive creatures for the mere amusement of hunting (especially in this instance, as this doe was with fawn). However we took the haunches off, strung them over our horses, and leaving the rest to the kiotas [coyotes], again started in pursuit. We rode 5 or 6 miles along the edge of the woods and on our return starting a number of both deer & antelope, but it was now too late in the day, as after their morning meal they are more on the lookout. At length I saw a band of antelope close huddled together approaching us from the plains with a kiota (Wolf) in pursuit of them. I proposed getting off my horse and secreting myself behind a tree in hopes that in their hurry they might come within shot. My companion said it was useless as they would not come near. I thought otherwise notwithstanding the opinion of the old hunter and giving him the bridle to hold, I threw myself on the grass and crawling to a tree took up a position there unobserved. As the kiota pursued and tried to head them they were drawn towards me, and in a few minutes came up in beautiful style. Within about 40 yards of my tree they branched off a little and got a glance of me, and away they scud some one way and some another. I took good aim at the largest buck and fired. His next bound ended in a plunge head foremost to the ground "dead as [?]." [49] The ball entered just behind his fore shoulder passing through the liver and out the other side. We were now quite satisfied with blood, and loading our horses with the hams of the buck, we returned home to dinner about 3 PM with an excellent appetite and but little fatigue. To the *Elk stakes* [steaks] ample justice was done and they were excellent. At sunset I bid Mr. Sinclair adieu, and rode to Capt Sutter's, taking with me as much vension as a pack horse could carry which I intend taking to the ship. As I intend returning to the ship tomorrow Capt. gave orders for a War dance to be got up this evening for my amusement. After supper we went out and found about 30 Indians almost naked and hideously painted dancing around a huge fire. Their performances were the same as I before described. Capt. S. told me many interesting stories re-

---

[49] Two words are illegible in the original manuscript at this point.

specting the customs and traditions of the Indians, one dance in particular which is performed but once a year, but is too immoral to commit to paper.

WED. 6th.   After breakfast I visited the improvements in the neighbourhood in company with Capt. S. Every thing looks well and thriving. Owing to his want of seed he will not have a great variety of garden stuff this year, or near the quantity of field produce which he would probably have had that not been the case. However, he has now 300 acres of wheat growing in one field and it looks very thriving, also about 160 acres of Indian corn, Rye Beans, and Potatoes. The kitchen garden is about half a mile in length and 100 yards wide, being the north bank of a stream of water which passes near the walls of the inclosure. This is under the management of a German gardener and is handsomely laid out. In it are 5 or 6000 grape vines planted this year, a large number of fruit trees, and a good variety of salad radishes, leeks, and strawberries. The *tobacco* plant seems to be doing well here, and cotton is just making its appearance. *The Live Stock* to which he has made an addition by purchasing from the Russian settlement at Bodega (since I was last here) is also doing finely. It now consists of 3400 head of cattle (not counting calves), of which there appears to be a great many). There are 500 milch Cows & 46 pair of *Working Oxen*. Of horses Capt. counts about 1500 of which 300 are *saddle and working horses*. Sheep, about 1600; 40 mules; and 350 hogs. Taking into consideration that it is but about two years that Capt. Sutter first landed on the Sacramento, he has done wonders. Owing to the heavy rains and the river being unusually high, his trappers have

not taken much fur as yet, but on the fall of the waters
he hopes to do a good business.

At 11 AM Capt Sutter accompanied me to the boat
and took leave of me when we set out on our return
down stream. At Capt S's I met with Messers. Flugge
(a German gentleman) and a Mr. Farwell from the
U. States both of whom were intelligent and respectable people.[50] The first intends being interested with
Capt. S. and the other proposes taking lands higher
up the river. About an hour after leaving Capt. S. I
shot a large land otter under the bank and on taking
him into the boat found that one leg was *fast* in a *trap.*
This game of course was not lawfully mine. Therefore
as I passed the Rancheiria of the fishing Indians, I left
a note for Capt. S., telling him what I had done, requesting him to credit the Trapper with the otter &
charge the same to me. Nothing particular occurred
in our passage down the river. We stopped at dark to
cook supper and immediately after took boat again,
and, keeping a watch on the look out to keep the boat
in the middle of the stream, the rest of us stowed
away as best we could in the bottom of the boat &
slept soundly, while the noiseless current was bearing
us rapidly to the sea. At sunrise we were abreast the
last camping place in the river. Here we

THURS. 7th.   stopt about ½ an hour, made coffee and

---

[50] Charles W. Flügge arrived in California by the overland route in
1841. Sutter seems to have known him earlier and employed him as clerk
and advisor. An intelligent and educated man, he was later a land grantee,
Los Angeles merchant, and active in 1845-46 in Honolulu. In 1852, however,
his eccentric character seems to have turned to insanity, and he wandered
away from home and was found dead. Bancroft, III, pp. 741-42.

Less is known of Edward August Farwell, who arrived from Honolulu in
1842 in the *California,* perhaps as mate, but he seems to have been a printer
as well as sailor. Bancroft, II, p. 735.

took breakfast. Beat down about 10 or 12 miles against a strong westerly wind, and at 11 AM we landed to await the ebb tide at the place were I killed the wild cow last summer. While stopping for a change of tide we took dinner and slept a couple of hours on beds of flowers. Here was the greatest profusion and variety of wild flowers I ever saw. Within ten steps I gathered 17 different kinds. The only ones which I knew were the Violet, which here grows much larger than with us, and the Hollyhock of which there were two colours. The soil and scenery here was good, as far as the eye could extend a lovely and fertile country, without the least sign of cultivation. Splendid farms might be established here which would equal any in the universe. At 1 PM made sail and continued working down with strong breezes untill the tide failed, when we camped at sunset on a point of land about 10 miles above the Carquines. Here we found two canoes belonging to the Hudson's Bay Comp'y. The crews consisted of a half breed and an Indian for one canoe, and a Canadian and his wife (who was a half breed) for the other. Their traps were set near by, but the weather had been so rough for the last week that they could not visit them with their slight canoes. A small tent was pitched under which they all domesticated. Their provisions were all expended with the exception of part of a seal's carcass which they had shot a few days previous and from which the good lady when I landed was cooking some stinking but to them savory morsels. Our fire was also soon underway and supper prepared, after which I entered the tent of my neighbours and spent an hour chatting and smoking with them. From these people I learnt much respecting the habits of the

Beaver and of their mode of trapping them. The woman appeared to understand *trap* as well as her husband. Declining their invitation to spread my blanket in their tent, I made my arrangements on the sand beach and slept soundly untill 4 AM, when rousing the boats crew we started with the ebb tide and pulled down for the Carquines.

FRID. APRIL 8th. 7 AM stopped at a camping place on the south side of the Straits, where we breakfasted and awaited the turn of the tide, and at 11 AM with a light breeze and the ebb tide continued on our way. Middle part of the day strong breezes from NW. Beat down to Angel Island during this tide. When taking the first of the flood we ran across the passage and arrived at the Ship at 4 PM.

SAT. 9th. The Boats which had been scouring the Bay under the direction of Mr. Mellus in pursuit of hides during my absence were now all returned, but had not been very successful. Therefore having nothing further for them to do at present, they were got ready to wood and water the ship &c. Weather squally throughout the day.

SUN. 10th. Winds variable and squally with heavy showers of Rain. Crew at Rest. Ends the same.

MON 11th. Strong Breezes from NW and pleasant weather. Dispatched the launch to Whalers Harbour for water, the pinnace for fire wood, and the cutter to kill bullocks on the north side of the bay. This morning I shot a large number of beautiful quail.

TUES 12th. Pleasant weather and strong winds. Launch and pinnace returned with wood and water, and were again dispatched in the afternoon. Bark *Tasso* sailed in the afternoon.

WED. 13th. Wind fresh from NW with pleasant weather during the day. The launch returned with a load of water, the pinnace with wood, and the cutter with the beef of the bullocks. The carpenter at work, making new brace bumpkins.[51] Ends with strong breezes.

THURS. 14th. Weather as yesterday. Boats employed the same.

FRID 15th. Weather as yesterday. Finished wooding and watering.

SAT 16th. Winds light and variable with pleasant weather. All hands employed in various duty on board ship.

SUN 17th. Fresh breezes and pleasant weather through the day. Part of the crew on liberty on shore, the remainder at rest.

MON. 18th. Weather as yesterday. Mr. Mellus gone with the Cutter to St. Antonio to be absent a number of days. Having nothing to do on board, I took a passage to Whaler's Harbour to pass a day or two with Capt. Richardson. Arrived there in the pinnace at 10 AM. Found Cap. R. at home. Dispatched the boat to return to the ship with a load of wood, with orders to come for me on Wednesday. Afternoon rainy and cold. Spent the time in reading and conversation in the house.

TUES. 19th. Morning pleasant. After breakfast rode

---

[51] Brace bumpkins are short booms, rigged on the ship's quarter to take one of the main brace blocks.

with Capt. Richardson over the mountains and along the seashore towards Puerto los Reyes. Returned about 2 PM after a pleasant ride of about 15 miles with an excellent appetite and found an excellent dinner awaiting us. In the afternoon walked up the valley with Capt. R. and his daughter Marianna to pick strawberries; found plenty of them but not many ripe.

WED. 20th. Morning pleasant. After an early breakfast Capt. & myself mounted horses and took another ride, proposing to visit Mr. Reed [Read] at the next farm about 16 miles dist. About half way there we saw appearances of much rain and concluded to return before reaching the house it rained violently. Found the boat waiting for me. After dinner the rain ceasing returned to the ship. Ends pleasant.

THURS. 21st. Weather pleasant with strong breezes from NW. Took in the launch and got ready for sea. Ends the same.

FRID. 22d. Squally throughout the Day with spits of rain. Nothing doing.

SAT. 23d. Morning pleasant. Crew repairing old sails. Carpenter making blocks. 4 PM the cutter returned. Ends with strong winds.

The Seventh Passage

San Francisco to San Diego,
Return to Monterey, and a Second
Visit to the Pueblo of Los Angeles

SUN 24th [APR. 1842]. Morning pleasant & calm. At daylight unmoored ship. 11 AM fine breezes. Got under way and beat out with the ebb tide. 2 PM passed the Bar and bore away for Monterey. Pleasant breezes all night.

MON. 25th. Morning fine with light winds. 7 AM anchored at Monterey. No other vessel in the harbour. Found letters from home, "per *Delaware*."

TUES. 26th. Weather pleasant with light winds from NW. Sent the pinnace to fish off Point Pinos. Returned at 3 PM with a good Fare. Crew employed variously.

WED. 27th. Morning pleasant. Carpenter caulking the quarter deck. Crew shifting and repairing sails. Cleared out the sail room and aired the sails. Latter part fresh breezes. Taking off hides.

THURS. APRIL 28th. Morning pleasant with light NW breezes. Crew variously employed. Carpenter caulking the deck. At 8 AM accompanied Mr. Mellus to the Mission of John [San Juan Bautista] distant about 11 Leagues to hunt up hides. We were supplied with excellent horses and accompanied by a man who owned the animals to take care of them. The ride was

pleasant and the country after getting about six miles
from Monterey had a fertile and pleasant appearance,
but not to be compared with the region around Sacramento. A little past noon we stopped at the farm house
of Don Joachim Gomes [Gomez], formerly head man
of the Custom House department. Found the old gentleman at home, partook of an excellent dinner; the
table being cleared, coffee and cigars were brought on.
The ladies (consisting of Mrs. Gomes & Mrs. Hartnell
who had stopped here on her way to St. Johns)[52] were
the first to light their cigars, and of course we followed
their example (Ladies do set bad examples sometimes,
but in this instance I do not say that we should have
waited long for one). At 3 PM we remounted and
rode over the mountains about nine miles and reached
the Mission about 5 o'clock. We remained here about
an hour and having transacted all the business we had
to do, returned to pass the night at Don Joachim's.
Of this Mission I saw but little. It appeared to be in
a ruinous state. Most of the houses were without inhabitants and falling into ruins. There are a few traders here to supply the Indians with rum, and collect
the hides and produce of the neighbouring Ranchos,

---

[52] José Joaquín Gómez was a Mexican customs officer and holder of other
offices in Monterey in the 1830's, and was the holder of Verjeles rancho,
on the Monterey-San Jose road, in the 1840's.

William Edward Petty Hartnell played a major role in the California
hide and tallow trade from his arrival in 1822, as partner in McCulloch,
Hartnell & Co., until the firm's breakup in 1828. His subsequent careers
as land holder, teacher, customs officer, inspector of missions, and the like
are discussed in Susan Dakin, *The Lives of William Hartnell* (Stanford,
1949). Although perhaps less successful financially than some of his con-
temporaries, Hartnell was an important early settler. Baptised as a Catholic
and naturalized, he married in 1825 María Teresa de la Guerra, and his
father-in-law, Don José de la Guerra y Noriega, was a constant support
to him.

By St. John's, Phelps means Mission San Juan Bautista.

but the place looks miserable and nothing is presented to induce a stranger to remain a longer time here than we did. It is astonishing what amount of labour and fatigue the California horse can undergo and with how little food. When we returned where we put up for the night, our horses were to all appearances nearly as fresh and when we started in the morning. We had rode 45 miles, mostly on the gallop, and over many hills. They were tied up the night previous to our leaving Monterey and kept *without food* to prepare them for the journey and they had eaten nothing all day, yet they did not seem as fatigued as a horse in the States would be after travelling 10 miles, and the owner of them said they were in good condition to return to Monterey the same night if we wished. A bountiful supper and excellent beds were provided for us, to all of which we did ample justice. Don J. has a tolerable good farm and more of the comforts of life than most of his countrymen, and is very hospitable but the wild Indians give him much trouble and steal many of his horses, even out of the Korral close to the house.

FRIDAY 29th. Morning partially clear; wind SW. After Coffee (for the Californians never provide breakfast), started on our return. Experienced a smart shower which lasted about an hour, after which we weather cleared and continued fine during the remainder of the day. Rode about twelve miles across a fine plain covered with rich clover, so high that we could break off the honeysuckle on horseback, and at 10 AM arrived at a farmhouse near the bank of the Monterey River. Here we were hospitably entertained, with broiled beef, Indian cakes, cream and cheese, and

again put out (as the western folks say). Arrived at
Monterey ½ past 12 M (horses quite fresh).

SAT 30th.   Begins with fresh breezes from SW with
cloudy weather. Employed in taking on board hides
& various other work. Latter part wind NW & pleasant
weather.

SUN MAY 1st.   Morning moderate breezes and fine
weather. Shortened in the chain & got ready for sea.
Latter part crew at rest. Wind strong from NW. Robert Elwell, Esq., and Don Augustine Sanchez came
on board as passangers for Santa Barbara.[53] At 5 PM
passed Point Pinos and bore away. Fresh breezes
through the night.

MON 2nd.   Pleasant breezes and hazy weather. Noon
moderate & variable winds. 5 PM ship off the anchorage at St. Luis Obispo. Sent the pinnace & quarter
boat on shore. Ship laying off & on. 6 PM boats returned with Mr. Robinson, Dan'l Hill and 130 hides;
hoisted up the boats and made sail. Night light airs
and much swell.

TUES. 3rd.   Light breezes from NW at daylight ship
off Pt. Arguello. 10 breeze freshening. 1 PM passed
Pt. Conception. Latter part calm. Anchored at sunset
in 9 fathoms.

WED. 4th.   Morning calm. 10 AM hove up and made
sail with a light breeze from NW. 1 PM anchored
at Refugio. Latter part calm. Killed a bullock for
ship's use. The cattle are now very fat. The one we

[53] Robert J. Elwell was a master of several vessels trading from Honolulu
to California in the 1820's, then settled at Santa Barbara, was naturalized,
and married a Californian, becoming a merchant and land grantee. Bancroft,
III, p. 790.   Don Augustín Sánchez cannot be further identified.

killed this afternoon cost $6. in goods (on about $4 cost) which at home would have brought $50 or 60.

THURS. 5th. Weather moderate & pleasant. Rec'd a boat load of hides. Messrs Robinson & Mellus gone to the Mission of St. Yness [sic]. Part of the crew on shore washing their clothes. So ends.

FRID. 6th. Morning calm & foggy. Messrs. R. & M. returned from St. Yniss [sic] being unsuccessful in getting hides. 3 PM made sail for Sta. Barbara. 5 PM off Sta. Barbara. Very thick fog. Stood off shore & hove too for the night.

SAT. MAY 7th. Morning light airs from WSW and very thick fog. Stood in shore to 5 fathoms water and sent the boat on shore to ascertain our situation. 10 AM boat returned reported the land opposite to be 8 miles east of Sta. Barbara. Middle part pleasant breezes from NW & clear weather. 5 PM calm. Anchored in 7 fathoms. 8 a light breeze from the East. Hove up & made sail. 10 Anchored at Sta. Barbara. *California, Fama, Tip-Coon,* & *Julia Ann* in port.

SUND. 8th. Moderate & pleasant. Part of the crew on liberty. Part at rest on board.

MON. 9th. Light winds & foggy. Employed in taking off hides and repairing sails. Ends the same.

TUES 10th. Light winds & foggy. Employed in watering ship. Carpenter commenced caulking the upper works. Killed a bullock. Ends clear.

WED 11th. Morning light breezes from SW, sky overcast. Got ready to sail. 5 PM hove up and made sail for St. Pedro. Midnight ship off Pt. Conversion. Calm & cloudy.

THURS 12th.   Morning light variable winds. 10 AM wind light from ENE. Saw & exchanged signals with Capt Wilson, Bark *Index,* bound up the coast. Afternoon, breeze freshening from NW. 5 PM anchored at San Pedro. Ends pleasant.

FRID. 13th.   Morning light airs and foggy. Messr*s* Mellus & Robinson gone to the Pueblo. Afternoon arrived bark *Tip-Coon* (alias) *Quiplacuaun* [*Guipuzcoana*] from Sta. Barbara. Crew employed in fitting topmast rigging. Carpenter caulking the upper works.

SAT. 14th.   Weather as yesterday. Crew employed the same. Received a few hides from Pueblo.

SUN 15th.   Weather as yesterday. Crew at rest.

MOND. 16th.   [Weather] Do. Crew at work on sails & rigging. Carpenter caulking.

TUES 17th.   Weather & winds as above. Employed as usual.

WED 18th.   Morning clear & pleasant. Wind NE. Crew variously employed. Rec'd a quantity of hides & tallow. Afternoon fresh breezes from NW.

THURS. 19th.   Wind & weather as yesterday. All hands variously employed.

FRIDAY MAY 20th.   Morning calm and cloudy. Received 200 hides from the Pueblo. At 9 AM light breezes from SW. Got under way for St. Diego. Latter part moderate breezes from NW. Midnight calm. Ship off St. Juan.

SAT. 21st.   Morning calm & foggy. Middle & latter part light breezes from NW. 4 PM passed & exchanged signals with the Bark *Tasso,* bound up. 9 PM anchored inside of Pt. Loma. Night calm.

SUN 22nd. Morning light breezes from west. At 12 AM hove up and proceeded up with the flood tide. Anchored & moored ship abreast the hide house. Latter part crew at rest.

MON 23rd. Weather as yesterday. Crew employed in landing hides. Carpenter caulking the upper works. Went up to the Presidio, and spent the night at Capt. Fitch's. Found the people of the place (i.e., the women, for the men are all absent at their farms or planting places), in much trouble and highly offended at the manner in which they have been treated by his Reverence the Bishop. It seems he was ordered by the Pope to repair to this country, and established himself at San Diego, this being the center of the California Missions. Consequently he came here first, and landed off his effects, and proclaimed his intention of rebuilding the Mission of St Luis Rey and erecting a Palace, &c. His arrival was hailed with great joy. The whole population came to the beach to receive and escort (or rather carry) him to the Presidio. His sedan chair was landed; his reverence was placed in it; and the men carried him on their shoulders half way to the town, when the women took possession and lugged his holiness through the sand the remainder of the way, a distance of 2½ miles, and deposited their precious burthen at the Mission. After a short stay at San Diego the bishop went up to Santa Barbara, leaving his effects, among which were many rich ornaments and other material for the new Palace, at S.D. promising soon to return hither himself, but it seems he has changed his plans, and having concluded on locating himself at Santa Barb., had sent down by the *Tasso* for his goods to be sent him, but the women have refused to give them up, and have risen *to a man* with the determination that he shall redeem his former promise or they will keep his goods. The Capt. of the *Tasso* brought an order from the Bishop to the Alcalda to have the articles sent him, but that the officer told the Capt. that the women were masters of the place and he could do nothing about it. The Ladies however sent the old gent's duds to him, with a strong letter of remonstrance.

TUES. MAY 24th.   This forenoon I called at a number of the houses and found a collection of females at most of them discussing the question which has so much excited this community of heroines. Some of them think they have gone too far, and the *ringleader* and chief of the revolutionists, Donna Tomala Pico (*the lady who furnishes our ship with bullocks*) fears excommunication will be the reward of her part in the rumpus.[54] During the day I understood that they had determined in council to send by me a peace offering to the Bishop when I return to Sta. Barbara. 4 PM returned to the ship. Crew employed as yesterday. Ends pleasant.

WED. 25th.   Morning foggy & calm. Carpenter caulking the upper works Crew cleaning and painting ship inside. An acquaintance (an Englishman) on the point of being married to a lady of this place, came down from the Presidio today and invited me to accompany him to the Presidio in order to attend church service tomorrow at the Mission, it being the festival of Corpus Christi. At the same time his banns are to be published. Rode up in the afternoon and passed the night at Capt. Fitch's house.

---

[54] Doña Tomala [Tomasa?] Pico cannot be further identified.

THURS. 26th. After breakfast mounted horse and rode to the Mission in company with 8 or 10 Cavalleros. The distance was about 5 miles from the Presidio. All the women of the place had arrived the night previous, bringing with them materials for a "Pic Nic". The Mission building is very large and contains many apartments. The enclosure also contains many buildings for the Indians and a tolerable church, but it is fast going to decay and there are but few Indians now belonging to it. The Priest, Padre Vincente, who resides here, has been here about 26 years.[55] He has the name of being about the best padre in California, but among his virtues he does not rank temperance as he gets "corned as a shad" every day.

On our arrival we were entertained with a cup of coffee. Aguadiente was also placed before us, but only the padre and some of the Rancheros partook of it. At 9 the devices of the church commenced. The priest had taken three drams while the rest of us were taking coffee, and on his entering the church appeared to be far from sober. This is the first service I have attended in the country, and tho' I could not expect to receive much edification from the lips of a drunken priest, I felt that I was in the Lord's house and I knelt with reverence among the multitude. Mass was said, and anthems were sung. The orchestra consisted of about a doz. Indians who sang with good voices and performed on a hand organ & base & kettle drum, two fiddles and a tambourine. After a while a sermon was preached, text from the parable of the marriage feast: "the feast was prepared & the guests were invited but

---

[55] Padre Vicente Pasqual Oliva was the priest at San Diego Mission 1820-1846, and was therefore the last missionary at this station; he died in 1848.

they all began to make excuses, &c.," and the sermon was adapted for the occasion. The Padre was very violent in his denunciations of those who had absented themselves from the feast, and in the course of his harangue, gave us foreigners a shot, saying that we came to the country to get all we could from the Missions, without giving any thing to the treasury of the church. The old gentleman forgot to credit us with the supplies furnished by the ships in return for the hides and tallow received. After the service was over we returned to the dining hall and again partook of coffee and cakes which were provided by the ladies. As the Catholic feasts are more like fasts than feasts, I expected this was all the dinner that would be afforded us and we had our horses brought up to return to St. Diego. But as the weather was extremely warm we did not like to go away in the heat of the day if there was any prospect of our getting any provender at the mission. Therefore to satisfy my doubts on that subject I looked in at the cookhouse and on uncovering sundry pots and pans, found lots of fat things in preparation, and at 1 PM sat down to an excellent dinner with Father Vicente and about 25 others, mostly females, and the gentry of the place. Taking a siesta of about two hours in a cool bed room, we were again ready for the performances of the afternoon, which consisted of a procession carrying flags, preceded by the Host, the padre and a band of music, going from house to house preaching at each, intended to represent the manner of the apostles of old. After each discourse, the host was elevated and the music made most discordant sounds. At one elevation of the sacred symbol the organ played "shove her up." I tho't there must have been a mistake and the wrong notes taken, but the whole band chimed in and away they went. Surely, thinks I, "there is but a step from the sublime to the ridiculous." I had seen enough, so lighting a cigar I took a stroll around the gardens for an hour or two, and at sunset rode back to St. Diego.

FRID. 27th. Returned to the ship, and got ready for sea. The ladies have sent down to the ship a large quantity of cakes, cabbages, onions, and lettuce for me to take to the Bishop, which he will get (if they keep). We have now cured and stored in the hide house 21357 hides, and hard work it has been to get them. Dana complains of his hardships and sufferings in having to go up the coast twice. We have already made five trips & ½ and will make one more before we complete the cargo, but I hear no talk of hardship from my boys.

SAT. MAY 28th. 1842. Morning pleasant & calm. Unmoored ship. Rode up to the Presidio to hurry down my passangers to the ship, consisting of Donna Isadora Pico Foster,[56] and a young Mexican lady, Mrs. Foster's children & servant girl. At 10 AM after much exertion they got under way in a bullock cart, and proceeded to the beach, escorted by a number of Caballeros on horseback and a second bullock load of their female friends. After dinner on board they took leave, and the friends parted with many tears. The breeze freshening at the same time, we hove up the anchor and made sail out of the harbour. Midnight becalmed off Punta Loma.

---

[56] Doña Isadora Pico Forster married John Forster (see above, page 64, n. 12) in 1837, and died shortly before her husband in the 1880's; her brother, Pío Pico, was sometime Governor of California.

SUN 29th. Morning light breezes from NW freshening toward noon. Weather pleasant. Night calm.

MON 30th. Fresh westerly winds throughout the day. Beating to windward. Caught some fine fish by trailing a line astern. Ends moderate. Ship of [off] St. Juan.

TUES 31st. Winds light and variable with fine weather. Crew employed in scraping the decks. Carpenter repairing boats. Latter part fresh breezes from NW.

WED. JUNE 1st. Weather pleasant through the day with westerly winds. Employed in beating to windward.

THURS 2nd. Light easterly winds in the morning with pleasant weather. Saw and exchanged signals with the *Tasso* and *Tip-Coon,* both coming out of St. Pedro. 11 AM came to anchor. After dinner landed passangers. Strong breezes from NW.

FRID 3rd. Weather pleasant and moderate. Crew painting ship inside & varnishing the decks. Carpenter caulking the stern. So ends.

SAT. 4th. Morning calm & pleasant. Part of the crew painting & varnishing. Sent a boat to catch deep water fish, and another to get lobsters; both were very successful. 130 lobsters were taken; some of them would weigh 7 or 8 lbs. The only difference between them and our lobsters at home is in the absence of the two large claws and having a rougher shell.

SUND. 5th. Fine weather and strong winds. Crew at rest 4 PM took horse and rode up to the Pueblo. Arrived at Don Abel Sterns at 7 PM after a pleasant ride.

MON. JUNE 6th. Forenoon very warm weather. Kept [to the] house. Don Abel has entered the matrimonial state since I was here last. His lady is young and very interesting and, having a sister with her as a companion, the domestic arrangements of the old Don's house are much better than heretofore.

Afternoon cooler. Mr. Mellus and myself rode a few miles around the vineyards calling at a number of houses. The vineyards and wheat fields all look very favourable.

TUES 7th. Weather extremely warm. We intended to have started for the ship after breakfast, but the heat was such (90° in the shade) that we concluded to stop untill tomorrow.

The Pueblo is nearly deserted at present by the male population. Some are at their ranchos preparing for the killing season, and all the loafers and vagabonds are collecting gold at a mine which has lately been discovered about 40 miles from here [Placerita Canyon, near present Newhall]. Don Abel shew [sic] me about a lb. of it which he had received at the store in payment for goods at the rate of $16 per oz. The quality looks well. He tells me there are about 200 people at work there, every one on his own account, and that each one obtains about $150 to 450 per day. I intend to visit the place when I return here. Took another ride just before sunset on a pleasant road.

WED. 8th. Morning calm and foggy. After breakfast our horses were brought up and at 7 AM we (viz. Messrs. Robinson, Mellus, and myself) started on our return to the ship. Arrived on board at 11 AM, and at 3 PM got under way with a westerly wind for Santa Barbara. Midnight moderate breezes from the Eastward. Ship running up by the Island of Catalina.

THURS. 9th.   Morning light breezes from ESE with overcast weather. All usefull sail set. Middle & latter part fresh breezes from NW and clear weather. At night off Pt. Dume.

FRID. 10th.   Morning moderate breezes from East, sky overcast. 8 AM in the passage between Anacapa & Santa Cruz. Wind light & weather pleasant. Lowered a quarter [boat] and went in shore to fish. Caught a few fine fish, but perceiving that the ship was drifting fast towards the shore with the current I hastened on board and got the boats ahead towing but they were not able to stop her stern-way, and there being no wind I got ready to anchor in a bad place, but fortunately a westerly breeze sprang up and we worked through the passage & at 9 in the evening anchored at Santa Barbara.

SAT. JUNE 11th. 1842.   Morning foggy with light easterly winds. Got the launch out to soak. Middle & latter parts pleasant. Crew employed in scraping the Larboard side & stern. Carpenter cutting timber to repair the boats. Spent the day on shore. Dined at the house of Capt. R. At dinner a child of about 18 mos. old sitting at table, was presented by its mother with a tumbler ½ full of wine. At first the poor little thing refused it, but after repeated attempts to make it drink, it seized the tumbler and drank the whole of it. I requested that it should be taken away, but the parents were highly amused and considered it a most laudable action. In the few moments the child was tumbling about the floor in a beastly state of intoxication. I cannot discemble [sic] what my feelings were. What could the feelings of such parents towards their offspring be I could not imagine. If this child does not die a drunkard it will not be the parents' fault.

SUND. 12th. Morning foggy, with light variable winds. Part of the crew on liberty, the remainder at rest. Rec'd an invitation to attend mass & dine on shore, which I declined. The Bishop is making every exertion to establish a Seminary at this place. He also proposes building a new church and a Palace for which purpose he is soliciting subscriptions from every one. The women seem to be the most zealous in the cause and turned out about a fortnight since in a large body to carry stone for the foundation. I was shown yesterday a number of large piles of stones which the women actually gathered and carried on their heads to the place. But I think that with all their zeal, the affair will be a failure, as we hear from Mexico that Santa Ana has seized upon the Fonda Religiosa (or pious fund) from which the Missions of this country had annually received $6,000 for their support and it is not expected that the Californians will be very good Catholics when their pockets are drawn upon for the support of their religious institutions. By the way, these *cakes* and *cabbages* – I shall have to render up a "Flemish account" of them to his Reverence as my steward appropriated them all to the use of us "Hearties" on the passage up.

MON. 13th. Morning foggy & Calm. Crew employed in filling water, repairing sails, and killing beef. Ends pleasant.

TUES 14th. Morning pleasant & calm. Employed in filling water and painting ship. Received letters from Home by the way of Mazatlan, Ship *Barnstable* 125 days out from Boston, for the coast to *assist us,* but as we have almost made our voyage without any assistance and have in fact help load two other ships, we feel rather indifferent at receiving help at this late hour. However it will save us making any more trips to St. Francisco and but one more to Monterey where we expect to meet the new ship and be again gladdened by receiving later news from absent friends. Got ready to proceed up the coast for the last time (we hope). Ends pleasant, wind NW.

WED. 15th. Morning foggy and calm. Employed in taking on board provision and vegetables. 4 PM fresh breezes from West. Got under weigh. Passengers Messrs Robinson, Mellus & Gamble, the latter a young Philadelphian ('una naturalista') [i.e. naturalist]. Midnight pleasant. Ship near Sta Cruz [Island].

THURS 16th. Moderate breezes from WNW and pleasant weather throughout the 24 hours. Beating up the Canal of Santa Barbara.

FRIDAY 17. Weather as yesterday. Watch employed in painting ship & various other work. Midnight calm.

SAT 18th. Morning strong breezes from WNW & cloudy. Ship beating to windward under single reeft topsails. Tacking as occasion required. Ends the same.

SUN 19th. Strong gales from NW with squally weather. Ship beating to windward when it was possible to carry sail. At other times laying too under close reeft Main Topsail. The wind has not changed a point for the last 8 days. The only changes have been from a steady gale to strong squalls, blowing hardest at night.

TO SAT. 25th. At daylight blowing heavy with no prospect of a favourable change, bore away and made sail for a port. At 11:30 AM anchored in 5 fathoms of water at St Simeon. Found it to be a very snug cove well protected from the NW winds. After dinner went on shore with Merrs. Robinson and Mellus and walked about 4 miles to a Rancheiri, where they obtained horses after much trouble and started off for Monterey. Engaged a bullock to be sent down tomorrow & returned on board. Mr. G., the naturalist, had amused himself in making collections of plants. He informed me that he had obtained about 30 new specimens.

SUN 26th. Pleasant with strong winds. Opposite the ship, there being a fine stream of fresh water, the crew requested & obtained leave to go on shore and wash their clothes. At sunset all returned on board. At noon saw a vessel in the offing standing in. She proved to be the *Joven Quipsicana* [*Guipuzcoana*] (or as my crew call her, the *Tip Coon*) belonging to Don Antonio Aguire [Aguirre][57] of Sta. Barbara (he was on board) from St. Luis bound to Monterey. She backed her Mn. Topsail near us and I went on board. They merely stood in to see what ship the *Alert* was. I advised the Capt. to anchor as he could not gain any to windward while it blew so hard but the owner tho't different. So after getting a quarter of fresh beef from us, they stood out again. Ends with strong winds & squally. Lat. at the anchorage 35°39′15″.

MON. 27th. Weather as yesterday. All hands employed in filling water at stream opposite. While were

[57] Don José Antonio Aguirre was of Basque descent, born about 1793; he had esablished himself as a successful trader a Guaymas. The owner of several vessels including the *Joven Guipuzcoana* (1840-43), he visited California frequently. After 1838 he settled in Santa Barbara, marrying into the Estudillo family, and became a well-liked grantee. Although he was often in government employ, he was mainly a trader, and was sometime partner of William H. Davis.

thus employed Mr. Gamble and myself went up the valley through which the stream descended, to gather plants. After filling his *vasculum* we found a beautiful deep basin of clear water with a hard sandy bottom, shaded by high trees, and in it we enjoyed a fine bath. 3 PM moderate breezes and pleasant. Having filled the water casks and got ready for sea we hove up and stood out. Strong breezes continued through the night. Tacked every 4 hours, keeping in shore, the water being smoother.

TUES. 28th.   Fresh breezes and clear weather. Wind NW. Ship beating to windward under single reeft Topsails. At 5 PM while standing off shore we passed to windward of the *"Tip Coon"* standing in. Night calm.

WED 29th.   Morning calm and foggy. Middle and latter part of the day light breezes from SE. Sent up royal yards and set studding sails.

THURS. 30th.   Morning wind & weather as yesterday. At noon ship off Point Anno Nuevo. 6 PM anchored a Monterey. Ends foggy. Bark *Don Quixote* in port.

FRID. 1st.   Morning foggy with light southerly winds. Employed in taking on board hides. Middle Part pleasan. Ends foggy.

SAT. JULY 2nd.   Morning foggy. Wind light from NW. Crew employed as yesterday. Noon pleasant. Ends foggy (caught 16 fine fish).

SUN. 3rd.   Winds & weather as yesterday. All hands on board. Crew at rest.

MON 4th.   Morning fresh southerly breezes and pleasant. At daylight hoisted the flags in honour of the day and at noon fired a salute of 21 guns. The bark *Don Quixote* likewise fired a national salute. Noon & afternoon calm & pleasant. In the evening a ball was given on shore by Messrs Paty,[58] Robinson, Mellus, & Larkin, at which the principal residents, native and foreign, were present. The Gov't Hall was decorated with flags & portraits of Washington & Layfayette [sic] and an excellent supper was prepared by the cooks and stewards of the ships, while the tables were waited upon by the ship's boys. A large quantity of liquors and wines disgraced the occasion and the Governor got drunk before midnight and most of the natives followed his example before morning. About 4 in the morning I was desirous of leaving, but found soldiers stationed at the door by order of the Gov. with orders to let no person pass out. He said the Americans invited him hither to celebrate the 4th of July and he should keep it up untill he was tired and no person should leave before he did, and in fact the dancing was not discontinued untill 9 AM. I was invited by Mr. R. and requested to superintend the tables, but had it not been on this particular occasion should have remained on board. I had hoped to have spent the day at sea, but was disappointed and could not avoid being present, although I could not partake of their revelries, and I hope never to witness any more such celebrations. My heart more than ever yearns for the land of steady liberty & cold water society.

[58] John Paty and his brother, Henry A. Paty, were both merchant-masters in the Boston-Honolulu-California trade. John is meant here (Henry commited suicide in 1841); he made frequent trips from Honolulu as master and owner of the *Don Quixote.* Although a San Francisco area land grantee, he was better known as a sort of senior captain in the Hawaiian navy.

TUES 5th. Moderate & pleasant throughout the day. Crew variously employed on ship board. So ends.

WED. 6th. Strong westerly winds and foggy. Crew employed as usual. Sent 2 boats fishing. A noon they returned having been very successful, bringing large quantities of fish. Ends pleasant.

THURS. 7th. Morning foggy. Light winds from WSW. A 10 AM arrived the ship *Barnstable* Capt. Hatch 148 days from Boston bringing a spendid cargo for the coast and what was far better a large package of letters from loved friends all speaking of love, health and happiness and may my heart be made to feel the deep obligations I am under to Him who thus protects and blesses those who are so dear to my heart. "Surely goodness and mercy have followed me all my days" and may my future life be spent more to the honour and glory of God than it has yet been. Spent the afternoon and evening in reading letters from my dear distant family and friends, and a rich treat they afforded.

FRIDAY JULY 8th 1842. Moderate and pleasant throughout the day. All hands assisting on board the *Barnstable* breaking out cargo and getting ready to enter the ship [i.e., in customs records]. So ends.

SAT 9th. Weather as yesterday. Employed in assisting the *Barnstable* to land goods at the Custom House. Today the ship and cargo was entered, paying $28,000 ($4000 cash). Latter part employed in transhipping goods to the *Alert*.

SUN 10th. Weather pleasant with strong westerly winds. Crew at rest. So ends.

MON. 11th. Wind and weather as yesterday. Employed in transhipping goods from the *Barnstable* to the *Alert*.

TUES 12th. Winds light & variable; weather pleasant. Crew employed as yesterday.

WED. 13th. Moderate & foggy in the morning. Afternoon clear and pleasant. Rec'd a few hundred hides from the shore and some fire wood. *Don Quixote* sailed for Sta. Cruz.

THURS 14th. Weather as yesterday. Taking in hides and discharging tallow & receiving goods from the *Barnstable*. So ends.

FRIDAY 15th. Weather pleasant with light winds. Employed as yesterday. Ends the same.

SAT 16th. Fine and pleasant with moderate breezes. Received a supply of stores from the *Barnstable* & took off 300 hides from the shore. Carpenter repairing the boats.

SUN. 17th. Wind & weather as yesterday. All hands at rest.

MON 18th. Morning moderate breezes from WSW. Took on board some goods on freight for Leeward. At 11 AM got under way and at 8 PM anchored at Santa Cruz. Ends pleasant. Passangers on board Messrs A. Robinson & Wm P. Avis [59] of Boston.

TUES 19th. Morning calm & foggy. Employed in taking on board hides, tallow & lumber. Killed a bullock for ships use. At 6 PM got under weigh with a fresh westerly breeze bound to St. Luis Obispo.

[59] Little information is available on William P. Avis, who arrived in California in 1842 with introductions, intending to go into business as a commission merchant; after some success, he returned to Boston in 1846. Bancroft, III, p. 706.

The Eighth Passage

Monterey to San Diego
and North to Refugio

WED. JULY 20th. [1842]. Light variable winds & cloudy throughout the day. The watch employed variously. At night ship off Bay de Esterly [Estero, or Morro Bay]. Calm.

THURS. 21st. Morning moderate breezes wind NW. 10 AM anchored at St. Luis. Found the brig *Bolivar* at anchor. 2 PM the *California* arrived. Mr. R. took horse in the afternoon in pursuit of hides. Crew employed in fishing. Ends pleasant.

FRID. 22nd. Fresh westerly winds and fine weather. Crew employed in watering ship. Mr. Avis & myself went to hunt quail but were not very successful. Ends calm.

SAT 23rd. Weather as yesterday. Embarking hides and tallow.

SUND 24th. Fresh westerly [breezes] & pleasant. Crew at work part of the day in taking on board hides & landing goods. Latter part of the day at rest. *Bolivar* & *California* sailed.

MOND. 25th. Morning foggy & calm. Employed in embarking Hides & tallow. Killed a bullock. Latter part, filling water.

TUES. 26th. Morning fresh breezes and foggy. 10 AM hove up and made sail. 4 PM passed Pt. Conception. Latter part strong squalls off the land which brought us to double reeft topsails. 7 PM calm. Anchored in 10 fathoms.

WED. 27th. Morning calm & pleasant. 10 AM light southerly winds. Got under weigh and at noon anchored at Refugio. Afternoon employed in wooding. Rode up to Mr. Hill's house and returned on board at dark. Ends pleasant.

THURS 28th. Moderate and pleasant throughout the day. Employed in embarking hides & tallow. To day we were visited by three priests from the missions of St. Yness & Purissima.[60] They purchased many goods, and are now having a good quantity of hides &c. brought down to pay up old debts. The matanzas or killing time has commenced and we now begin to make good collections. The Mission of St. Yness has about 7000 head of cattle. Purissima has much less, but they are governed by the best priests on the coast and although they will never be what they have been yet will probably outlive the other missions. The priests dined on board, and were quite temperate and decorous in their behavior. Ends calm.

FRID. 29. Weather as yesterday. Employed as above. Mr Avis and myself rode up the valley and passed the afternoon with Donna Madelina & her pretty daughters at their farm. We found them seated under trees bending with Pears & Apples in the midst of a fine vineyard and passed an agreeable visit.

---

[60] Before "Purissima" Phelps has crossed out "St. Juan."

SAT. JULY 30th 1842. Light breezes from SW and pleasant. 8 AM got under weigh from Refugio and at 4 PM anchored off Santa Barbara. Ends clear & pleasant.

SUN 31st. Weather as yesterday. Most of the crew on liberty. Mr. A. and myself dined with the Commandant by invitation. Ends pleasant. All hands on board.

MON. AUG 1st. Light variable winds with overcast weather througout the day. Crew employed in landing lumber and repairing sails.

TUES 2nd. Pleasant throughout with light westerly winds. Employ'd in selling & landing goods and receiving hides & tallow. Many visitors today.

WED 3rd. Weather as yesterday, wind "tambien" [also]. Employed variously in filling water, receiving hides & horns &c.

THURS 4th. Morning light westerly winds, sky overcast. Crew boating hides. The Com'd'ts Lady, two daughters and a granddaughter came on board (a shopping), dined and spent the day on board. In the afternoon went on shore with the ladies, took a walk in the garden, and partook of some very good fruit such as figs, apples, &c. Spent the night on shore.

FRID. 5th. Morning calm & foggy. Crew variously employed in repairing sails, filling water &c., &c. Ends with fresh westerly winds and fine weather.

SAT 6th. Morning light easterly winds & overcast. Crew employed as yesterday. Ends pleasant. Wind NW.

SUN. 7th. Winds & Weather as yesterday. Crew at rest.

MON. 8th. Morning calm. At noon got under way with a fine breeze from NW and made all sail for San Pedro. Passengers on board Messrs Robinson & Avis, and Donna Conception Carillo and two daughters; one of them, named "Espirito Santo," figures in Dana's book.[61] She has another daughter named "Maria Jesus." It is quite usual for the Californians to give these and similar names which we should consider sacrilegious to their children, but the most absurd case of the kind I have known is of an old Indian at the Mission of Santa Barbara who rejoices in the name of Santissima Trinidad. Ends pleasant.

TUES AUG. 9th. Morning light airs from the SW. Sky overcast, weather smooth. Ship off Pt. Dume. At noon a moderate breeze from NW & fine weather. Evening wind light. At midnight off the port, but being too dark to find the proper anchorage; stood in shore and anchored for the night in 6 fathoms.

WED. 10th. Morning calm & pleasant. At daylight lowered a boat and landed the lady passangers. After breakfast Mr. R. started for the Pueblo. 10 AM westerly winds. Hove up and run in to a birth [berth]. Latter part, crew employed in stripping the main topmast to overhaul the rigging and fit new crosstrees. The boys employed on shore carting hides from the house to the beach.

THURS. 11th. Winds fresh from the westward and

---

[61] The identity of Doña Concepción Carrillo is uncertain, but probably Phelps had in mind the wife of Domingo Antonio Ignacio Carrillo, who held various offices in San Diego in the 1830's and was later in Santa Barbara; that Doña Concepción was the sister of Pío Pico, and thus had important connections. "Espirito Santo" is mentioned by Dana, without further identification, as a pretty young dancer at a fandango; *Two Years,* Ch. XXVII.

fine weather. Employed embarking hides & tallow & refitting Mn. topmast rigging &c. Some ½ a doz. women came on board to day to trade. Sold them considerable. Ends pleasant.

FRID. 12th. Wind & weather as yesterday. All hands variously employed, in boating off hides, tallow & horns. Refitting topmast rigging, &c., &c.

SAT 13th. Wind & weather as yesterday. Crew employed the same.

SUN 14th. Moderate & foggy in the morning. Crew at rest. Ends pleasant.

MON 15th. Moderate & pleasant. Employed in boating off hides & tallow. The matanzas now being over, the Rancheiros are carting down the produce of their cattle to pay up their arrears to the shipping, and as the *Alert's* debts are of longer standing than the other vessels we come in for the largest share.

TUES 16th. [to] THURS 18th. Winds and weather as usual. Crew employed in boating off Hides and Tallow.

FRID 19th. [same]. *California* arrived.

SAT 20th. [same]. *Bolivar* sailed.

SUN 21st. Moderate & pleasant. Crew at rest. Strong breezes.

MON. 22nd. [to] WED. 24th. Pleasant & moderate. Employed as last week. Killed two bullocks.

THURS. 25th. Pleasant breezes from NW. 10 AM got under weigh for St. Diego, having on board about 6000 hides & 200 bags of tallow. Night light breezes. Ship off Pt. Dume.[62]

FRID. AUG 26th. Morning moderate breezes from East. 8 AM wind hauling northerly. Stood in for the port of St. Diego. Beat in on slack water and anchored at 10 AM & moored ship. Found a brig just arrived from Mazatlan, having on board a new Governor & General sent by the Mexican Gov't. to rule in California. His name is Don Manuel Micheltereno [Micheltorena] who fills both offices.[63] He comes attended with a large suite. Also backed by 4 or 500 troops, who sailed in company with him on board of 3 other vessels but have not yet arrived. At noon the Govt. landed with his suite. At the same time we saluted him with 17 guns. Got out the Launch and commenced landing hides. Ends with strong breezes from NW.

SAT. 27th. Strong breezes and pleasant throughout the day. Crew landing hides. Carpenter at work on shore making stud. sail booms. Found that a great mortality had prevailed among our pigs since we were last here; 5 fine hogs and a number of pigs had died of starvation or from other causes, some probably bit by rattlesnakes which are unusually numerous this year.

SUN. 28th. Weather pleasant, wind moderate in the morning, and fresh in the afternoon. Crew at rest.

MOND. 29th. Weather as yesterday. Crew employed in landing cargo. Rode up to the presidio intending to pay my respects to his Excellency but tho't better of

---

[62] Since Phelps was underway from San Pedro to San Diego, probably Dana Point is meant here.

[63] Manuel Micheltorena, a native of Oaxaca, and Mexican Brigadier-General, was named Governor of California in 1842, only to be expelled three years later by revolution. The troops he arrived with were in fact recruited from Mexican prisons. Micheltorena's reign is discussed in Bancroft, IV, Ch. XI-XXI.

it and did not call. He is represented to be quite gentlemanly in his appearance and of good habits, has served against Texas, and can probably run as fast as any Mexican soldier or he would not have left Texas alive.

TUES. 30th.   Moderate and pleasant through the day. Crew employed as yesterday. Sent the carpenter to repair some damages sustained by the Mexican brig in her spars on the passage up.

WED. 31st.   Moderate & pleasant. Employed as yesterday.

THURS. SEPT. 1st.   Wind & weather as yesterday. Employed the same. This morning arrived one of the transport vessels, a small brig of about 120 tons. Seeing the Gov. waiting on the beach for a boat to go on board of her in, I sent him one from the ship which he made use of & generously gave the boys each a dollar and myself many thanks. In the afternoon I went on board to enquire for letters, and with the exception of a slaver, I never saw a more miserable looking set of creatures on board of any vessel. They were all convicts, *to be made soldiers in California.* 110 of them were stowed in the hold of this small vessel, some of them with only a rag round their waists. Some of the best clothed were minus a shirt, others ditto trousers. Falstaff's soldiers were gentleman compared to them. It appears that the 500 troops consist of 100 soldiers of the line *and 400 theives,* the sweepings of Mexican prisons. These last are sent here to reform, and become soldiers. I fear California will rue the day she permits these ragamuffin freebooters to set foot on her soil. Among the cargo of sin and misery were about a dozen females; whether they were the wives of some of the prisoners or are prisoners themselves I did not remain long enough to ascertain, as I felt anxious to hurry on shore to take some precautionary steps to protect our property at the hide house previous to the landing of the newcomers.

FRID. 2nd. Morning mild & pleasant. Landed the remainder of hides & tallow and put on shore stores for the hide house. For the better security of the property I put two extra men on shore and furnished the house with additional arms and ammunition. This morning the troops disembarked, and such a troop of miserable looking vagabonds I've not seen for a long time. Falstaff's company had a shirt and a ½ among three of them. I do not think a perfect shirt could be found among all these Mexican heroes. They are ordered to camp on the beach untill the vessel which has clothes for them arrives. Later part unmoored ship and at 3 PM made sail out of the harbour. Ends calm. Ship near the islands.

SAT 3rd. Calm & pleasant the first part. PM light breezes from WNW. Passed between the Islands and stood off shore to avoid the SE current. Midnight calm.

SUN. 4th. Moderate & variable winds throughout the day. Working up the coast. Ends calm.

MON 5th. Winds & weather as yesterday. Water smooth. At sunset ship off St. Juan.

TUES. 6th. Morning fresh westerly breezes, weather fine; beating up. Latter part gentle breezes from SE.

WED. 7th. Morning light winds from SE & cloudy. 6 PM anchored at San Pedro. Mr. Robinson went to the Pueblo. Crew employed variously on ship's duty.

THURS. 8th. Calm & pleasant. Employed in boating off hides & tallow & selling goods. Carpenter caulking the bends.[64] Ends with strong NW winds.

FRID. 9th. Wind & weather as yesterday. Crew employed as above. Carpenter caulking, and the boys making candles on shore.

SEPT. 10th. SAT. Morning clear and pleasant. Crew variously employed. After breakfast took horse and rode up to the pueblo. Being alone and the road being lonely, I proceeded upon a gallop most of the way and arrived at my old quarters at Don Abel's in two hours & 40 minutes, dist. 33 miles. In riding over the plains, saw a drove of perhaps 5 or 600 wild horses. After dinner, and a siesta, went with Mr. Robinson to the vineyard of Don Manuel Requena [65] and had a glorious tuck out of grapes & peaches. Evening: a dance at Don Abel's house.

SUN 11th. Weather pleasant. In this place with a population of about 7 or 800 inhabitants there is at present no public worship on the sabbath. The church is out of repair. There is no priest here and the day is spent in horseracing, cockfighting and gambling. After breakfast I walked down to the farm of Mr. Wolfskill (A Kentucky trapper) and passed the day with him. Mr. W. is a hard working, steady and excellent man married in the country and very pleasantly situated, has a good house of his own erecting, a small farm but under excellent cultivation, and

---

[64] Bends, or wales, are planks extending the length of the ship's side at different heights to reinforce the deck.

[65] Don Manuel Requena, a native of Yucatan, arrived in 1834 as a trader from Guaymas, but stayed on to become prominent in Los Angeles politics until his death in 1876, aged 72.

abundance of fruit trees, kitchen vegetables, &c. His vineyard contains 11,000 vines, mostly of his own planting and all now in full bearing, vines which are but 18 months old are well filled and more forward than any I ever saw in the Mediterranean. I counted 47 bunches of grapes on one vine of three years and estimated the average number of bunches to each vine to be about 14 of 4¼ lbs each. Pears, peaches and figs are also excellent, but the apples very inferior. A fine field of Indian corn adjoining the vineyard invited my attention. It appeared very thrifty and among it I found a great quantity of musk & watermelons, pumpkins & beans. In other places were Irish and sweet potatoes, cabages, onions, beets, and tomatoes, all of excellent quality and very abundant. After dinner took a book and stretched out under the trees. In the evening returned to Don Abel's.

MON 12. The weather to day has been exceeding warm. Kept house most of the day, reading & conversing. Towards sundown visited the vineyard of Mr. Prior [Pryor], another American, and tried the quality of his fruits.[66]

TUES 13. Weather as yesterday. Passed the day in visiting various vineyards and fields. The grapes are not yet quite ripe but there are enough that are eatable in the sunniest places. The wheat and corn bid fair for an abundant crop.

WED. 14th. Morning warm and sultry. After breakfast bid Don Abel & family good bye and mounted

---

[66] Nathaniel Miguel Pryor arrived from Kentucky in 1828. A clockmaker and "platero," or silversmith, he was as often an otter hunter, and not always within the law. He was in charge of Abel Stearns' hide warehouse and San Pedro business, 1834-39. Wright, *Stearns*, pp. 39-40.

to return to the ship. Stopping at Mr. Wolfskill's, he urged me to stop to dinner with him, which I did and as the weather was quite hot, I concluded after dinner to spend an hour or two in the vineyard and rode down in the cool of the day. Therefore after cramming myself with grapes & peaches I laid under a tree and slept until 4 PM when ordering a quantity of dried fruits to be put up for sea use I bade farewell to Mr. W. and the Pueblo, expecting that I shall never see either any more. As I passed by the vineyards, I observed that in the middle of each a scaffolding is erected on which an Indian boy is stationed in the morning and remains throughout the day with a hat full of stones and a sling, with which he keeps away the crows and blackbirds who otherwise would destroy half of the grapes. After a pleasant and rapid ride arrived at the ship about sunset.

THURS. 15. Morning foggy and calm. Crew employed in boating off hides & tallow. Carpenter caulking the Bends. Ends with a strong NW winds & fine weather.

FRID. 16th. Weather & winds as yesterday. Employed the same.

SAT. 17th. Morning clear and pleasant. Employed in painting the masts & bowsprit. Ends fresh NW winds.

SUN. 18th. Wind light from SW & foggy. Crew at rest. Latter part fresh breezes & pleasant.

MON. 19th. Morning calm and foggy. All hands employed in boating off hides & tallow. Carpenter caulking the bends. Ends with strong NW winds.

TUES 20th. Weather as yesterday morning. Getting

ready for sea. At noon fresh breezes from West. Got under weigh for Sta. Barbara. Passangers Donna Conception Carillo & daughter. Latter part of the day and night ship becalmed off the east end of Catalina.

WED. 21st. Light and variable airs throughout the 24 hours with fine weather, during which the ship made scarcely any progress.

THURS. 22nd. Morning light airs or calms. Middle & latter part light breezes from WNW. Ship working to windward between the Islands of Catilina [sic] & Clementia.

FRID. 23rd. SEPT. Morning calm with much swell from WNW. The watch picking oakum; carpenter repairing the cutter. Latter part moderate breezes for about 4 hours from NW and calm during the night. Sta. Barbara Island at dark bore NW about 8 miles. Made preparations for an Elephant hunt tomorrow morning should we be becalmed.

SAT. 24th. Morning calm & pleasant. The island west about 5 miles dist. At 6 AM started from the ship with a large quarter boat and 4 men armed with a whale lance, Gun clubs & knives. On arriving at the Island, found the landing place (a small beach) so thickly covered with Eliphant & seal that we had to wait sometime for the seal to clear out before we found room to haul the boat up. The seal are all of the hair kind and not valuable. Therefore we did not trouble any of them. The Eliphant were rather numerous but not very fat. I killed thirteen of them and with the blubber of twelve loaded the boat as deep as she could swim. We also caught a number of fine large fish and started for the ship. About ½ way off we found the boat was leaking badly and as there was a number of large sharks round it would not answer to raft any of the blubber in order to lighten the boat. Therefore I made a signal for another boat from the ship which was immediately dispatched to our assistance. Arrived on board, discharged and hoisted up the boats at 1 PM. 3 PM light breezes from WNW. So ends.

SUN. 25th. Begins calm and pleasant & continued untill 8 PM when with a fresh breeze from NW we passed under the lee of Anacapa and stood over to the main. Fresh breezes through the night.

MON. 26th. Morning light breezes from ESE. At 10 AM came to anchor at Santa Barbara. Found lying here a Mexican brig, the barks *Index* & *Tip Coon* and Amer. whaling Bark *Cherokee*. Latter part crew employed in filling water. Carpenter caulking the Bends. Boys trying out oil on shore.

TUES 27th. Wind & weather as yesterday. Crew employed as above.

WED. 28th. Morning foggy & calm. All hands boating off hides & tallow. Carpenter caulking the bends. PM fresh NW winds & clear.

THURS 29. Morning calm & pleasant. All hands variously employed boating of [off] hides, tallow, water, &c. Carpenter repairing boat. Ends pleasant NW winds.

FRIDAY SEPT 30th. Pleasant and moderate through the day. Employed in landing freight and &c. Killed a bullock.

SAT OCT 1st. Morning as yesterday. Hove up and moored the ship outside the kelp to discharge ballast. Latter part fresh westerly winds. Employed in discharging ballast.

SUN. 2nd. Moderate & foggy. Crew at rest. Ends calm.

MON 3rd. Weather as yesterday. Employed in discharging ballast. 8 PM light winds from NE. Got under weigh and ran up the canal.

TUES. 4th. Moderate breezes from WNW. At 11 AM anchored at the Refugio. Latter part all hands on shore cutting fire wood.

WED. 5th. Moderate & pleasant weather through the day. Crew cutting fire wood and carting it to the beach. This morning I shot 4 geese (the first of the season). Afternoon rode to Mr. Hill's Rancho; found him gathering his grapes. The old veteran sailor of whom I have before spoken as living here, has died since I was last here. His name was James Swift, Ae. about 60, belonged to Plymouth, Mass. A few days previous to his death he embraced the Catholic faith and was baptised by Mr. Hill.

THURS. 6th. Morning pleasant breezes off the land, and fine weather. All hands boating off hides & tallow. So ends. Received a fine basket of grapes from Donna Madelina.

FRID. 7th. Continuation of the weather of yesterday. Crew employed as above. Rode up to Donna Madelina's Rancho to buy our sea stock of Potatoes, Onions & beans for the homeward passage. While the Indians were digging the potatoes I enjoyed an hour under the

shade of the large grape vines, the rich clusters of the
fine fruit hanging around my head in a most tempting
manner, and I only regretted that some of my friends
at home could not reach them. Afternoon very warm.
Returned on board at dark.

SAT. 8th.   Morning calm & smooth. Crew boating off
wood, vegetables, &c. Fresh NW winds.

SUND. 9th.   Winds & weather as yesterday. Crew at
rest. Afternoon received a visit from four of Donna
Madelina's daughters & two other ladies. Wished them
at home. Put them on shore at sundown.

The Ninth Passage

Refugio to San Diego, and Preparation for the Home Voyage to Boston

MOND. OCT. 10th. [1842]. Morning fresh breezes off the land (NW) and fine weather. Taking off fire wood. 4 PM got under weigh for Santa Barbara, thankfull that we have no more beating up the coast to do this voyage. Night calm.

TUES. 11th. Morning calm & foggy. Lay two [sic]. At noon fog clearing with a light breeze from NW. Ran in and anchored off Sta. Barb. at 4 PM.

WED. 12th. Winds & weather as yesterday. Crew employed variously on board.

THURS. 13th. Weather as yesterday. Discharging ballast.

FRID. 14th. Morning clear & pleasant. Light airs off the land. Crew [employed] in boating off hides & tallow & discharging ballast.

SAT. 15th. Weather as yesterday. Repairing main topsail &c. Latter part light NW winds. Weather warm.

SUN. 16th. Cloudy with SE winds through the day. All hands at rest.

MON. 17th. Morning pleasant and calm. Crew employed in getting water & killing bullocks. Latter part cloudy.

TUES 18th. Morning cloudy with light westerly winds. Received the welcome orders to proceed to St. Diego & commence loading for home. At 11 AM hove up the anchor and made sail from Sta. Barbara. Saluting the place with 13 guns, we squared away from a place from the inhabitants of which I have ever received the utmost politeness, but I hope never to see it any more. Soon we'll spread our sails for Yankee land, and already home is on the lips of all on board. At midnight ship off Pt. Dume.

WED. 19th. Morning light breezes & pleasant. Wind NW. At noon passed near the anchorage of St. Pedro & exchanged signals with the vessels lying there; bade a last adieu to St. Pedro. Latter part fresh breezes from NW.

THURS 20th. Moderate winds & variable throughout the day. Ship making slow progress. Saw the *Tasso* bound up. Two years more for you, my poor fellows (Thinks I) and no doubt they looked at the *Alert* with envious eyes. A fig for the southeasters now.

FRID 21st. Morning calm Noon light breezes from NW. At 4 PM passed Pt. Loma. Finding the tide strong against us came to anchor. Sent down T. Gallant yards & masts & got the Pinnace out. So ends.

SAT. OCT 22d, 1842. Morning calm. Hove up the anchor and warped up the harbour. Moored ship abreast the hide-house Unbent all the sails and stowed them away in the house, also the spare rigging, water casks & salt provisions, &c.

SUN. 23rd. Moderate & pleasant throughout the day. Crew at rest.

MOND. 24th. Morning calm & foggy. At early daylight commenced landing the hides. Finished landing at dark. We have now about two months hard work before us to cure the remainder of the hides, discharge ballast, put the ship in order and load. We have about 4500 hides now unsalted, and expect the *Barnstable* will bring us down about 5000 more. I have two extra men to help cure them and we hope that the rains will not commence untill late; it is time however now to expect them. The division of labour now is the carpenter is caulking the bends, with a man to assist him; 6 men on shore curing hides, with a boy to cook for them; the rest of the crew clearing out the hold and getting ready for stowing. Went up to the Presidio to get a bullock but did not succeed. The woman who supplies the ship has gone to the "Pueblo los Angelos" with all her family and nobody else in the place has any cattle. This makes it rather bad for us as we have no meat on board but some dried beef besides the salt provisions, and the latter is kept sacred for the homeward passage.

"Russel," one of my hired men at the hide house (the same mentioned by *Dana* as Don Tomas, Capitana la casa, &c.),[67] being absent to day I rode up to his house to enquire for him, and found him engaged in his yard, making two coffins for children which had died the day previous. He said they were laid out in

---

[67] Thomas Russell, as Dana explains, had served on the *Pilgrim,* the brig on which Dana arrived in California; later he was naturalized and married a native Californian. See *Two Years,* Ch. XIX, for several references, and XXVIII for his dismissal for misconduct and subsequent arrest.

a house which he pointed out and that the people
were *waking them* [i.e., holding a wake]. I went to
the house and found the room filled with people dancing and singing, as they had been the whole previous
night. On one side of the room laid out on a table
were the corpses of the two children, both of one year
old, belonging to two mothers, both born the same
day, and both died the same day. They were totally
dressed, bedecked with tinsel and ribbons, a crown of
gilt paper on their heads, and their tiny hands holding
a little cross on their breasts. They looked pleasant in
death, and as I gazed on their beautiful countenances,
I tho't of my own sweet ones far far away, and turned
away & wept. The custom of the country is that when
children die in infancy, the parents, friends & neighbours celebrate the event by dance and singing. The
child they say never sinned, and is now rejoicing in
Heaven, and we should rejoice at its happiness. Both
the mothers were in the room and had been dancing.
I saw no sign of grief on their countenances, and if
their hearts had felt sorrow they now exhibited no
trace of it. One told me that as her child breathed its
last she whispered to it to pray for her when she arrived at Heaven. The wax candles were replenished
while I was in the room, and were kept burning on the
table by the bodies, and they were recommencing the
dancing which had been suspended for about an hour
to take refreshments and were to be continued through
the day. It was expected that I would stop and assist,
but I assured the party who made the request that I
never felt less disposed to dance than I did at present,
so jumping on my horse I rode back to the beach,
thinking of the inconsistencies I had witnessed among
which not the least was that these parents were quite

poor, and the present fooleries must have cost them (or somebody) over $200.

TUES. 25th. Morning foggy & calm. Started at 2 AM with two boys in the cutter to fish outside the harbour. Returned at 11 with over 40 fine fish. Crew employed in putting on shore the *Barnstable's* bread and other articles, discharging ballast and whitewashing the Forecastle. Carpenter caulking. Latter part strong NW winds & clear weather.

WED. 26. Clear and pleasant through the day. In the morning got chronometer sights. Crew discharging ballast. Carpenter caulking. Arrived brig *Catalina* from St. Pedro to load for Mazatlan.

THURS. 27th. Weather as yesterday. Employed in discharging ballast. Carpenter caulking bends, & people curing hides on shore.

FRID. 28th. Morning cloudy & calm. Employed as yesterday. *War. War. War.* At noon just as we had set down to dinner a friend came on board showing me a letter from Mr. Park an Amer. Gent. in Sta. Barbara,[68] stating that the U.S. Frigate *United States,* Com. Jones, and the Sloop of War, *Cyanne* [*Cyane*] had arrived at Monterey bringing news of war between Mexico & the U. States, also that they had taken Monterey and garrisoned the Fort. Upon receipt of the news, I turned the crew too and informing them

[68] Thomas B. Park, after several earlier visits to California as assistant supercargo or agent, took up permanent residence after 1835, and in due course succeeded Alfred Robinson as principal agent for Bryant, Sturgis & Co. on the California coast. Naturalized in 1844, he often occurs in business records. His alcoholism, however, resulted in his dismissal on Phelp's recommendation when, as agent for the *Sterling,* Park came under Phelps' overall supervision. Phelps to Joseph B. Eaton, 6 November 1846, Phelps Papers, vol. 6.

how matters stood, we were not long putting the ship
in a good state for defense. Fly we cannot, as the ballast is nearly all out and the sails & provisions on shore.
The large guns were loaded with round & grape shot
& run out, blunderbusses & muskets cleaned & loaded
& boarding pikes & cutlasses placed convenient for use.
At 5 PM a courier arrived from Mr. Robinson con-
firming the previous news and advising me to leave
St. Diego for a more northern port, but at present it
is impossible to do so as it would take a week to ballast
the ship.[69] Therefore I have concluded to remain and
defend the ship and property on shore in the best way
I can. We have on shore at a pistol shot from the ship
property to the amount of over $120,000 and I cannot
think that Mr. R. wishes me to abandon all this property while there is a chance to protect it. At all events
I shall do my best to protect both ship & property.

Hoisted up the boats at dark and doubled the watch,
keeping matches lighted & the guns primed. I also ordered the people at the hide house if they were molested
during the night, to fire an alarm and come on board,
leaving a small boat on shore for that purpose. The
Catalina is the only vessel in port with us as she is
Mexican & commanded by an officer of the navy, a
hotheaded ignorant fellow and it is necessary to keep
an eye on him. The people of the town I am not in the
least afraid of but Mr. Warner (Mr. Robinson's courier) informs me that when he left the pueblo yesterday
it was rumoured that a party was forming there to come

---

69 "You must be wide awake and the least appearance of an attempt to
molest you in this Ship, direct your steps this way, that is proceed for some
northward port – it will be better to come here direct," wrote Robinson in
obvious haste from Santa Barbara. Robinson to Phelps, 24 October 1842,
Phelps Papers, vol. 10.

ALFRED ROBINSON'S LETTER OF OCTOBER 24, 1842, TO PHELPS
INFORMING HIM OF COMMODORE JONES' OCCUPATION OF MONTEREY
By permission of the Houghton Library, Harvard University.

ALERT off CAPE HORN

A WATERCOLOR OF THE "ALERT," PRESUMABLY BY CAPTAIN PHELPS
By permission of the Houghton Library, Harvard University.

down & take the *Alert*. Also that the new Gen'l & his vagabond troops were returning towards this place. We are certainly in the most unprepared state for a "bobbery" now that we have been in since on the coast, but we must make the most of it and I'd rather run than fight. I have no fears of them taking my ship.

SAT. 29th. At early daylight, the crew were sent to bring the provisions, sails, & water casks from the shore. Took all hands on board from the hide house and bent a part of the sails to enable us to run out if circumstances should require it. During last night Mr. Warner having rested himself again started for Sta. Barbara with a letter to Mr. Robinson to whom I wrote that it was impossible for me to leave here at present with the ship and that I should remain and defend or secure the property as long as possible. To day 5 boats with otter hunters who have been hunting on the coast arrived and encamped at the entrance of the harbour. Being well acquainted with the heads of the party Messrs Sparks & Nidever,[70] I visited them & informing them of the state of affairs induced them to put their furs of which they had $4000 worth on board the *Alert,* all hands of them excepting Mr. Sparks (who is naturalized here but is Yankee at heart) promising to be on board at 5 minutes notice, and defend their property. And indeed they appear extremely anxious for a brush, most of them being men who have travelled through New Mexico and over the Rocky Mountains and all having a mortal hatred to Mexicans & therefore with the addition of nine hunters with

[70] George Nidever was a well-known otter hunter who had settled in Santa Barbara in 1833. See Bancroft, IV, pp. 753-54. Isaac J. Sparks arrived in California in 1832. Long an otter hunter, he ended his career as a prosperous rancher in San Luis Obispo country.

their rifles I feel quite secure. This afternoon got the fore hold cleared out and dunnage [71] ready to take on hides on Monday. At night no further news from the seat of war. The people of the Presidio sent me down a bullock in the evening so it appears we have friends among our enemies.

SUNDAY OCT. 30th 1842.   Morning pleasant. At 8 AM perceiving some military movements on board the *Catalina* such as firing pistols and the Capt. displaying his uniform & talking largely & loudly to the crew, I hoisted our Ensign & pennant & shipped the blunderbusses on the gangways as an offsete [sic] *to his* display. Shortly after breakfast he mounted horse and rode up to town dressed in uniform; at the same [time] I started in a boat with my carpenter and 4 hands, took possession of the fort at the narrow entrance of the harbour, spiked all the guns consisting of 5 beautiful long brass 18 pounders & 3 iron 24d. Out of a pile of shot we also picked out all that would fit our own guns & returned on board. These guns at the fort were part of them dismantled but could soon have been put in service to annoy us in our passage out.[72] Of course there was no garrison to oppose us,

[71] Dunnage is material placed under the cargo to prevent its shifting in the hold, and also to raise it above the floors and sides and thus keep it dry. In the California trade, it was common to use brush, or cattle horns, or salted (as opposed to dried) hides.

This page of Phelps' journal is most difficult to read, since after writing in the normal horizontal way, Phelps has turned to book 90° and written across the page.

[72] The *Alert's* 12-pounder guns seem to have been at least a fair match for the fort. Fort Guijarros on Point Loma, built in 1797, had, according to Phelps, only eight cannon, "of which only a few were serviceable" (Bancroft, III, p. 610). It is not likely that Micheltorena had sent to seize the *Alert,* but – in Bancroft's view – he probably did send men to secure the cannon, only to find that Phelps had taken matters in hand as he describes. Bancroft, IV, p. 320.

but had the general left a small garrison here on his way up, we should have warm work to have got the ship out. Hearing that the mate of the *Catalina* was an American, I wrote him a note warning him of the consequence of being found in arms against his country and also offering to receive him & any other Americans who might be in that crew on board the *Catalina*. He shortly after came on board and stated that he had urged his Capt. to discharge him, which he had refused, but that on the least hostile movements he would be found under the flag of his own country.

At dark the otter hunters came on board to camp, bringing their rifles, fearing that we might be attacked in the night they could not remain easy at their own encampment. Nobody has been down from the Presidio during the day, consequently we are without news.

MON. 31st. Morning cloudy with light southerly winds. No enemy being in sight we commenced at daylight taking on board hides & the carpenter continued caulking. Took in & stowed away 1500 hides. No news from above has reached us today. A person from the Presidio says that 10 runaway soldiers passed through there last evening having their arms with them. The Alcaldi yesterday read a banda (official order) in church, calling upon all citizens to take up arms in defence of the country, or they would be considered traitors. Our situation is certainly rather a singular one (laying in an enemy's camp taking in cargo in time of war). We are ready to run out however, should we be compelled to do so. The topsails are kept loose and the provisions were all brought on board to day, but unless large guns are placed on the hills which overlook us I cannot be made to abandon the anchorage. Any force which the country can bring against us to attack from the beach we can easily disperse. Springing the [ship] broadside to the shore with a battery of 4 12-pounders & blunderbusses & muskets I think will keep such enemies at a distance.

TUES NOV. 1 1842. Weather cloudy & southerly winds. All hands employed in taking on board & stowing cargo. Carpenter caulking the bends. Ends pleasant, wind NW. Capt Hanson [Hansen] of the *Catalina* found on visiting the fort with the Alcaldi yesterday (for the purpose of putting the guns in order) that the whole battery was rendered useless, and having ascertained by whom it was done, a courier was dispatched to inform the General who is somewhere between the Presidio and the Pueblo.

WED. 2nd. Weather pleasant. All hands employed as yesterday. No signs of enemies yet. In the afternoon a person from the town brought word that Com. Jones had rec'd dispatches from Mexico which caused him to give up possession of California & cease hostilities. I hope this is not true, but that the American Govt. will hold on to this country and will take ample satisfaction of Mexico for her oft repeated insults & aggressions on our flag.

THURS. 3rd. Weather as yesterday. Discharging ballast from the after hold. Carpenter caulking. A gentleman at St. Luis Rey sent down a copy of Com. Jones' official communication to the Governor which confirms the report of yesterday, in consequence of which I had the sails unbent again and put on shore. Got sights for the Cme. [chronometer].

FRID. 4th. Continuation of fine weather. Discharging all the ballast. Carpenter finished caulking outside.

SAT. 5th. Weather as above. Employed taking on board hides & horns & stowing tallow in the after hold. Two men sick & off duty.

SUN. 6th. Moderate & pleasant throughout the day. Crew at rest.

TO SUN. 13th. The weather during the past week has continued quite warm, clear & pleasant, with but little wind which we have improved to the best advantage in curing hides and taking them on board. We have now stowed away 200 bags of tallow & 10,000 hides. We have also sent down & overhauled the topsail yards and got them up again, stripped the bowsprit, refitted the rigging, &c, &c. The carpenter has been employed on shore, making new long fore & mizen topgallant masts. No arrivals & no news from windward. All hands well.

SUN 20th. The weather throughout the week has been pleasant. All hands have been busily employed in curing hides and loading ship. The *Barnstable* arrived on Wednesday bringing about 5000 hides for us. Mr. Robinson came down in her to take passage for Acapulco in the *Catalina*. He intends returning home by the way of Mexico; has with him his little daughter.

During the past week we have taken on board about 7000 hides & tomorrow commence stowing the lower hold. Mr. Robinson informs me that Com. Jones has returned affairs to their former standing, but that the flag ship will remain at Monterey for the present probably with a view of again taking possession of the country if his next advices should be of a hostile nature.

Mr. R. saw the Gov. Gen'l at the Pueblo who told
him that Com. Jones was on his way to St. Pedro in
the *Cyanne* to give him an interview. He also informs
Mr. R. that my spiking the guns at this place would
be a *national affair* and for which the Commodore
must be accountable. The *Index* arrived yesterday
from windward.

SUN. 27th.   The weather during the past week has
been tolerably good & favourable for our business of
curing hides & stowing them. A strong gang has been
steeving the hold to the cheerful tune of "It's time for
us to go, my boys," and twelve men from the two ships
have been curing hides on shore. The cooper of the
Barnstable had overhauled & repaired our water casks,
and they are now being filled at the Presidio. The
Mexican bark *Clovila* from windward arrived yesterday. Ends pleasant. All hands on board.

SUN. DEC. 4th.   The weather has been fine during the
week. All hands employed as usual. taking on board
& steving hides. Crew at rest.

SUN. 11th.   The early part of the week we had a few
rain squalls and cloudy days which impede the work
on the cargo, but as we filled and stowed the water and
took in the fire wood in that time, no time was lost.
Two men have been laid up sick, but are now at their
duty. Exchanged stewards with the *Barnstable* & received from her a lot of stores & provisions for our use.
Finished steving the lower hold.

SUN. 18th.   The work has gone on slowly but well.
The dining room has been taken down and its place
filled with hides. The hides on shore are cured and the
gang taken on board to assist in steveing. Some hands

have been employed in taking off fire wood and filling water. The Carpenter employed on shore making hog pens and hen coops. Sent up top gallant & royal yards and studdingsail booms. Crew at rest.

SUN DEC 25th 1842. *Christmas day* begins with fine clear pleasant weather. Yesterday we completed loading the ship at sunset. Took in the launch and gave three hearty cheers. Discharging the Kanackers and gave up the hide house to the *Barnstable*. The cargo on board consists of 33,000 hides, 200 bags of tallow, 10,000 horns & 2 casks of beaver.

Gave the crew a good Christmas dinner on board, and dined myself at the house of Capt. Fitch at the Presidio where all the capt's & supercargoes were invited. Returned on board at dark.

MON. 26th. Clear & pleasant. All hands employed in getting ready for sea. Bent all the sails, and took on board the live stock consisting of 7 large hogs, 24 pigs, 12 sheep, 2 goats, 11 doz. fowls, and 2 turkies. So ends.

TUES. 27th. Weather as yesterday. Employed in lashing spars and clearing the decks and filling water for the stock.

WED. 28th. Weather pleasant with fresh westerly winds. Employed variously. Afternoon ship ready for sea.

THURS. 29th. Morning pleasant & calm. Unmoored ship & dropped down the harbour to await the breeze. 2 PM hove up and made sail. In wearing ship in a narrow channel the anchor caught the bottom, & keeping the ship from paying off, she swung with her stern on the same bank on which the *Alert* grounded in going out loaded in Dana's voyage.[73] Hove all aback, but would not do. Ran out a kedge anchor; hove taught on the hawser and waited for the flood tide to float her off, which it did at 8 PM. Anchored for the night with the small bower in 6 fathoms water.

FRI. [DEC.] 30th.   Got under weigh in the morning with fine breezes from NW and got out safe. The *Barnstable* left St. Diego yesterday and passed us while we were on shore. She also touched but worried over. Capt. Hatch hove too outside and sent his boat in to our assistance. We also rec'd help from Capt. Arther in the *California's* boats. The *Barnstable* lay off and on untill we came out this morning, when passing close to her we exchanged salutes, and then made sail on our respective courses, we for Home, they for 2 years hide droging.

Set all the starboard studding sails to a fresh breeze and at sunset took a last look at California. Thirty months we have [spent] cruising up and down this coast, selling goods and collecting hides, and with the exception of losing one of the boys, have been very fortunate in not meeting any serious accident, Thanks be to a Merciful God.

At 4 PM the Corronades Islands bore due North 25 miles dist. from which I take my departure. During our being on the coast we have been seven times to St. Francisco, thirteen times to Monterey, three times to Santa Cruz, four times to St. Louis [San Luis Obispo], once to St. Simeon, 17 times to Santa Barbara, 17 to St. Pedro, 5 to Refugio, and returned to St. Diego 9

---

[73] Dana, Ch. XXIX; the *Alert,* passing over the bar at the same time as the *California,* passed too far to the south and, being fully loaded, grounded, but was soon lifted off by the rising tide for a second try.

times, anchoring frequently along the coast to take in
hides and wait for wind. We have hove up the bower
anchor 131 times, and killed and consumed 203 bullocks, and not a man a boy has been seriously sick although they have been exposed night and days in the
boats, sleeping in them or in the woods frequently, and
during the winter months frequently wet night and
day when away from the ship. Add to this their constant exposure carrying hides through the surf on
every part of the coast during the day, and then standing watch at night, the fatigue of working the ship up
and [down] the coast, anchoring often and handling
the heavy sails so much, it is wonderful that they have
withstood so much fatigue and not given out. I ascribe
it under God to the exceeding salubrity of the climate,
and to the absence of ardent spirits, their always being
well fed and never sent away in the boats without a
change of clothing with them.

Lat. at noon 30°51′ N. Lon. 117°15′ W. [Approxi-
mately 50 miles off the coast of northern Baja California.]

Appendices
Bibliography
and Index

Appendix I

Copy of Rules and Regulations to be Observed by the Officers & Crew of Ship *Alert*[1]

1st.   All profanity is expressly forbidden and no Man or Boy is to be called out of his name by any Officer.

2d.   The Crew are to treat the Officers with becoming respect, to always answer, when spoken to, and by no means to give improper replies. They will always be allowed their Forenoon watch below at sea, unless the duty of the Ship requires all Hands. The watch to be called at 7 bells in the morning. The watch below to get their breakfast and relieve the deck at 8 bells. All Hands to dinner at noon and turn too without being called when the bell strikes two. The Watch below to get supper at 3 bells & relieve the Watch at 6 o'clock, at which time the decks are to be cleared up and cleanly swept.

3d.   During the night one man to keep a look out on each side of the Forecastle, one in each waist, & the others as may be directed by the Officer of the Watch, no one to sleep in his watch, or lie down.

4th.   The *Officer* of the watch will always report to the Capt. at the expiration of his watch, the Bell to be struck by the man at the wheel every half hour & to be repeated by the bell forward.

5th.   The Ship to be scrubbed & washed inside and out every morning when the weather & other duty permits. The Masts to be greased every Saturday Afternoon.

6th.   The Officer of the watch will never shorten sail without leave of the Capt. (except in case of sudden squall). He will during his

---

[1] The Rules, like the last entry in the journal, were written in pencil and written over in ink. Since they are given on the page immediately following the last entry, they must have been added after the journal was complete, either as an afterthought, summarizing the rules Phelps had tried to apply, or as a copy of rules recorded elsewhere at an earlier time.

watch on deck, pay particular attention to having the sails well trimmed and every advantage taken to drive the ship along.

7th. Saturday Afternoons will be allowed the crew for washing & mending their clothing. No unnecessary work to be done on the Sabbath.

When in Port

8th. No Man or Boy shall be allowed to go on Shore on liberty without permission of the 1st Officer, and to return on board at the expiration of his time, under the penalty of having his liberty stopped. Drunkeness will be subject to the same penalty & if repeated the offender will be turn out of the ship.

9th. No Boat shall at any time be sent away on duty or otherwise on the *Sabbath* unless there be urgent necessity for the same and by consent of the Captain. Nor shall a boat be dispatched from the Ship at any time without *orders* from the Capt. when he is on board or within communication. Boat crews will be detailed for each boat on arriving at San Francisco and are not to be changed to other boats, except with the Capts permission. The *Cockswain* of each boat to have sole charge of his boat and all belonging to her. The crew with him to be subject to his orders, and all to be respectfull & obedient to the Supercargoes or whomever may go in the boat to do the business.

10th. *The Boys at Sea* will muster for inspection in clean clothes every Sunday Morning at *1 Bell,* & if found wanting in cleanliness of person or clothing will be punished by Mastheading for one hour. It shall be their duty to keep the Forecastle & Steerage clean, to take the provisions to the Forecastle from the Galley & return the Kids [2] and pans to the cook after meals.

11th. The Mizzen Topsail, Royal & Top. Gt. Yards are also to be considered as belonging to their care, to Reef Furl & send up or down. And deviation from the above orders & regulations will be considered as insubordination and neglect of duty which will be punished accordingly.

WM. D. PHELPS
Master

[2] Kids are tubs or pans in which the rations were carried to the fore-castle.

BOAT CREWS

Launch Mr. Bumpus 2d Mate in charge.

Crew: Henry Hackett, John Bray, Lowell H. Druce, Lemuel Clark

Pinnace Wm Anderson Cocks'n

Crew: Andrew Naldie, J. L. Philbrick, John Williams

Cutter: Joseph Abbott, Cocks'n John Robinson, Dan'l Vorralt, Thos Knight

Whaleboat: Edward Robinson, Cocks'n & 2 Sandwich Islanders

Gig's Crew: Wm. Dommalt, Cocks'n, Sam Hooton, John Hill

Appendix II

Common [?] Cloaks	$35.00		Quills pr 100	1.00
Looking glasses	$15. 20. 30. 40.		Steel pens doz.	1.50
Rugs (Wilton) Hearth	9-12		Manifold writers ea.	12.00
Blond Lace [no figure given]			Blank books $1.50 to 5.00	
Figured Satin, pr vara[1]	$2.50		Ink pr Botl.	.75
Pongee Hdkhs handkerchiefs			Letter paper (ream)	10.00
(piece)	12.00		Segar "	8.00
Black "	20.00		Wicking lb.	1.00
Cotton "	7.00		Boots fine 8 to 10 pr pair	
Ladies " linen Cambric 2 to 3			Brogans 2 to 3.50 "	
Linen Thread pr lb.	4.00		Shoes	2.50
Sewing Silk	18.00		Hats (ea)	14.00
Tape pr dozen	1.50		Umbrellas (silk)	12.00
Calicos $17. 19. 22 & 25 pr.			Cotton shirts (ea)	2.50
Striped Cambric pr			Spool Thread doz.	2.50
ps [piece]	14.00		Cloth jackets	$30.00
Sheeting (bleached)	$30.00		" pants	15.00
Brown Cottons	16 to 18		Satinett pants	9.00
Gingham	18		Twilled (common)	6.00
Velvet pr vara	1.25		Coffee mills ea.	2.00
Broad Cloth "	10.00		Sauce pans $1 to $6	
Satinett "	2.00		Tea Cannisters	1.50
Cotton Hose doz.	15.00		" Scales, pair	8.00
Towels, drape [?] doz.	6.00		Watering pots	2.50
Ribbons 1.50 to 4.00 ps.			Lanthorns (com)	2.—
Confectionary lb.	1.00		Tin pots	1.—
Needles pr M [1000]	6.00		Candle moulds	2.—
Suspenders $1.50 to 2 pr.			Tunnels[2]	$.75
Pencil Cases (com)			Pans 1 to 2	
[common]	2.00		Dish covers ea.	2.—
Artificial Flowers box	$15.00		Dimity[3] pr. ps.	35.00

[1] Vara: Spanish yard [36-43"]. [2] Tunnels: another name for Funnels.
[3] Dimity: a cotton fabric, white or dyed, in which is woven a stripe of heavier yarn.

Shawls	15.00	Shot belts	$1.50 & 2 each
Patch [?] ps.	20.00	Flat irons pr pair	$2.00
Pocket knives	$1 to 3	Gouges (sett)	$1 to $8.00
Bowie *"*	4	Chisels (sett)	1 to 8
Jack *"*	50¢ to 1.00	Wrench Hammers [?] (ea) 5.00	
Scissors	.75	Buttons (groce)	[no figure]
Thimbles	50¢ to 25¢	Gen. [general?] locks (ea)	4.00
White cotton	$18. 20. 24	Chest locks	.75 to 2.50
Blue Calico ps.	16.00	Trunk *"*	1.00
Spanish cigars M	30.00	Dead *"*	$1. to 3.00
Plug tobacco lb.	1.—	Brass candlesticks (ea)	3.00
Trace chains pr.	5.00	Nails (arobe, 25 lb.)	9.00
Dog *"* ea.	2.—	Sickles doz.	15.00
Hoes ea	1.50	Sugar (arobe)	8.00
Pick axes	1 to 2.50	Rice *"*	3.00
Screws (groce) [gross] $3 to 6		Maccaroni *"*	6.00
Clout nails pr M	1.50	Coffee *"*	9.00
Brass tacks M	2.50	Pepper *"*	6.00
House hinges pair	.50	Molasses pr gall.	1.00
Razors (sett)	$6 to 12	Lemon Syrup box	15.00
Knives & forks	$6. 9. to 30	India R[ubber] shoes pr.	2.50
Carvers pair	2.00	Chocolate (arobe)	15.00
Hooks & eyes, box	.25	Nutmegs lb[?]	3.00
Table spoons box	2.00	Cloves *"*	3.00
Tea *"*	1.50 to 3.00	Tea	2.00
Snuffers	1.50 to 2.00	Muscat wine box	10.00
Pins pr. bundle	$3.00	Port *"* gall.	2.50
Shoe [?] knives doz.	4.00	Madeira *"* *"*	2.50
Butchers *"* *"*	$4-9.00	Brandy *"*	4.00
Scalping *"* *"*	6.00	Cordial box	12.00
Spoke shaves (ea)	1.50	Almonds arobe	9.00
Shot	$8 pr bag	Raisins box	7.00
Powder	1.50 *"*	Tumblers doz	3 to 6.00
Files	$4 to 12 pr doz	China Tea Setts	8.00
Hand saws (ea)	3.00	Basin & Ewars pr	3.50
Ladles	$1	Chairs doz. $25 to 50.00	
Forks	$1	Paint oil gall.	3.00
Norfolk Latches doz	6 to 10	White lead cwt.	36.00
Powder flasks (ea)	3.50	Black paint *"*	36.00

Appendix III

VESSELS ENCOUNTERED ON THE CALIFORNIA COAST

(Source: Adele Ogden, "Trading Vessels on the California Coast, 1786-1848," Bancroft Library, University of California, Berkeley; with thanks to Ms. Ogden for her suggestions.)

VESSEL	RIG	TONS	FLAG	MASTER
Alciope	ship	377	U.S.	Curtis Clap

Owner: James Hunnewell, etc., Boston; chartered by Alpheus B. Thompson

Ayacucho	brigantine	125	Mexico	J. Blanca

Owner: Bizat & Roussel, Bordeaux (Joseph Y. Limantour, supercargo)

Barnstable	ship	373	U.S.	James B. Hatch

Owner: William Appleton & Co., Boston

Bolivar	brig	224	U.S.	Gorham H. Nye

Owner Alpheus B. Thompson, etc., California

Braganza	ship	469	U.S.	Charles C. Waterman

Owner: (whaler) Pope & Morgan, New Bedford

California	schooner	85	Mexico	John R. Cooper

Owner: Govt. of Calif. (at San Francisco, 10 Oct. 1840)

California	ship	369	U.S.	James P. Arther

Owner: Bryant, Sturgis & Co., Boston (1839-40 voyage): Benjamin T. Reed, Henry Price, Joseph B. Eaton, etc., Boston (1842-44 voyage)

Catalina	brig	161	Mexico	Christian Hansen

Owner: Henry E. Virmond, Acapulco

Cherokee	bark	261	U.S.	Adams/Pease

Owner: (whaler) Hathaway & Luce, New Bedford

Clarita	bark	210	Mexico	Charles C. Wolter

Owner: Henry E. Virmond, Acapulco

Columbia	bark	300	Britain	Charles Humphreys

Owner: Hudson's Bay Co., London

VESSEL	RIG	TONS	FLAG	MASTER
Cowlitz	bark	345	Britain	William Brotchie

Owner: Hudson's Bay Co., London

Cyane	sloop-of-war (18 guns)		U.S.	C. K. Stribling
Don Quixote	bark	260	U.S.	John Paty

Owner: Paty & Co., Honolulu (William H. Davis, Jr., supercargo)

Duxbury	?			
Fama	ship	362	U.S.	Cornelius Hoyer

Owner: Benjamin T. Reed, Boston; Alpheus B. Thompson, California

Fly	schooner	92	Britain	John Wilson/
				Edward Stokes

Owner: John Wilson and James G. Scott, California

Guipuzcoana: see *Joven Guipuzcoana*

Index	bark	203	Britain	James G. Scott and
				(sometimes) John Wilson

Owner: James G. Scott and John Wilson, California

Joseph Peabody	brig	224	U.S.	John C. Dominis

Owned at Salem, Mass.

Joven Guipuzcoana	bark	194	Mexico	Joseph F. Snook

Remarks: Former *Roger Williams,* alias *Tipcoon;* purchased March 1840 by José Antonio Aguirre, Santa Barbara

Juan José	brig	217	Ecuador	Thomas Duncan

Owner: Antonio Menéndez, Antonio J. Cot, and Miguel F. de Pedrorena, Peru; also called *Miguel* or *Don Miguel,* after Pedrorena, supercargo and part owner

Julia Ann	schooner	99	U.S.	William A. Leidesdorff

Owner: John C. Jones, Jr., California

Leónidas	brigantine	206	Mexico	Edward Stokes

Owner: José Antonio Aguirre, Santa Barbara

Lama	brig	145	U.S.	Owen Jones

Owned at Boston; shippers: James Hunnewell, Boston, and Peirce & Brewer, Honolulu

Maryland	brig	99	U.S.	Henry A. Peirce

Owner: Peirce & Brewer, Honolulu

Miguel: see *Juan José*

VESSEL	RIG	TONS	FLAG	MASTER
Monsoon	ship	327	U.S.	George W. Vincent

Owner: Bryant, Stugis & Co., Boston

Morse: see *Nymph*

Nymph	schooner	98	Mexico	Henry Delano Fitch

Owner: Henry Delano Fitch, John Temple, Abel Stearns, California
(formerly the *Morse* owned by Fitch and Peirce & Brewer, Honolulu)

Orozimbo	ship	588	U.S.	David H. Bartlett

Owner: (whaler) Barton Ricketson, New Bedford

Roger Williams: see *Joven Guipuzcoana*

St. Louis	sloop-of-war (18 guns)		U.S.	French Forrest
Sapphire	ship	366	U.S.	Alexander Cartwright

Owner: (whaler) Stephen C. Phillips, Salem

Tasso	bark	286	U.S.	Samuel J. Hastings

Owner: Curtis, Stevenson and Price, Boston

Tipcoon: see *Joven Guipuzcoana*

Vincennes	sloop-of-war (18 guns)		U.S.	Cadwallader Ringgold
Yorktown	sloop-of-war (16 guns)		U.S.	John H. Aulick

Select Bibliography

Adams, E. D. "English Interest in the Annexation of California." *Amer. Hist. Rev.,* XIV (1909): 744-63

Babson, John J. *History of the Town of Gloucester, Cape Ann, including the Town of Rockport.* Gloucester, 1860; reprint, Peter Smith, 1972

Bancroft, Hubert Howe. *History of California,* Vols. I-VI. San Francisco: History Company, 1886-88

———. *California Pastoral, 1769-1848.* San Francisco: History Company, 1888

Bentley, William. *The Diary of William Bentley, DD, Pastor of the East Church, Salem, Mass.* Gloucester: Peter Smith, 4 vols., 1962

Cleland, Robert Glass. *The Cattle on a Thousand Hills, Southern California 1850-80.* San Marino: Huntington Library, 2nd ed., 1951

Cutter, William Richard. *Genealogical and Personal Memoirs relating to the Families of Boston and Eastern Massachusetts,* Vol. II. New York: Lewis Historical Pub. Co., 1908

Dakin, Susanna Bryant. *A Scotch Paisano: Hugo Reid's Life in California, 1832-1852.* Berkeley: Univ. of Calif. Press, 1939

———. *The Lives of William Hartnell.* Stanford Univ. Press, 1949

Dallas, Sherman F. "The Hide and Tallow Trade in Alta California, 1822-1846." Unpublished Ph.D. dissertation, Indiana Univ., 1955

Dana, Richard Henry, Jr. *Two Years Before the Mast: a Personal Narrative of Life at Sea,* 2 vols. Ed. by John Haskell Kemble. Los Angeles: Ward Ritchie Press, 1964

Davis, William Heath. *Seventy-Five Years in California.* San Francisco: John Howell, 1967

Fernald, Helen Clark. *The Jonathan Harrington House.* Lexington, Mass., 1937

Fritzsche, Bruno. " 'On Liberal Terms': The Boston Hide-Merchants in California." *Business Hist. Rev.,* XLII (1968): 467-81

Gale, Robert L. *Richard Henry Dana, Jr.* New York: Twayne Pubrs., 1969

Geiger, Maynard. *Mission Santa Barbara, 1782-1965.* Santa Barbara: Franciscan Fathers of Calif., 1965

Gleason, Duncan. *The Islands and Ports of California.* New York: Devin-Adair Co., 1958

Gudde, Erwin C. *California's Place Names.* Berkeley: Univ. of Calif. Press, 2nd ed., 1960

Hudson, Charles. *History of the Town of Lexington,* Vol.II. Boston: Houghton Mifflin, 1913

Jackson, Sheldon G. "Two Pro-British Plots in Alta California." *Southern Calif. Quar.,* LV (1973): 105-40

Jore, Leonce. "Jean Louis Vignes of Bordeaux: Pioneer of California Viticulture." *Southern Calif. Quar.,* XLV (1963): 289-303

Kelley, Beverly Allison. *Lexington, a Century of Photographs.* Lexington, Mass: Lexington Hist. Soc., 1980

Kroeber, A. L. *Handbook of the Indians of California.* Washington, 1925; reprint, New York: Dover, 1976

Larkin, Thomas Oliver. *The Larkin Papers:Personal, Business, and Official Correspondence,* Vols. I-V. Ed. by George P. Hammond. Berkeley: Univ. of Calif. Press, 1951-1955

Lucid, Robert F. "The Composition, Reception, Reputation and Influence of Two Years Before the Mast." Unpublished Ph.D. dissertation, Univ. of Chicago, 1958

————. *The Journal of Richard Henry Dana, Jr.* Vol. I. Cambridge: Harvard Univ. Press, 1968

Lyman, George D. *John Marsh, Pioneer.* New York: Scribner's, 1930

Morison, Samuel Eliot. "Boston Traders in the Hawaiian Islands, 1789-1823." *Mass. Hist. Soc. Proceed.* LIV (1920): 9-47

Northrop, Marie E. *Spanish-Mexican Families of Early California, 1769-1850,* Vol. I. New Orleans: Polyanthos, 1976

Ogden, Adele. "Alfred Robinson, New England Merchant in Mexican California." *Calif. Hist. Soc. Quar.,* XXIII (1944): 193-218

————. "Boston Hide Droghers along California Shores." *Calif. Hist Soc. Quar.,* VIII (1929): 289-98

————. "Hides and Tallow: McCulloch, Hartnell and Company, 1822-1828." *Calif. Hist. Soc. Quar.,* VI (1927): 254-64

————. "New England Traders in Spanish and Mexican California," in Adele Ogden, ed., *Greater America: Essays in Honor of Herbert Eugene Bolton.* Berkeley: Univ. of Calif. Press, 1945, pp. 395-413

Parker, Robert J. "Larkin, Anglo-American Businessman in Mexican California," in Adele Ogden, ed., *Greater America: Essays in Honor of Herbert Eugene Bolton.* Berkeley: Univ. of Calif. Press, 1945, pp. 415-429

[Phelps, William D.] *Fore and Aft; or, Leaves from the Life of an Old Sailor, by "Webfoot."* Boston: Nichols & Hall, 1871

Posner, Russell M. "A British Consular Agent in California: the Reports of James A. Forbes, 1843-1846." *Southern Calif. Quar.,* LIII (1971): 101-112

Pringle, James F. *History of the Town and City of Gloucester, Cape Ann, Massachusetts.* Gloucester, 1892

Robinson, Alfred. *Life in California during a Residence of Several Years in that Territory.* New York: Wiley and Putnam, 1846; reprint, N.Y: Da Capo Press, 1969

Ruschenberger, William Samuel Waltham. *A Voyage Round the World . . . in 1835-37.* Philadelphia: Carey, Lea, & Blanchard, 1838

Simpson, Sir George. *Narrative of a Journey Round the World during the Years 1841 and 1842,* 2 vols. London: H. Colburn, 1847

Smith, Dorothy Blakey, ed. *James Douglas in California, 1841: Being the Journal of a Voyage from the Columbia to California.* Vancouver, B.C: Public Library Press, 1965

Stanton, William. *The Great United States Exploring Expedition of 1838-1842.* Berkeley: Univ. of Calif. Press, 1975

Thompson, Alpheus B. *China Trade Days in California: Selected Letters from the Thompson Papers, 1832-1863.* Ed. by D. Mackenzie Brown. Berkeley: Univ. of Calif. Press, 1947

Underhill, Reuben L. *From Cowhides to Golden Fleece: A Narrative of California, 1832-1858, based upon Unpublished Correspondence of Thomas Oliver Larkin, Trader, Developer, Promoter, and Only American Consul.* Stanford Univ. Press, 1939

Williams, Glyndwr, ed. *London Correspondence Inward from Sir George Simpson, 1841-42.* London: Hudson's Bay Record Soc., 1973

Wilson, Iris Higbie. *William Wolfskill, 1798-1866: Frontier Trapper to California Ranchero*. Glendale: Arthur H. Clark Co., 1965

Wright, Doris Marion. *A Yankee in Mexican California: Abel Stearns, 1798-1848*. Santa Barbara: Wallace Hebberd, 1977

Zollinger, James Peter. *Sutter: the Man and His Empire*. New York: Oxford Univ. Press, 1939

Index